Women, Work, and the Web

Women, Work, and the Web

How the Web Creates Entrepreneurial Opportunities

Edited by
Carol Smallwood

ROWMAN & LITTLEFIELD
Lanham • Boulder • New York • London

Published by Rowman & Littlefield
A wholly owned subsidiary of The Rowman & Littlefield Publishing Group, Inc.
4501 Forbes Boulevard, Suite 200, Lanham, Maryland 20706
www.rowman.com

16 Carlisle Street, London W1D 3BT, United Kingdom

British Library Cataloguing in Publication Information Available

Library of Congress Cataloging-in-Publication Data

Women, work, and the Web : how the Web creates entrepreneurial opportunities / edited by Carol Smallwood.
p. cm.
Includes bibliographical references and index.
ISBN 978-1-4422-4426-9 (cloth : alk. paper) – ISBN 978-1-4422-4427-6 (pbk. : alk. paper) – ISBN 978-1-4422-4428-3 (ebook)
1. Self-employed women. 2. Internet and women. 3. Businesswomen. 4. Small business. 5. Electronic commerce. 6. Internet marketing. 7. Internet publishing. I. Smallwood, Carol, 1939–
HD6072.5.W65 2015
658.1'141082–dc23
2014032086

Printed in the United States of America

Contents

Foreword

Christine A. Olson

"No Guts, No Glory," read the card from my friend. It sat next to the flowers my husband had sent on this, the opening day of my consulting practice. It was October 1984 and I was officially starting up Chris Olson & Associates in the extra bedroom of our house. On my agenda for the day was renting a typewriter from a local office supply store, speaking to a designer about a logo for my new business, and phoning contacts who might be interested in hiring me for my marketing and communications services.

The Internet was in its infancy and light years away from where I was sitting. I had worked on the DOD ARPANET network a few years earlier and I was an information professional, so I knew what was in the wings. But as a fledgling consultant I was in no position to leverage the network to my advantage. I didn't even own a computer! Like other entrepreneurs at the time, I assumed I would rely on phone calls, faxes, in-person meetings, and courier services for conducting business.

So much for assumptions. Within three months I had purchased an IBM desktop computer for the sum of $10,000. It used floppy disks, a black-and-white monitor, and a dot-matrix printer. I was on my own to figure out the spaghetti of cables that came with it and the software programs to make it run. Suddenly I had a business asset that consumed time and saved time. In 1985 being connected to the Internet still wasn't an option, but I had electronic mail, and that became the beginning of adding electronic tools to my business mix and the new opportunities that would open as a result.

Incorporating the Internet into my consulting practice didn't happen until February 1996 when I registered my own domain, Chrisolson.com. At the time, the Internet was comprised of 100,000 websites and I joined them that same year. I taught myself HTML and worked out network problems as I encountered them. It was time consuming, but I was now connected to the electronic network that my prospective clients were beginning to explore.

Being linked to the Internet and having a presence on it became an important aspect of my consulting practice. Not only did I use my website to promote my knowledge, experience, and abilities, but I was able to locate and communicate with potential clients. For me the Internet became a two-way communications channel that outpaced and outperformed other business communications tools. As the Internet developed and grew, so did the entrepreneurial opportunities that opened up. For example, I took advantage of Internet-based electronic mail services by converting a paper-based newsletter to an electronic one distributed via e-mail and my website. I extended my workshops by leading virtual sessions using Internet-based conferencing services. I utilized video conferencing services to augment in-person meetings and expanded my consulting counseling sessions with clients by using Internet-based conference calls and desktop sharing. Today my business tool set is being expanded with survey-research, graphics, editing, and file-sharing applications based in cloud computing services that are easily accessed via Internet connections, regardless of platform, time zone, or geographic location.

The Internet has opened doors and delivered opportunities to my consulting business doorstep, and I have leveraged them to my advantage to meet goals and objectives. And so have the contributors to this book. The book's twenty-eight chapters offer candid glimpses into the role the Internet has played and currently plays in endeavors led by women. Arranged into five themed parts, "Fostering Change," "Running a Business," "Educational Applications," "Personal Aspects," and "Writing and Editing," the chapters give you a front-row seat to the stories behind the initiatives and businesses impacted by the Internet.

Each chapter has nuggets of advice and insight to be gleaned by anyone, male or female, looking to leverage the Internet for starting a business, identifying an opportunity, augmenting an existing venture, exploiting and expanding personal knowledge, contributing to society and humanity, fostering change, leading causes, teaching, researching . . . the list of possibilities is as vast as the Internet itself. In fact, the very existence of the Internet and its electronic environment has spawned unique entrepreneurial opportunities for women. Before the Internet there was no such thing as "blogging", Facebook, or Twitter, all of which now offer women ghostwriting and editing opportunities. eBay, Etsy, and similar electronic storefront services provide opportunities for women to be shopkeepers without geographic limitations. Without the Internet the world might not be the oyster for women that it is today.

To call out specific chapters for attention would emphasize one story over another. To be honest, I found every chapter to be fascinating reading. Every story teaches and inspires in its own voice. No matter where you open the book, there is a chapter that can't be put down until it's finished. It doesn't matter if you read the chapters in order or at random, the stories are addictive reading, and many are penned by awesome women who have broken through traditional entrepreneurial barriers with the help of the Internet.

Collectively, the chapters provide a valuable list of recommendations for all entrepreneurs. Women looking to leave the workforce or who want to focus energy into different directions will find this book to be inspiring and insightful. The authors have made a point to share the lessons they have learned, outcomes from their experiences, and resources they found critical to their success. Many are familiar, causing me to conclude that there are aspects of being an entrepreneur that are timeless—Internet or not.

Take for instance the silence of working alone. I remember how quiet the house was when I first started my consulting business. In fact the whole neighborhood was quiet. Everyone left to go to offices in distant locations while I took my cup of coffee upstairs to my "office/former bedroom." The commute was nice but the silence was deafening. I had to play a radio to keep myself alert. Apparently the silence that comes with working by yourself at home is still a challenge, as several of this book's chapter authors explain how they handle it.

A piece of advice for aspiring entrepreneurs is "love what you do because you'll be living it twenty-four hours a day." This dovetails with another observation by many contributors to this book: as an entrepreneur the buck stops with you. You are the chief cook and bottle washer, and you also take out the trash. While the Internet may relieve some organizational and management tasks, a whole new set of Internet-generated tasks crowd the entrepreneur's desk. Unfortunately, the number of hours in a day is still set to twenty-four. The Internet hasn't changed that.

As a marketing and communications consultant I have seen firsthand how the Internet has altered the mix of promotion activities needed for maintaining and growing a successful venture, be it a business or social endeavor. The marketing savvy demonstrated and discussed by the chapter authors is commendable, and you will be wise to note, study, and act on their recommendations. They not only describe their approaches and results, but many authors explain and provide pointers to resources they found valuable.

When I began my consulting business I relied on market research that I conducted myself, by hand. Sending out several hundred survey questionnaires required many hours of licking stamps, filling envelopes, and handaddressing labels. The Internet brings market research applications to an entrepreneur's desk and provides the tools for dissecting and analyzing results so that communications can be targeted to preferred groups of people. Many chapters in the book provide insights and guidance for conducting market research using Internet-based resources.

Back in 1984 being a woman entrepreneur was the exception, not the norm. When I named my business I purposely chose my nickname, Chris, because it was not gender specific. It turned out to be a wise decision that ensured no doors were closed to me immediately because I was a woman. To this day, I continue to surprise some phone callers because they assume I am a man, making the ensuing conversation rather enlightening as I listen to profuse apologies. The brand names used by chapter contributors prompts me to point out how important it is for aspiring entrepreneurs to be thoughtful when naming their endeavors. The Internet has made branding a significant task. A name has to be unique for a website domain name and should be able to carry over as the name for Facebook, Twitter, and LinkedIn accounts too. As of this writing the Internet has more than 265 million registered domain names making the creation and identification of a unique brand name rather daunting, but necessary.

And lastly, don't overlook the brief bios at the end of the book, as these provide snapshots of the chapter authors and in many cases add context to a chapter's points or scenario. Here's to the Internet and women everywhere who dream and create, and who put the Internet to work to benefit themselves, their loved ones, their causes, and their communities. Bravo!

Preface

Carol Smallwood

In a tight economy women entrepreneurs are making progress in a field that has been traditionally (along with science, math, and engineering) one in which women haven't been well represented—technology. *Women, Work, and the Web: How the Web Creates Entrepreneurial Opportunities* is by contributors from the United States and Canada sharing how the Internet has opened doors, leveled the playing field, and provided new opportunities. How the Internet has helped women with young children, caretakers of disabled family members, women with disabilities. How it has helped female veterans gain employment; put women into work boots; and allow women to publish in a male-dominated world, become editors, online instructors, and hold the First International Day of the Girl. The twenty-eight chapters are divided into five parts: "Fostering Change," "Running a Business," "Educational Applications," "Personal Aspects," and "Publishing and Writing."

It is exciting to see how the creative contributors of different ages, backgrounds, and goals are using the web to further their careers and the status of other women as they progress online. I extend my thanks to everyone who contributed for generously sharing their experiences.

Acknowledgments

Thanks to:

Dorothea J. Coiffe, Media Librarian, A. Philip Randolph Memorial Library, New York City

Lynne Davis, Writer, Yahoo Contributor Network

Ada Fetters, college teacher and editor, *The Commonline Journal*, www.commonlinejournal.com

B. Lynn Goodwin, managing editor, *Writer Advice*, www.writeradvice.com

Rebecca Marcum Parker, contributor, *Library Services for Multicultural Patrons: Strategies to Encourage Library Use* (2013)

Christine Redman-Waldeyer, founder/editor of *Adanna*, a literary journal for and about women

Karla J. Strand, Gender and Women's Studies Librarian, University of Wisconsin

Linda A. Wade, unit coordinator of digitization, Western Illinois University

Part I

Fostering Change

Chapter One

Blogging to Create Change

Amanda Peach

At first glance, *Plain Jane Activism*, http://plainjaneactivism.blogspot.com, might appear to be just another of the many 365-day challenge blogs permeating the Internet these days. Like those, Plain Jane's readers can depend on a daily infusion of new content from its author. Frequency of publication is where the similarities end, however. Plain Jane's author, Mae Suramek, uses her blog to challenge her readers to commit new small acts each day, such as "Act # 13: Challenge the status quo: Talk to a man about rape", all aimed at improving the lives of women. Where many 365-day blogs are concerned merely with self-reflection or capturing the minutiae of everyday life, either in photos or words, Mae's blog is concerned with the frank treatment of larger issues that impact women's safety, welfare, and quality of life, such as human trafficking, racism, and domestic violence.

The idea for the blog was born out of a family discussion of New Year's Eve resolutions; the conversation led Mae to commit to find a way to live more intentionally in the New Year. After some reflection, she decided journaling might be the answer. To force herself to remain consistent, she decided to commit to a 365-day blog format that would require her to publish every single day. She was not an experienced blogger when she decided to undertake the project and wasn't entirely sure where content would come from on a daily basis, but she knew she was tired of being silent.

Mae had spent nine of the last ten years in a very high-profile administrative position with her alma mater, Berea College, a small liberal arts school in Berea, Kentucky. As the director of Alumni Relations at Berea, she served as the face of the school's 17,000 alums. It was her job to bring alumni into the fold to financially support the school's mission, and to that end, she put a lot of pressure on herself to please everyone. Ironically enough, with each year she served in the position, she found herself further removed from the politically conscious activist she had become as a student at Berea. The college, which prides itself on its commitment to social justice and on producing graduates who are concerned with the welfare of others, had cultivated in her a deep need to serve others. After graduating from Berea, she had served in both Kentucky and North Carolina in a variety of settings: an Americorps program, at a refugee resettlement center, in a domestic violence shelter, and with a human rights organization. Her life prior to becoming director of Alumni Relations had been dedicated to speaking out about social injustice in its many forms, but nearly a decade into her position at Berea, she realized she had somehow found herself with opinions she no longer felt comfortable voicing.

As she turned forty, Mae decided it was time for a serious change, and so she left her position at Berea College, not knowing what would come next. About the change she said, "I knew one thing for sure, which was that I would never again be silent or compromise my thoughts and views, no matter what I did." After some soul-searching, Mae found herself in a position that was the perfect marriage of her need to speak out while also doing good: she became the director of the Bluegrass Rape Crisis Center. Still, the burden of nine years of silence was not alleviated by her work alone, and so Mae created her blog.

When she began writing the blog, Mae assumed she would only garner the attention of a few readers, mostly friends and family who shared her worldview. Most of her blog content is comprised of those topics that tend to not make polite dinner conversation: politics, religion, sexuality, the sex industry, and everything in between. She was surprised to find, then, that the bulk of her readers are actually twenty-something females, many of whom look to her as a sort of role model. She feels honored to be embraced by these emerging feminists that remind her so much of her younger self, and she has never quite gotten used to it. They write her privately asking for advice or telling her how much she inspires them. It is that feedback that, more than anything else, lets her know that she is on the right track.

GETTING STARTED: ADVICE FROM
ONE BLOGGER TO ANOTHER

When I asked Mae what advice she would give others who might want to create a blog, she suggested that potential authors:

- Set aside a block of time to write every day and stick to it; this is the easiest way to be accountable.
- Limit how much time you spend on your entries. It is very easy to get stuck in a permanent state of editing if you don't reel yourself in.

- Be yourself. Your unique voice is what makes your readers seek you out.
- You don't need to be a techie to do this.
- Use free tools like Twitter and Facebook to promote your blog.

Mae writes every morning when she first wakes, from 5 AM to 6 AM. Rather than spending the entire day reconsidering her every word and endlessly editing, Mae allows herself only that one hour to write, and then she walks away. She uses a free blog, hosted on Blogger, and simply plugs her content into a ready-made template as she creates it. As she writes, she tries to frequently remind herself of her initial intent in starting the blog, which was to write from her heart about things that matter to her. She tries not to worry about what her audience will think, freely admitting to me that in those entries where she has succumbed to some imagined pressure, it has resulted in entries she is not proud of. Her readers don't like those posts any more than she does: on those rare occasions when she has departed from her most authentic and genuine self, readers have not engaged with her work, revealed by their low rates of comments and links to her posts. Mae shares links to her blog on her other social networking accounts on a daily basis and so a typical day will find her posts liked and shared or re-tweeted repeatedly via Facebook and Twitter. She actually had to create a Facebook page for *Plain Jane Activism* because friends' requests from readers of her blogs became too overwhelming on her personal account.

OTHER THINGS TO CONSIDER

Your blog, like Mae's, is a part of yourself that you will put out into the world for anyone to read and respond to. Your writing may inspire strong reactions in your readers, whether positive or negative; this is especially true if you plan to write about potentially divisive topics, such as those addressed in *Plain Jane Activism*. The following are questions potential bloggers may want to consider before undertaking blogging. In theory, your blog is one place where you should have complete autonomy to say what you feel, but the reality is that there will be an audience of readers whom your words will impact. You should consider the various possible ramifications of that impact and whether you could tolerate the outcome. Ask yourself:

- How will your family feel about your blog?
- Would your employer support your blogging efforts if they were to discover them? Could you be penalized or punished for the stance you take?
- Are you strong enough to withstand criticism from strangers?
- Will you have to censor yourself as you write? Will you censor the comments of others?

• Would you accept paid advertising, should you be approached by a potential sponsor?

Mae makes sure to try and keep her blog and her work separate. She only writes on her own time, never at work, and is sure to have a very visible disclaimer on her blog that assures the reader that her views do not represent any of the views of the organizations she is affiliated with. Still, she works in such a progressive environment that she believes that the board members she answers to in her role as director of the Rape Crisis Center would likely personally support every blog that she's written. She describes her workplace as an environment where her colleagues talk about these issues openly and in which they constantly consider their own role in the social justice movement. She says, "We talk pretty frankly because how can we not? I work in a rape crisis center. It is going to be raw sometimes." Still, she acknowledges that may not be the case for everyone and concedes that if she were still alumni director at Berea College, she might not be permitted to write her blog, even if it was personal, because it might alienate too many people that had different beliefs.

Mae has an incredibly supportive family, and they have never second-guessed her choice to blog or her choice of blog content. Her husband remains her biggest fan, and her mother gladly reads her posts, even though English is her second language and it takes her much longer than it would if it were written in her native Thai. Even in the face of such acceptance and love, there have been tough emotional moments she did not anticipate when she first started writing. When Mae wrote in her blog about her being bullied as a child or about being abused by her high school boyfriend, two subjects she had kept secret from her mother at the time that they were occurring, her mother was deeply saddened by the new knowledge. Mae hadn't considered that her mother might feel responsible for these secrets once she learned of them, but that is exactly what happened, and Mae found herself in the unexpected position of having to comfort her mother.

The majority of Mae's readers have responded positively to her writing. In fact, she says that even when they do disagree with her, they have been afraid to be negative in their responses, cloaking their criticisms in polite disclaimers, such as, "Mae, I just want you to know that I really respect you and the work that you do in the blog BUT. . . ." Typically they only let her know their feelings via private e-mail. Mae always encourages them to respond publicly in the comments section of her blog, welcoming the opportunity to engage in friendly discussion and debate, but her readers usually refrain from doing so. Mae doesn't believe in censorship of herself or others, and so even if a reader were to leave a comment on her post that was blatantly racist or sexist, for example, she believes she would leave it posted, allowing it to serve as a talking point.

For Mae, *Plain Jane Activism* is a "daily project to commit to simple, seemingly insignificant, acts that won't earn anyone a Nobel Prize, but might somehow encourage intentional living and a deeper investment in the world." She sees a connection between her blog and the work she does training bystanders to fight sexual violence at the Bluegrass Rape Crisis Center or her volunteer work with the Human Rights Commission, fighting to pass a local ordinance to have sexual orientation protected. Each of these efforts has the same aim, which is to engage regular everyday citizens to be more active in creating change.

BIBLIOGRAPHY

Armstrong, Jerome, and Markos Moulitsas Zúniga. 2006. *Crashing the Gate: Netroots, Grassroots, And The Rise Of People-Powered Politics*. White River Junction, VT: Chelsea Green Pub. Co.

Moulitsas Zúniga, Markos. 2008. *Taking on the System: Rules for Radical Change in a Digital Era*. New York: Celebra.

Chapter Two

Creating Opportunities for Women on the Web

A Mother's Quest

Denise Powell

I started my online venture in November 2012, about six months after having my first baby. It was then that the smoke cleared from the first few months of motherhood, and I was ready and able to allow my idea to come into fruition. The Voices Project www.thevoicesproject.org is a nonjudgmental online venue where women and girls of any age, education level, or background can share their personal stories and observations through poetry in order to promote social change. I have written poetry for most of my life and have an extensive editorial background from working at publishing companies in New York. I have also traveled to forty-two different countries around the world throughout my life, although over half of those I visited during a year abroad in 2008. During my travels, I observed the various roles of women around the globe, which inspired me to start The Voices Project. For example, in the rural villages of West and Southern Africa, the women of the family were not only the caretakers of the children, but they were also very skilled at making things (crafts, jewelry, clothing). They were also good business people, selling their handmade goods at local markets with their babies strapped to their backs. Also in Africa and other areas of the world, including India and Southeast Asia, I observed that when women were in charge of the money for the family, the money went to basic needs for the family. Often, when the men were in charge of the money, especially in rural areas of the world, it often went to alcohol or gambling. Women also seemed to value education for their children, even if it made more financial sense to have the child work instead of go to school. It was the women who appeared

9

to carry much of the responsibility in the family. Those who managed their own businesses or were taking classes to learn a trade, spoke positively about their futures and the future of their children. We can all learn from the stories of women like these, and others.

I believe that if you empower a woman to speak her voice there is a chance for positive change in her family and community. Harnessing the increasing opportunities the web provides while combining my academic training and career experience allowed me to follow my passion—to bring forward the literary work of women and girls all over the globe. As the project evolves, I am seeking a combination of microloans, click-through dollars, and other enabling technologies to help me determine how women writers can not only be empowered, but also make money through publishing their creative works on my website. The Voices Project now has over seventy-five contributors and more submissions come in everyday.

The web provides all the tools you'll need to get started with your own online project, a lot of them free. You do not have to spend a lot of money to begin. You have at your fingertips a way to:

- Design and launch your own website.
- Advertise and partner with other online companies, blogs, magazines, and forums.
- Build your own online community.
- Make some money, depending on your project/business.
- Have flexibility and work from home.
- Find work-life balance with young children.

Many people are aware that being a mother with young children while trying to keep a sense of your own identity or uphold a career is very hard work. For those mothers who have the desire to have a more flexible schedule in order to spend more time with their children, while still fulfilling their own entrepreneurial visions, I have a few tips on how to get started based on my experience.

THE LOGISTICS: HOW TO GET STARTED WITH YOUR ONLINE VENTURE

Start with an Idea

No matter what your idea for a new business or creative endeavor may be, I believe it's important to not only use your current skill set, but to follow what you're passionate about (as mentioned above). For me, it was poetry and women's issues. Identify what it is for you and how you can turn that into a product, services, or a creative project. Write down your vision and how you see it coming into fruition. What will it look like? What problem will it solve for people?

Create an Online Presence

There are a few web-hosting companies out there that charge a small monthly fee for hosting your website. They provide templates that you can use to design your own website with your very own personal flare. Most sites are very user-friendly, have a plethora of designs to choose from, and step-by-step instructions on how to create one. You can also choose an option to create a new e-mail address through a package on the same site. For example, the one I created was editors@thevoicesproject.org. You can create one or multiple e-mails to accompany your website. I also have info@thevoicesproject.org to direct people who have any general questions regarding my project. To look more professional, it's a good idea to have an e-mail address with your company name after @, rather than a Yahoo or Google address. I currently use Weebly for The Voices Project and have had a good experience.

There are a few notable companies to choose from that I have either used myself or for which I have heard good reviews. I've noted the free resources below, along with a couple that require a monthly fee:

Free hosting sites:

1. Weebly (http://www.weebly.com)
2. Blogger (http://www.blogger.com)
3. WordPress (www.wordpress.org). Note: you may need to know a little more about graphic design or Photoshop to use this site. If you are seeking to, and have the skills to do more with your site, this one may be for you.

Sites that charge a small fee:

1. GoDaddy (www.godaddy.com)
2. Network Solutions (http://www.networksolutions.com)

Note: For creative/crafty projects, like making clothes or selling a handmade product, you can create your own store on etsy.com.

Advertise Your Online Project

Now that you have your website launched, it's time to get the word out. Here are a few steps you can take to drive traffic to your website:

1. **Send an e-mail to friends and family with a *brief* description of you project with a link to your website.** Your family and friends make up a key network of people who know you and want to support your project. Ask them straight-out to post it on their social media sites and encourage their own networks to check out your website. Depending on the type of project you have, research various online venues on which you can advertise.

2. **Create a social media page dedicated to your business.** Create a Facebook page exclusively for your business. Include details on your mission and a brief description of what you do. Also create a Twitter page for your business. Post everyday if you can. There are ways to link to your social media sites from your website if you also have a blog on your website that you post on regularly. That way, you only need to post once as your website blog post feeds into Facebook and Twitter. Cross-promote your business on your personal social media sites.

3. **Partner with other companies of interest.** Reaching out to colleagues in a similar industry with a common goal is a good way to advertise. Do your research before you reach out and make sure partnering with a certain company will not be a conflict of interest for either party. Often, the owners of other sites will be happy to exchange advertising on their site for advertising on yours, as sort of a cross-promotional effort by both parties. It's a win-win for everyone involved. For example, I created a "resources" page on The Voices Project site, and list all my partners on that page, sometimes including logos or widgets provided by those partnering sites. In turn, they provide me with a free classified ad on their site or include me on their list of resources.

4. **Post a classified ad.** Again, depending on what the focus of your project is, you can look into other venues, or online magazines, that offer classified listings for websites like yours. To advertise my "call for entries," I found that NewPages.com was a great venue that offered me an option to post a free simple classified ad. For new moms, *Literary Mama* also offers something similar. A lot of sites may offer a simple free ad, or you may need to pay to post an ad with a logo or an ad with more verbiage. Find sites that will support your niche and see what they offer in terms of classifieds.

5. **Using Google AdWords** (http://www.adwords.google.com). Creating an account with Google AdWords is fairly easy. (Note: If you choose to use AdWords, proceed with caution. If you do not monitor your account closely, especially the first few days, you are at risk of paying more money than you bargained for. You can always change the amount.) AdWords agents are available to help if you need it. If you

do not have a little money to spare for advertising, AdWords may not be for you. First, you create an account online. Then, create your first ad campaign by taking the following steps:

    a. Choosing where your ad will appear on your site
    b. Decide on a budget, or how much you're willing to pay each time someone clicks on your ad (I recommend starting small—maybe 10 cents per click)
    c. Pick key words that can help your ad show in searches. Agents are available to walk you through the process if need be. Do an experiment and see the kind of response you get. You can check your stats on your AdWords account. You can always pause the advertising should you feel it's not working they way you want it to.

Making Money

There are a few ways you can earn a little money by taking advantage of advertising opportunities on your website. Bear in mind, you'll need to do your research and really learn what it is your specific audience will find valuable in terms of ads you place on your website. To get the most click-through, you'll want to test the ads and note what does not work, and keep refining your strategy. Advertising may not earn you big money, but it can certainly help, especially if you focus on your audience and keep your ads targeted.

1. **Use Targeting Advertising with Google AdSense** (http://www. google.com/adsense/). The Google AdSense program allows you to make money advertising on your site by placing targeted text ads generated by Google on your pages. They appear in rectangular boxes running down the side or across the bottom of a web page. First, you'll need to create an AdSense account. This is very simple and you just need to follow the step-by-step instructions provided by Google Ad-Sense. Once you are signed up, you can place your ads on your page. Weebly allows you to drag and drop the Google AdSense box onto each page so you can place the ads where you want. You'll link your bank account directly to AdSense and any money you make will go direct to that account. You can monitor your earnings on your account page. Keep in mind, this is not a way to make big money, but you may make some. With The Voices Project, I am experimenting to see if I may be able to divvy up what I make from AdSense to my contributors as a way to help them earn something too.

2. **Promote an affiliate product on your site.** Joining another company's affiliate program is another way to get started with Internet advertising. Affiliate links are not ads; they allow you to make money by promoting someone else's product. You have an opportunity to earn a commission each time someone you've referred makes a purchase. Posting a banner on your site that links to the affiliate site or publishing a newsletter article about their product can help encourage sales. Do your research to find a program that best fits with your site. Different affiliate programs offer different payout options. Some, for example, offer 10 percent commission for each sale, while others pay up to 50 percent. For more on this option, check out the following links:

   Amazon Associates (https://affiliate-program.amazon.com/)
   iTunes Partner Program (www.apple.com/itunes/affiliates/)
   The Affiliates Directory (http://www.affiliatesdirectory.com/)
   Refer It (http://www.ecommerce-guide.com/)

3. **Sign up for a blog-specific ad program.** If you have a blog, you can sign up to feature blog-specific ads on your site. You'll want to think about the types of ads your audience will find interesting and valuable. A couple notable affiliates follow:

   Amazon Associates (https://affiliate-program.amazon.com/)
   Crisp Ads (http://ww38.crispad.com/)

4. **Providing products and services.** Use a "lean start-up" model, an incremental and customer-interactive approach that lets you gain a deep personal firsthand understanding of your potential customers' needs before locking into a specific path and a precise product. Before spending money building your product, first test the product or services to make sure they may be marketable by offering them before they are available. Build, test and search for a business model while iterating and evolving based on customer feedback. The goal is to test, refine, and scale ideas fast and affordably. The key questions to ask at every step:

   - What insight do I need to move forward?
   - What is a simple test I can run to get that insight?
   - How do I design an experiment to run that simple test?

GENERAL TIPS FOR MOTHERS WITH YOUNG CHILDREN SEEKING TO LAUNCH AN ENTREPRENEURIAL VENTURE

The following are tips for women who are seeking a work-life balance while also having young children at home. Not all women have the same goals for their life and career. These tips are meant to help guide women who have the desire to start a new creative or business venture from home while they raise young children. The first three are ones most new moms have heard before. I think they are worth repeating.

1. **Do something for yourself everyday, no matter how small.** Take a class, go for a walk, sit alone with a cup of tea. Clear your head. Ideas will start to flow if you have a good daily rhythm and can get small breaks from your child. I know I am a better and more present mother when I am able to get breaks and have something of my own.

2. **Get help with your child if you can.** Even one day a week may help you gain back some of your identity as you remain immersed in the all-consuming role of motherhood.

3. **Get some sleep.** If you're running on empty or are burnt out, you likely won't be motivated to start your online venture.

4. **Make a list of what you want and don't want out of a career.** Once the baby is on a schedule and you are feeling comfortable with motherhood and have a handle on it, take twenty to thirty minutes for yourself during the baby's naptime to write down what it is you want. Be specific. Focus on what it is you *want*, rather than what your skills are. Do you want to work part-time? Make your own hours? It's good to home in on what it is you really want and don't want. How can starting your own online company help you get to those goals?

5. **Reconnect with your passion.** When you focus on what it is you truly feel passionate about, you home in on what truly makes you happy. Life's too short to ignore what really drives you.

6. **Brainstorm ideas for your online venture.** Once you've determined what you want, start using your time to brainstorm ideas for your online venture. Ask yourself these questions: What will it take to get started? How many hours per week are you able to work on it? Who can help with the baby? If no one can help, consider using nap times and after the baby is in bed. How viable is the idea, and how might you test it without spending money? Who can you partner with? How will you advertise? Is this something that has potential to turn into a money-maker for you, even if it's a small amount?

7. **Get your elevator speech down.** Once you're determined what your project will be, come up with two to three sentences or a mission statement for your venture. Keep it short, to the point, and very clear. This is your new endeavor that you are excited about. Make others excited too, and make them believe in it as you do.

TAKE ADVANTAGE OF TECHNOLOGY

This bold new world of the Internet creates opportunities that we never had even five or ten years ago. Women with young children have the ability to create their own business online and run it from home.

Raising a child is one of the most important tasks a woman will ever undertake and parenthood is not to be taken lightly. It's a tough job. For me, personally, I knew that in order to be a better mother and be more present with my child, I also had to be in touch with myself and have something of my own I was working toward to create positive change in the world and set an example for my daughter. Through creating The Voices Project, I am able to manage my work from home, during the hours I make for myself. At times it is hard and I still have many goals I wish to achieve with regards to the future of the project. It's a work in progress, like many other things in life. The present day is an interesting time to live, when we can drive our future and create our own outcomes by taking advantage of the technology at our fingertips. Use it to create yours.

Keep Up the Momentum

Life gets busy, especially for people with a family. Set aside thirty minutes, at the very least, every day, to post on your website blog or social media site, reach out to a potential partner, or talk to someone about your project. Think about what you often do in thirty minutes that seems a time-waster. Instead of going to fold laundry or answer e-mails, put that on hold. Ask yourself, "If this is the only thing I accomplish today, will I be satisfied with my day?" If you prioritize properly, there is no need to multitask. You don't always need to be focused on finishing everything. Focus on one attainable task at a time, so as not to get overwhelmed.

If you have an idea, and a little time set aside, why not test it with the online tools available to you? When you're ready to begin, these tools can help make your life a little easier by allowing you to work from home and still be attentive to your family.

Chapter Three

Girls' Human Rights and Virtual Empowerment

Celebrating the First International Day of the Girl with a Virtual Summit

Emily Bent

Over the last twenty years, the girls' human rights movement has continued to gain momentum and recognition at the United Nations. From the girl child's early emergence in the Convention on the Rights of the Child to her more recent identification at the Fifty-first Session of the Commission on the Status of Women, she remains a powerful figure in the human rights community. On December 19, 2011, the United Nations General Assembly adopted Resolution 66/170, declaring October 11 as the International Day of the Girl Child. October 11, 2012 (or 10.11.12) marked the first commemoration of this historic day. This chapter documents the online celebration of the first International Day of the Girl vis-à-vis the Day of the Girl (DOTG) virtual summit.

The DOTG summit is a virtual event that brings thousands of girls and girl-serving organizations together to celebrate the International Day of the Girl. Developed by Sage Girl (n.d.), a nonprofit organization that delivers girl-positive programs to the community, in collaboration with iTwixie (n.d.), the DOTG virtual summit engages online technologies to connect girls around the world. This chapter details the creation of the virtual summit website, and identifies several key partnerships, strategies, and activities associated with this signature initiative. It also illustrates how girls and girls' organizations utilize the Internet to advance girls' human rights in their communities.

THE STORY OF THE INTERNATIONAL DAY OF THE GIRL

The United Nations adopted Resolution 66/170 on December 19, 2011, declaring October 11 as the International Day of the Girl Child. This day, the General Assembly (2011) noted, "would help galvanize worldwide enthusiasm for goals to better girls' lives, providing an opportunity for them to show leadership and reach their full potential" (para. 33). Four years prior, members of PLAN International (Canada-based children's rights organization) and School Girls Unite (Washington, D.C.–based girls' advocacy group) began mobilizing support for this particular resolution (Bahr 2012). More than one hundred countries joined this original campaign to petition the United Nations General Assembly to establish an annual event dedicated to girls around the world. According to School Girls Unite (2013), their campaign was about "highlighting, celebrating, discussing, and advancing girls lives and opportunities around the globe . . . [because] October 11 is not just a day, but a movement" (para. 1). International Day of the Girl advocates sought to not only celebrate girls as powerful agents of change, but to also recognize the unique struggles and challenges faced by girls in their everyday lives.

Because of the successful campaigning of School Girls Unite, PLAN International, and many other organizations, the General Assembly (2011) agreed to observe the International Day of the Girl Child every year beginning in 2012 and to "raise awareness of the situation of girls around the world" (para. 5). In the formal declaration, the General Assembly (2011) also recognized:

> The empowerment and investment in girls . . . as well as the meaningful participation of girls . . . is key in breaking the cycle of discrimination and violence and in promoting and protecting the full and effective enjoyment of their human rights, and recognizing also that empowering girls requires their active participation in decision-making processes and the active support and engagement of . . . the wider community (para. 3).

It is with these specific objectives in mind that Sage Girl decided to organize a virtual event to commemorate this historic day. Because the Internet provides access to girls around the world at little to no cost, we opted to create the virtual summit in an effort to establish a vibrant online community of girls' rights activists. In the next section, I outline our goals for the Day of the Girl virtual summit and describe key partnerships and strategies that ensured its success.

CREATING THE DAY OF THE GIRL VIRTUAL SUMMIT

The Day of the Girl (DOTG) virtual summit is a signature initiative of Sage Girl. To create the virtual summit, we partnered with iTwixie, a girls' organization that provides a safe and empowering virtual space for tween girls. Throughout the length of the project, Sage Girl and iTwixie executive directors shared the administrative and creative responsibilities associated with the virtual summit. We likewise collaborated with School Girls Unite, the lead organization in the U.S.-based campaign for the Day of the Girl. Because School Girls Unite owned www.dayofthegirl.org, it was necessary to ensure visual consistency between the Day of the Girl campaign website and the virtual summit site, www.dayofthegirlsummit.com.

Our mission for the virtual summit was to bring thousands of girls and girl-serving organizations together to celebrate the International Day of the Girl on October 11. To accomplish this task, we identified the following goals and objectives:

- Inspire and empower girls in the celebration of the first International Day of the Girl
- Provide safe virtual space for girls to connect with one another across the globe
- Raise awareness and build momentum for girls' human rights using virtual technologies
- Garner 10,000–25,000 virtual summit participants between August 1 and October 11
- Partner with at least twenty-five different girls' organizations to promote the virtual summit
- Produce a sixty-minute live video broadcast on the virtual summit site on October 11
- Increase DOTG publicity via social media (Facebook and Twitter)
- Secure corporate sponsorship and donations to underwrite cost of virtual summit

Based on our shared goals, we then negotiated individual and shared responsibilities for the virtual summit. Sage Girl managed participant registration, website content development and monitoring, social media posting, organizational partnership outreach, video solicitation, and e-mail communications. iTwixie created the marketing materials (DOTG avatar, web banners, ads, etc.), managed the website structure, secured technologies necessary for the live video broadcast and online chats, and produced the DOTG events map. Sage Girl and iTwixie also collaborated extensively in the weeks and months leading up to October 11. As previously noted, the virtual summit website mirrored the style of the Day of the Girl campaign site owned by

School Girls Unite. School Girls Unite in turn contributed social media access and a Day of the Girl e-mail account to ensure recognition of virtual summit activities. They also posted a link to the virtual summit on the Day of the Girl homepage to increase traffic to the summit site.

To build momentum for the DOTG virtual summit, we contacted national and international girls' organizations to encourage their support and participation in the site activities. A record number of forty-four girl-serving organizations joined the virtual summit celebration. Partner organizations promoted the virtual summit to their networks via social media, organizational webpages, and e-mail outreach. We in turn featured partner organization logos on the virtual summit website.

Partners included: Alice Paul Institute, Bella Abzug Leadership Institute, CALM Yoga, Chatham University, Circle of 6, Congregation of Our Lady of Charity of the Good Shepherd, Day of the Girl, Equality NOW, Girls for a Change, Girls Coalition of Southwestern Pennsylvania, Girls Inc. of NW Oregon, Girls Learn International, Girl Museum, Girls Rock NC, Girls on the Run, Girlvana Yoga, The Grail, Hardy Girls Healthy Women, International Council of Jewish Women, Inner Grace Dance, Institute of the Blessed Virgin Mary, ITVS, iTwixie, Loretto Community, One Simple Wish, National Council of Jewish Women, New Moon Girl Media, Say No UNiTE, School Girls Unite, She's the First, SPARK Summit, Strong Women, Strong Girls, 10 x 10, The Line Campaign, The Salvation Army, The Warhol Museum, UN Women, V-Girls, V-Day, Women and Girls Foundation, Women and Girls Lead, Women in Learning and Leadership at the College of New Jersey, Working Group on Girls, and the Women Worldwide Initiative.

A select group of girls' organizations also contributed funds to support the virtual summit; these organizations included Girls Learn International, School Girls Unite, and the Working Group on Girls.

Lastly to increase publicity and enthusiasm for the virtual summit, we organized a series of tweet-ups, Facebook postings, and shared tweets to direct participants to the DOTG virtual summit site. From October 1 to October 11, we tweeted and updated Facebook posts every few hours. These technologies allowed us to direct the virtual summit narrative and engage girls in our online activities (described in detail in part 4 of this book). It was also important to be consistent on all of our social media forums, ensuring a coherent message across technologies. Here are a few sample tweets and Facebook posts from October 1, 2012:

- 12:00 PM: Check out @Bacheletjeria of @UN_Women message for #girls, launching #11DaysofAction! http://dayofthegirlsummit.com/michelle-bachelets-message-for-the-1st-day-of-the-girl/
- 1:00 PM: It's Day 1 of #11DaysofAction! What does #dayofthegirl mean to you? Join us tonight at 7 PM ET www.DayoftheGirlSummit.com

- 2:00 PM: @Bacheletjeria of @UN_Women believes in #girls, do you? Join us at 7 PM ET of #11DaysofAction for #girls www. DayoftheGirlSummit.com
- 4:00 PM: Join us for #11DaysofAction! What does #dayofthegirl mean to you? Chat LIVE with us at 7PM ET www.DayoftheGirlSummit.com
- 6:45 PM: #11DaysofAction chat begins in 15 minutes at www. DayoftheGirlSummit.com What does #dayofthegirl mean to you?
- 7:00 PM: #11DaysofAction chat begins NOW at www. DayoftheGirlSummit.com What does #dayofthegirl mean to you?

Collectively, these technological efforts drew over eleven thousand participants from twenty-six countries from October 1 to October 11. On October 11, the virtual summit also attracted three thousand three hundred fifty unique visitors and the #DayoftheGirl hashtag trended twice on Twitter. We also secured hundreds of new Twitter followers and Facebook "likes" on the Day of the Girl pages.

The next section details some of the girl-centered activities organized as part of the DOTG virtual summit. These online activities served to propel the DOTG message using social media technologies and other Internet-based discussion forums.

GIRL-CENTERED DIRECTIVES AND RESPONSES

The virtual summit featured a wide variety of virtual activities designed to elevate the voices and needs of girls. These activities allowed girls to share their voices and experiences as well as speak to the importance of the day. To participate in these activities, visitors formally registered as virtual summit members. Registration included the first name, e-mail address, and location of the participant. Once approved as a virtual summit participant, members could post comments on the website and take part in the DOTG virtual activities. Sage Girl monitored the registration process to ensure privacy protection for minors.

In 2012, some of the signature activities included:

Day of the Girl Challenge: series of six interactive activities designed to promote the virtual summit and help raise awareness about girls' human rights. Girls changed their profile pictures to the DOTG avatar, shared information about the summit on Facebook and Twitter, and made announcements in their schools and local communities. After completing a challenge, girls completed an online form submitted to virtual summit organizers. A sample copy of the DOTG challenges included:

1. Change your avatar on social media sites (Facebook and Twitter) to the DOTG pic.
2. Tell 5 friends about the Day of the Girl virtual summit.
3. Tell us why you think the DOTG rocks! Submit a paragraph, upload a video or send in a picture or drawing.

11 Days of Action Campaign: virtual summit members took part in daily online chats (October 1–October 11 from 7:00 PM EST to 8:00 PM EST) hosted by partner organizations. The chats focused on critical issues for girls around the world such as education, ending violence against girls, and the impact of the media on girls' self-esteem. We used RumbleChat for the online chat feature, which costs $19.95 per month for unlimited chats. Registered summit members used e-mail accounts, Facebook pages or Twitter handles to join the chat room. Partner organizations hosting the online chat then posted questions to participants around the selected topic. This feature provided summit participants with a sense of community and collective action on behalf of girls. Sample chat date topics included:

1. October 1: What does the DOTG mean to girls? Hosted by Working Group on Girls at the United Nations
2. October 3: Girls Activism and Leadership, Hosted by Girls for a Change and SPARK Summit
3. October 9: Girls Ending Violence Against Girls, Hosted by the United Nations Say No UNiTE campaign

Live Chats and Video Broadcast: On October 11, 2012 at 7:00 PM EST, the virtual summit site went live with prerecorded and real-time videos featuring DOTG messages and celebrations from around the world. Virtual summit members watched the video broadcast and live-chatted with other girls on the homepage of the site. Girls from seven countries submitted short videos (30 seconds to 2:30 minutes) to express what the first International Day of the Girl meant to them. We used Google+ to stream the prerecorded and live videos (originally uploaded to YouTube); we also used this technology to incorporate a girl reporter who introduced each of the videos and provided commentary throughout the broadcast. This component of the site reached a global audience with girls from twenty-six countries viewing and commenting on the DOTG celebrations. Notably, former executive director of UN Women, Michelle Bachelet, produced a series of promotional videos to launch the DOTG virtual summit.

Proclamation Pledge Project: In partnership with School Girls Unite, virtual summit participants signed the DOTG Proclamation Pledge to petition their city or town to proclaim October 11 as the International Day of the Girl. The Proclamation Pledge was featured on the homepage of the site and participants joining the project received a *Day of the Girl Toolkit* with step-by-step instructions on how to petition the town council. School Girls Unite also provided one-on-one support.

Girls Hall of Fame: featured page on the virtual summit site that shared the biographies of twenty-four girl-activists from around the world. The biographies included their stories of struggle and triumph for social change; virtual summit members responded to questions posted about these inspirational girls.

Shout Outs: Girls left messages to one another and posted about what the DOTG meant to them on the virtual summit homepage. This feature showcased the participants' enthusiasm for the virtual summit as an online celebratory tool. Sample posts included:

> "I love this site. It makes me feel like more and more girls are getting appreciated for their strengths and contributions to society!!"—mgg2012
>
> "Girls Rock! This is an amazing summit!"—tarasom
>
> "I attended the virtual event last night and it was great to hear from other girls all around the globe. We have the power to make a difference!"—Megs
>
> "A big SHOUT OUT to the team that hosted this live party. You have set the stage for the Day of the Girl to become viral!"—LisaML
>
> "I want to give a shout out to everyone who put tireless hours into this. YOU ROCK! You people did this for us! We salute you!"—The Husner
>
> "This is a wonderful idea and such a proactive use of technology!"—amawhite

Global Map of DOTG Celebrations: members shared the details about their planned DOTG celebrations on the site's events map. Participants completed an online form describing their plans for the DOTG and then we added it to our virtual map. The virtual map visually captured the global scope of the day with a total of 245 DOTG parties registered in thirty-nine countries. On the website, visitors could view a map of the world with small pins stuck in the areas where a DOTG celebration took place. Because of privacy issues, we shared basic details on the location of each event.

UGG Boot Giveaway: UGG Australia donated 100 pairs of classic UGG boots to virtual summit participants. Participants could enter the UGG Boot Giveaway by registering for the virtual summit, completing DOTG challenges, posting shout outs on the homepage, and taking part in the 11 Days of Action. Winners were announced on October 12, 2012.

The first annual Day of the Girl virtual summit was a terrific success by many accounts. It proved to be an innovative and cost-effective use of technology that not only celebrated the first International Day of the Girl, but also empowered girls across the globe. The following underscores a few key accomplishments:

- Site garnered 11,372 visitors between October 1 and October 11 with 3,350 unique visits on October 11 from twenty-six countries
- 2,400 posts received from the 11 Days of Action online chats
- 1,623 girls entered for a chance to win a pair of classic UGG boots
- #dayofthegirl trended twice on Twitter on October 11
- 519 girls posted "shout outs" on the virtual summit homepage
- 322 DOTG Challenges were completed by virtual summit members
- 245 DOTG events were registered on the site from 39 countries
- 207 Proclamation Pledges were taken by summit participants
- Over 20 prerecorded videos were submitted by girls sharing the importance of the day; submissions were received from Canada, India, Jamaica, Mexico, Mozambique, Sweden, and the United States

Given these accomplishments, the next section outlines "next steps" in terms of preparing for a stronger virtual summit in October 2013. Our goals include enhancing the technological capacities of the site, continuing to successfully leverage social media to propel the DOTG narrative, and facilitating additional opportunities for online participation.

CONCLUDING THOUGHTS AND NEXT STEPS: INTERNATIONAL DAY OF THE GIRL 2013

The virtual summit is about bringing attention to girls' needs and capacities, and in doing so, affirming the necessity of their human rights. After the success of our pilot summit, Sage Girl intends to exponentially grow this initiative over the next three to five years. We are prepared to build a more expansive project for the 2013 International Day of the Girl that will:

- *Increase the number of girl participants from 10,000 to 100,000* by strategically targeting outreach to international girls' organizations, expanding participation numbers via social media, translating our website into multiple languages, and investing in our web presence to increase traffic.
- *Enhance the quality of web-based activities and in-person initiatives* by creating more digital images, video, and content around girls' human rights to propel the virtual summit narrative. We will also develop content tailored to specific audiences, and increase the number of featured live events, allowing us to expand to multiple locations to feature in-person celebrations.

- *Brand www.dayofthegirlsummit.com as "the place" to go to celebrate girls' human rights year-round* by facilitating topical discussion groups using video and organization presentations, host content across multiple platforms to attract girls' participation and diverse girls organizations, identify additional giveaways and other small incentives to increase retention, and allocate resources for measurement and evaluation via quantitative and qualitative metrics.
- *Secure diverse revenue streams* to support the technological advancement and enhancement of the virtual summit brand.

Our intention is to build upon the strengths and achievements of the first virtual summit to attract a more diverse and expanded global constituency. We look to build from the momentum of the first DOTG to ensure that the 2012 virtual summit is the first of many. Toward this end, our signature activities will be enhanced to better accommodate global audiences and participants (via language translation), and we will leverage our partnerships with girls' organizations to increase traffic to the site. Our principal goal is to make the virtual summit *the* gathering place to celebrate the International Day of the Girl. As women and girls continue to break barriers via the Internet, I conclude this chapter with the words of a virtual summit participant, krislipscombe: "A shout out from a Canadian girl trying to make it in the sometimes-tough world of sports media, specifically hockey. Cheers to girls and women around the world who are breaking their own gender barriers!" (Day of the Girl Summit, 2012).

REFERENCES

Bahr, Anna. 2012. "Young Feminists Have Their Day: The U.N. Recognizes Girl Power." *Ms. Magazine*, Fall.

Day of the Girl Virtual Summit. 2012. http://dayofthegirlsummit.com.

iTwixie. (n.d.) http://www.itwixie.com .

Sage Girl. (n.d.) http://www.sagegirl.org .

School Girls Unite. 2013. *Day of the Girl*. (May 1) http://www.dayofthegirl.org/about .

United Nations General Assembly. 2011. *UN Resolution 66/170. International Day of the Girl Child*. New York: Author.

———. 2011. *Draft Text Approved by Third Committee Recognizes Youth as 'Key Agents for Social Change', Affirms Investment in Youth Crucial for Sustainable Development*. New York: Author.

Chapter Four

Establishing Online Business Identities

How Female Small Business Owners Use Social Media to Market Their Business

Kara Poe Alexander

Social media have rapidly transformed our culture. Networks such as Facebook, Twitter, LinkedIn, and YouTube have altered how we get our news, how we understand the world around us, and how we interact, collaborate, and connect with others. Social media also offer new opportunities for businesses, nonprofit organizations, and government agencies to present themselves to the public, connecting with a larger audience more quickly, more efficiently, and for less money than ever before. Animal shelters, for instance, can post videos of dogs needing adoption to YouTube, in hopes of stirring the heartstrings of potential pet owners. Retail clothing stores and photographers can post pictures to Pinterest or their blog to entice returning and new clients. Politicians can use Facebook or Twitter to connect with their constituents, perhaps by linking to bills they've sponsored. In sum, groups such as these can use the Internet and social media to develop a professional image online, or an "online business identity" (OBI).

An online business identity is the impression a business conveys to their audience through online tools and platforms, including social networking sites, a website, and a blog. It is established both by (1) the business's engagement with the Internet and (2) the users' (clients, customers, audiences) online interactions with or about the business. This two-way approach contrasts greatly with traditional marketing approaches where a business's professional image was determined mostly by what it said about itself, or what a business led people to think about their brand (Turner and Shah 2011,

13). Dialogue between a business and its audience was mostly one-way, and the audience either accepted or rejected the image the business was putting forward but had no real say in the business's image or identity.

Social media, however, alters this dynamic by making a business's OBI a participatory endeavor. Through sites like TripAdvisor, Yelp, Facebook, and Urbanspoon, customers now engage in two-way conversations with businesses, offering feedback, participation, and response. Because users now influence the way a business is perceived, it is extremely important for businesses to convey a transparent, honest, and respectful OBI, a clear picture of who you are and what you do.

Although businesses recognize the potential of social media for online marketing, small businesses have been much slower to embrace these outlets (Bakeman and Hanson 2012; SMB Group 2012). For one, small businesses often do not have the funding, resources, or expertise to design and implement an online marketing plan or to hire someone to do it for them. In addition, gender, race, and age also appear to influence one's level of engagement with social media marketing. Women, for instance, are opening businesses at 1.5 times the national average, but these businesses receive fewer small business loans (Arora 2013), are smaller, and are in more "slower-growth industries" than male-led businesses (SBA Office of Advocacy 2013, 2). Moreover, a greater percentage of women-led businesses are run by minority women and/or older women who may not have the technological skills, financial resources, or time to develop these kinds of online business identities (NWBC 2012).

Yet social media also has the potential to level the playing field, offering smaller businesses opportunities to develop an online business identity that before were only available to larger organizations. In this chapter, I therefore consider how small businesses might establish, manage, and gain greater control over their online business identities so that they effectively engage customers, seize networking and marketing opportunities, and grow the business. Specifically, I explore the reasons female small business use social media and their strategies for doing so. I end with advice for how small businesses can better construct a professional online business identity.

METHODS

To better understand how professional women use social media to create online business identities, I interviewed twenty female small-business owners actively involved in social media. The participants ranged in age from twenty-six to fifty-nine, and in education from technical degrees to masters degrees. Thirteen participants were white, four were African American, and three were Hispanic. In all cases, the person I interviewed was the owner of the business, and the only person who posted, updated, and maintained the business's social media pages. The businesses ranged from photography studios, consulting firms, and a gym to retail stores, spas, and hair salons. All of the businesses had a website and a Facebook page. Half used Instagram and Twitter, and one-third used Pinterest and LinkedIn.

WHY FEMALE SMALL BUSINESS OWNERS USE SOCIAL MEDIA

Women-led business owners have three main motivations for using social media: connecting with others; increasing revenue; and establishing a positive business image. These motivations develop customer loyalty, drive new and repeat sales, and increase exposure to the business, and create a unified, transparent, and credible online business identity.

Connecting with others. These participants recognize that the web is social, and they use the tools offered to network with people, including both current and potential clients/customers. They often post questions or polls that encourage customers to respond. They also rely on current customers to help them gain new clientele. Word-of-mouth sharing through social media is an important element of gaining clients. Anytime a follower likes or shares a post, she is, perhaps inadvertently, referring and promoting the business. Finally, female small business owners also use social media to find out what other businesses are doing and learn from them. They scour social media sites of similar businesses—often following, liking, and friending—to discover what online marketing strategies are being employed and then they incorporate the best ideas into their own social media marketing plans. In sum, social networking is a strong motivation for going online.

Increasing revenue. Female small business owners also use social media to increase sales and revenue. Social media offers a quick and efficient way to grow a business, create a brand, and drive repeat sales. When clients are pleased, they refer their friends, and sales increase. Women who own small businesses ultimately want to increase their revenue, and social networking is one powerful way to do so.

Creating a positive impression. Small business owners use social media to create a positive online image. This image is maintained through honesty, transparency, and genuine interactions with customers. Turner and Shah (2011) claim, "By nurturing your relationship with [consumers], you can create brand advocates who will do the selling for you" (28). When customers are satisfied, they want to tell others about it, and, in effect, they are helping out the business and its image. Creating a positive online business identity brings respect and helps grow businesses.

USING SOCIAL MEDIA TO ENHANCE YOUR
ONLINE BUSINESS IDENTITY

Developing an online business identity benefits a business: it connects you with others, increases revenue, and establishes a positive image with others. This section explains the stages necessary to establish and enhance an OBI.

Stage One: Plan

The first phase of creating an online business identity involves planning. Research shows that when small businesses use social media, they often have no strategy for doing so (Goodman 2012), which proves ineffective. Therefore, before you can effectively launch an online presence through social media sites, you need to plan. This section examines some of the steps involved in the planning process: conducting research, formulating a social media marketing strategy, and gathering and developing content.

Conduct Research

The research phase is one of the most important for establishing a professional and credible online business identity and should not be overlooked. The research process can be lengthy but will pay dividends in the long run if you spend the necessary time collecting the following information.

Social media sites: What social media sites are available? Which ones are popular with businesses? What are the benefits and drawbacks of each? What sites are other businesses using, and how are they using them? What strategies do businesses employ? Which ones are effective/ineffective? Why?

> *Tip:* One of the best ways to research social media sites is to join them as a user. Join a variety of networks to get a feel for the "affordances" (potentials and limitations) of each—what works best and what doesn't work as well. Participating as a user while you are researching will aid you in the next step of developing an online marketing strategy for your business.

Your business: Even if you have not actively participated in social media, you probably still have an online presence (and you can bet your customers are checking you out). Check review sites to see what others are saying about you. Perhaps you have a website or a blog. Research the amount of traffic you get on your website or blog. Analyze the feedback you get on these sites.

> *Tip:* The first step in establishing yourself online is to have a website. A website can develop trust and credibility and, as "the hub of your digital world" is "perhaps the most important element in your whole digital marketing strategy" (Ryan and Jones 2012, 30). All of the social media sites you create can point users to your website and can be instrumental in establishing a

professional OBI. Purchase a domain name and evaluate web-hosting services to see which one you will use.

Your target audience: Who is your target audience? Who are you trying to reach? What are their characteristics? What are their greatest needs? How do they use digital technologies?

Your purpose: Why do you want to participate in social media marketing? In online networking? What are your motivations? What do you hope to achieve and accomplish? Once you have asked and answered these questions, you are ready to formulate your social media marketing strategy.

Formulate a Social Media Marketing Strategy

After you have conducted fairly exhaustive research about developing an online identity for your business, you are ready to formulate a social media marketing strategy. This strategy will guide you as you launch your business online and will keep you from stumbling or making egregious errors; it will also keep you from becoming consumed or overwhelmed by social media once you join them. This plan will vary according to each business's audience, purpose, and context and, therefore, should be tailored to one's need. In short, having a clearly defined marketing strategy will keep you focused on your audience and purpose, ensure your plan is aligned with your goals, and lead to a cohesive and unified online business identity.

Understand your market. The first step in formulating a social media strategy is to consider your audience and purpose. Whenever you post online, think first about your audience (who is going to read this) and your purpose (why are you posting/updating). Consider how your intended audience will perceive your postings and what impression/image you are conveying. Then, consider what image you are conveying through your posts and how they do (or do not) align with your purpose.

Decide which social media you are going to use. Rank the social media networks from best to worst in terms of meeting your goals and purposes. Then, choose one or two sites to launch at the beginning as your preferred destination(s) for your customers. Then, choose a handful of secondary sites you would like to launch later. Being connected to too many social media networks at the beginning can overwhelm a customer and distract you from meeting your goals. When deciding which sites are your preferred ones, analyze what works best for your customers. Go to where they are. Facebook, Twitter, and LinkedIn are the most often used, but Pinterest and Instagram are also becoming increasingly popular. Set a tentative date for when you would like to launch these preferred sites and another date for when you would like to launch your secondary sites.

Gather and Develop Content

After you have conducted research and developed a marketing plan, it is now time to gather, create, and develop content for your sites. Content might include images, logos, customer stories and quotations, short videos, blog posts, upcoming events, articles of interest to your audience, and other material that will allow the launch to go more smoothly.

Stage Two: Get Online

After you have planned and strategized, you are ready to establish an online business identity by following two steps:

Create social media pages for your business. Set up business pages on your preferred site, remembering to initially focus on a handful of platforms. Make your profile robust and include more detail rather than less. Finish your page before you make it public (or active). If you need to gather and develop more content, then do.

Participate! Be an active participant. Post regularly, purposefully, and thoughtfully. Remember that with each post you communicate something about your business, so aim to build trust by being transparent, honest, and intentional.

Stage Three: Generate Fans and Followers

After you have moved online, the next step is to increase awareness of your business by gaining followers, friends, and fans. In order to do this, you must be strategic. Here are some ways to generate a customer base:

- Invite your friends to "like," "follow," and share your pages.
- Participate in "socially visible" actions, or actions that increase exposure to your business, such as "tagging," "liking," or "following"; "checking-in"; or using hashtags.
- Reciprocate. When someone likes or follows your page, do the same with theirs. "Like" and "follow" the pages of others as well.
- Add social media links to your website and your print marketing materials (brochures, flyers, newsletters, business cards, etc.). Include a link to your website on your social media pages and print marketing materials.
- Participate in "like-gating," where you offer exclusive content or incentives to users (freebies, coupons, discounts, T-shirts, e-books, webinars, newsletters, etc.).
- Make it easy for customers to connect online. If your business has a physical location, get your customers connected to your social media networks while they are in your store (on their mobile device, the store computer, a piece of paper). If you don't have a physical location, come

up with other creative strategies to connect your customers to your pages (i.e., an e-mail invitation, a newsletter, an online form).

Building an audience takes time. If something isn't working, try something new. Regardless of how you approach it, your goal should be to increase the connective opportunities between you and your customers.

Stage Four: Engage and Respond

Even though social media is often free or cheap, establishing an online business identity still requires some investment—in time, money, resources, and engagement with your customers. In this section, you will learn how to engage and respond so that you continue to connect with and expand your customer/client base.

Engage with the Audience

When customers are engaged with your business online, your visibility increases. It is thus extremely important to engage with your audience.

Focus on your audience and purpose. The content you deliver should always appeal to the needs and expectations of your target audience and fulfill your intended purpose.

Use multiple media to deliver your messages. Use a range of media—both online and offline to increase exposure. These include social media, your website, your blog, e-newsletters, and print materials.

Create media-specific content. Since many people follow you in several media, create unique content for each site. Don't post the same thing to each platform. Instead, consider the affordances, or capabilities, of each media and choose content accordingly.

Deliver interesting and relevant content. Drive people to your pages by posting interesting and relevant content. Be intentional. Carefully choose when and what you will post. Sequence your posts and spread them out over time. Focus on quality engagement, not quantity. More posts does not necessarily mean better. What kind of content should you deliver?

- Promotions, sales, discounts, and coupons.
- News, announcements, and other information.
- Links—to your own sites or external sites your customers will find interesting.
- Events—webinars, online classes, videos, fundraisers.

Add value to the conversation. Make your customers want to stay connected with you. Say something that moves the conversation forward, raises a new or interesting point, or gets people excited. Every time you send a message out, your followers will determine whether or not they will read the next one, so take care in what you say.

   Seek referrals. Referrals are "the single most effective source for generating new customers" (Goodman 2012, 4). In short, when you engage with clients and customers, they engage with you. They increase your visibility and influence how you are perceived by others. They also tell others about you and, in effect, become a member of your marketing team. To generate referrals, encourage your customers to like and share your content with their social networks. When your customers endorse you, they help build trust, which leads others to want to do business with you (Goodman 2012, xxi).

Respond to the Audience

Social media invites a response by users. This response can be a positive one—people "like" your pages, retweet posts, respond to questions, or share your content. It can also be negative feedback. Regardless, businesses should respond to user feedback. The primary rule is to listen first (i.e., understand) and respond second once you are informed. Customers want to know that they are being heard, so always acknowledge their point of view and then respond to their questions or concerns. You might even consider implementing their criticisms or suggestions. When you listen and respond to your customers with genuine sincerity, you are building a trustworthy, transparent, and honest online business identity.

Stage Five: Assess and Revise Your Plan

After you have been active on your social media sites for a while (a few weeks to a few months), analyze the results of your approach and then revise your plan accordingly. Consider the return on your investment—what has happened as a result of your campaign? Ask the following questions:

   What's working and what's not working?
   What challenges do you face?
   What other opportunities might be available that you have not applied?
   What other platforms, tools, and technologies might be useful to add
      now?

   Once you have evaluated your social media marketing strategy, revise your plan accordingly. Make the necessary changes to your approach and then continue to assess and revise your plan as you use the networks. Remember: "Social media is about communicating across a wide variety of channels for a sustained period of time" (Turner and Shah 2011, 15).

CLOSING ADVICE FROM WOMEN-LED BUSINESS OWNERS

Find others to help you. Although you may not have the resources in money, time, or people to establish an online business identity, there are others out there who can help you, often for free or at very little cost. Contact faculty at your local college or university to see if they have an internship program. Start with the English, Communications, Journalism, or Business departments. Most likely, the department keeps a list of potential internships and your business could be added to the list. If no internship program is set up, ask if they know of students who might be interested in this kind of work. If you have funds to pay someone, consider finding young people in your community who have grown up in this social media environment and possess immense knowledge about the platforms and technologies. Alternatively, seek help online by posting on your individual page. Your friends might be able to point you to someone. When someone does help you, ask them to teach you what they are doing and to share their knowledge with you. Learn from them so that you know how to market yourself online after they have left.

Follow rules of online etiquette. It doesn't matter how well you establish a cohesive, unified, and trustworthy OBI if you don't demonstrate good online etiquette. Have good manners. Always demonstrate professionalism, respect for your customers, honesty, transparency, and ethical awareness. These characteristics enhance your trustworthiness and lead to a good reputation.

Don't be an opportunist. Remember that although you want to increase revenue, social media marketing is more about connecting with your customers by creating a community. It's more about "we" and less about explicitly selling your product. Your customers want to connect with you but don't want to feel as if you are always selling them something. This is a two-sided endeavor, so always put their needs and perspectives ahead of making money.

Engage with negative comments. Because this is a participatory web, the time will come when you might receive negative feedback. What should you do? You can either ignore the conversation or you can participate in it. Since you are the one most impacted by a negative comment, you should participate. You are the only one who can help "frame the issues and spread correct information about your brand or product" (Turner and Shah 2011, 76), and you should therefore attempt to respond. If someone is dissatisfied, then reach out to them and see what you can do to rectify the situation. Of course, there are occasions where a response would fall on deaf ears, but at least you could follow up or give your response so that others who see the feedback know how you have responded.

Adapt to change. Social media tools and technologies change just as fast as we use them. It is therefore extremely important to be willing to adapt to change. Be open-minded to experimenting and playing with new technologies as they come so that your business will remain relevant, connected, and interesting.

The rewards of engaging in social media and establishing an online business identity are far-reaching and numerous. Increased revenue, a positive image, connecting with others, gaining recognition, and self-actualization are just some of the rewards waiting for you as you enter into the online realm. It is an exciting time for you and your business, so take care in creating and establishing an online business identity that resonates with you and others.

REFERENCES

Arora, Rohit. 2013. "Women Business Owners Still Overcoming Gender Obstacles." *Fox Business*, March 19. Retrieved from http://smallbusiness.foxbusiness.com/technology-web/2013/03/19/women-business-owners-still-overcoming-gender-obstacles/.

Bakeman, Melissa Mary, and Lee Hanson. 2012. "Bringing Social Media to Small Business." *Business Education Innovation Journal* 4 (2): 106–11.

Goodman, Gail F. 2012. *Engagement Marketing: How Small Business Wins in a Socially Connected World*. Hoboken, NJ: Wiley.

NWBC (National Women's Business Council). 2012. "Women-Owned Firms in the U.S.: A Review of Important Areas of the 2007 U.S. Census Bureau's Survey of Business Owners." Retrieved from http://www.nwbc.gov/research/women-owned-firms-united-states.

Ryan, Damian, and Calvin Jones. 2012. *Understanding Digital Marketing: Marketing Strategies for Engaging the Digital Generation*. Philadelphia, PA: Kogan Page.

SBA Office of Advocacy. 2013. "Venture Capital, Social Capital and the Funding of Women-Led Businesses." 1–30. Retrieved from http://www.sba.gov/advocacy/7540/561201.

SMB Group. 2012. *Impact of Social Business in Small and Medium Business Study.* Retrieved from http://www.smb-gr.com/wpcontent/uploads/2012/pdfs/2012_Impact_of_ Social_Business_Study_Marketing_Overview.pdf.

Turner, Jamie, and Reshma Shah. 2011. *How to Make Money with Social Media: An Insider's Guide on Using New and Emerging Media to Grow Your Business*. Upper Saddle River, NJ: FT Press.

Chapter Five

Find a Hub

Kanina Holmes

Digital media raise a variety of issues as we try to understand them, their place in our lives, and their consequences for our personhood and relationship with others. When they are new, technologies affect how we see the world, our communities, our relationships, and our selves. They lead to social and cultural reorganization and reflection.—Baym (2010, 2)

New media are firmly entrenched in the daily routines and lives of North Americans. We rely on digital technologies to consume, to inform, to communicate, to network. For example, a survey conducted in late 2012 by the Pew Research Center's Internet and American Life Project found that more than two-thirds of all adults in the United States who go online use social networking sites. We have at our disposal hundreds of thousands of apps and previously unimagined interactivity, mobility, and evolving conceptualizations. The popularity of social networking platforms such as Facebook, Twitter, Pinterest, blogs, and personal audio and visual content-sharing sites such as YouTube, Vimeo, Instagram, Tumblr, and Flickr represent just a snapshot of how digital technologies and interactions are shaping the ways people communicate. Current developments harken back to earlier predictions by communication scholars such as Manuel Castells that the Internet would start to seem less like exotic wizardry to become routinely embedded into our lives. More recent analysis focuses on the permeation and transformation of space by information technologies and, more specifically, by software code (Kitchin and Dodge 2011).

When the Internet first began to become entrenched in many of our daily lives, many saw its potential for emancipation, opening up new social, political, and economic possibilities, especially for women. Others were apprehensive that the net could also create and exacerbate women's problems, including online harassment and hostility.

In many respects, the evolution of digital media and, more recently, social networking platforms, mirrors the ebbs and flows of the larger debate over the roles, benefits, and detractions of online technologies to society. The ideological pendulum has shifted back and forth, perhaps unwittingly, giving a parallel expression to the numerical binaries upon which computing is based. As mentioned, on one hand, there is a conviction that the World Wide Web and its many communication applications can invert entrenched inequalities and transcend boundaries of geography, gender, class, race, and sexuality, creating dynamic online communities and activism, notably among socially marginalized and disenfranchised groups. On the other side, there are those who are sometimes characterized as "techno-pessimists" because of their fear of increasing isolation and a reduction in collective sensibilities.

A more realistic, accurate and constructive portrayal of life with digital technologies treads the middle ground between these polemics and involves a vision of online activity where the boundaries between online and offline are porous and that seeks to better understand these virtual and physical intersections. In this context, it is also important to acknowledge the potential to perpetuate inequalities, create new imbalances and also open up new, more democratic spaces through, for example, Internet-based social networks (Parks 2011; Rainie and Wellman 2012.)

What happens when we consider the impact and dynamics of the Internet on our work environments? Given the amount of time and attention many devote to digital platforms, it is worth exploring how some of these technologies affect the way people work, in particular women. This chapter travels to Canada's capital, Ottawa, and looks at a new, online start-up company founded by two Canadian women and examines how the web both fuels their entrepreneurialism but also inspires and requires them to find offline ways to connect.

Instead of the bleary eyes, yawns, and general lethargy that one might associate with the beginning of a work week, especially after a three-day holiday marking the official start of Canada's summer, HUB Ottawa is a calm and constant hive of activity. By early afternoon about twenty people populate the workstations, made of repurposed doors. There are few walls in this space and those that do exist are transparent glass. Maybe it's the help-yourself coffee and free-flowing WiFi, but there seems to be something more to explain the energy in this modern, industrial, open-concept and conceptually new type of office space.

"We want to create a trusted environment so our members feel empowered to do great things and to create and ask for help and turn around and introduce themselves to another member," explains Vinod Rajasekaran, HUB Ottawa's cofounder and executive director. Rajasekaran says HUB Ottawa, part of a network of thirty-eight other hubs around the world, is one of the largest communities driving social innovation in Canada. The goal is to create a space and provide the infrastructure to bring together diverse, but like-minded entrepreneurs. People can purchase a range of memberships that give them a certain number of hours to work from the HUB, to hold meetings and participate in seminars.

"There's always going to be more talent, more ideas, better approaches outside your cubicle, your coffee shop, your kitchen, your office. HUB is an environment that helps facilitate those connections to those, both locally and globally," says Rajasekaran.

Some of these HUB-generated start-ups could be considered more traditional companies involving brick-and-mortar storefronts and face-to-face meetings. Many, however, are increasingly based online, taking advantage of the reach and resources offered up by the World Wide Web. If we pause for a moment and consider what constitutes a hub—a central part of a wheel or the center of an activity, region, or network—and what makes a web—a network of fine threads spun, in this context, out of the ability to connect servers and personal computers all over the world—then we can see how an initiative such as HUB Ottawa might form a home base or at least a kind of second home.

"There's no way of telling who is a seasoned expert or at the beginning of their journey. That's the beauty of the environment. Everything is really accessible," says Rajasekaran, noting an almost equal split between men and women working out of the HUB. Part of that accessibility is a conscious effort by HUB Ottawa to ensure everyone feels welcome. This is no small feat given that when it comes to working with information technologies—a key platform for social innovation—women only represent a quarter of the workforce (Edmiston 2012).

In some respects, an organization such as the Hub is not totally new. Linda Duxbury, a professor who specializes in organizational health, said the concept of a work hub can be traced back to the 1970s. Originally, hubs were designed to reduce commute times. Large companies started buying buildings in suburban locations, separate from their central offices, so that people could congregate closer to home. "Now the hub is more a way for entrepreneurs to get a legitimate address and legitimate piece of ground," says Duxbury, adding that one of the primary benefits of hubs now is that they make professional office space much more affordable.

For Bettina Vollmerhausen, cofounder of SMAKK, an online enterprise that promotes the purchase of gift cards from local merchants rather than big box stores, HUB Ottawa is "an incredible resource of connections, knowledge, encouragement, energy and support." Two years ago Vollmerhausen was a stay-at-home mom who schooled her two daughters until they became teenagers. Today, she's an active participant in HUB Ottawa's workspace and professional courses and finds herself at the helm of an innovative Internet-based business. SMAKK, which stands for sharing meaningful acts of kindness and karma, is an online portal that connects shoppers looking for specialized and individualized gifts who want to buy from businesses in their community instead of taking the more traditional route and using well-financed, publicity-savvy retailers, such as Amazon, Ikea, and the Future Shop. Using the site, customers can purchase everything from high fashion to high-calorie gourmet doughnuts, all made in Ottawa.

The founders of SMAKK have some big plans. The original idea for the company came from cofounder Heidi Fuller after she saw the impact of giving small gifts to her fellow teachers and staff at a middle school plagued by social tensions and drug abuse. When someone received a present, it was also accompanied by a playful note saying they had been "smakked," explains Fuller, who liked the combination of kindness and karma in the concept and in the label they attached to these altruistic acts. In addition to creating a new vocabulary, these two entrepreneurs also aspire to forge a community that revolves around grassroots products and services and, more important, local culture and initiatives.

"When you have small businesses, if you look at our society now and you have all these corporations that make huge sums of money, it's taking money out of the communities and sending it to headquarters," says Fuller, adding that SMAKK's emphasis is on relationship building. "People love to gift cards, but it can be a little bit impersonal. I wanted to make it more personal by supporting local businesses. You're actually getting to the heart of what that person actually likes."

Ironically, while Vollmerhausen is now in the business of helping others forge links, at the beginning of this entrepreneurial journey, she found herself extremely isolated. Fuller, who participated in the interview for this chapter with her seven-month-old son on her lap, can also relate to feelings of being on the outside.

"One of the benefits of doing an online business is that you can work at home, particularly for women, if they want to be home and they want to have that flexibility around their kids' schedules and stuff like that. But you end up working in a bubble," says Fuller. Both women say the online/offline separation is just one part of a complex digital dynamic, a potential pitfall, but one that can be overcome by joining groups such as HUB Ottawa.

The experience of working on SMAKK highlights the positive and negative push and pull of forces that shape the Internet in general. For example, there is certainly a tension between the freedom from fixed schedules offered in working online and, as Vollmerhausen and Fuller can attest, the cutoff from face-to-face social contact that often accompanies it. By way of offering some context, perhaps this can explain the strong and mixed reaction to the announcement in February 2013 by Marissa Mayer, Yahoo's chief executive. At that time, she halted all telework and ordered every employee to start working from its offices. "She's broadcasting that she doesn't trust her staff very clearly," says Duxbury, who teaches at the Sprott School of Business at Carleton University. Duxbury has extensively researched issues around work-life balance. She also wonders, "if she's (Mayer) going to stop them working at home during office hours, is she going to forbid them from doing work-related tasks on their own time when they're at home on the evenings and weekend?" In its coverage, the *New York Times* characterized it as a tradeoff. It is the ability to work from home and the flexibility that such arrangements offer pitted against the productivity and the innovation that some believe emerges, almost exclusively, from direct interaction with others in an office (Miller and Rampell 2013). Duxbury advocates a balance of telework or working from home on an ad hoc basis one to two days a week. Not only does it demonstrate an employer's confidence in an employee, it also reduces isolation while still allowing the benefit of face-to-face interaction and the exchange of ideas.

For an online start-up like SMAKK, the way to resolve the conflict between the desire for scheduling elasticity and the need for more concrete connection was a hub. Vollmerhausen takes courses through HUB Ottawa and spends time brainstorming with fellow members. The space is often open until 9 PM and is also available on Saturdays. She says getting out her home office, even if it's just for a couple of hours, has been key to providing both momentum for SMAKK and also some much-needed personal connection.

"Because we are innately instinctually needing the conversation, I think it [the Internet] allows that flexibility. But I think we still need that physical, personal connection," says Fuller, adding that perhaps the requirement for face-to-face connection is even more powerful for women.

Another requirement that Vollmerhausen and Fuller made explicit, from the beginning of their venture, was that their friendship survived the process of starting a new business. The women, who first met in 1996 when they were both living in western Canada, are at dramatically different stages of life. Vollmerhausen, who worked as a translator before raising her children, is now at a time where her daughters will soon be leaving home and she can devote more time and energy to outside activities. Fuller, on the other hand, is just starting her family after a career as a biology and chemistry teacher and international development consultant. However divergent their paths, both women say their priority is their relationship and their personal lives and finding ways to make the business fit into those. To support these priorities, Vollmerhausen and Fuller worked out a partnership agreement in which they wrote down things that were important to them, including finding a mediator if there ever was a disagreement or an issue they couldn't revolve.

"I'm not sure if it's gender based, but I definitely see collaboration and friendship being so much more important," says Vollmerhausen. "We place a lot of value on that."

While debates over the value and pitfalls of working from home and online will likely remain unsettled, Vollmerhausen and Fuller say it is clear to them that they wouldn't have been able to launch their business without web-based digital platforms such as Skype and social media sites such as Twitter. The two women live in different cities in Canada and communicate via online video conferencing frequently. In the past two years they've only met in person an estimated eight times with each visit lasting less than a week.

"Without the technology there would have been no way we could have started this business," says Vollmerhausen. She now regularly relies on social media, tweeting to get the word out about her company and connect with local vendors. "You can access so many people from so many different places. If you had a storefront, it's really sort of who passes by your spot."

James Wagner cruised by SMAKK when he was on Twitter a few months ago. In his spare time he runs a limousine service called Retro Rides that uses a 1966 Volkswagen bus, complete with oversized sunroof and seating for six. Wagner says he liked the idea of gift certificates with personality and he appreciated Vollmerhausen's enthusiasm for all things local. "I just think supporting local business and small businesses is a good way to live and keep our economy and our whole social structure intact." Wagner is now one of the businesses featured on SMAKK's website.

In the two years since they started SMAKK, the online company's founders say they've learned a lot, especially when it comes to doing business over the Internet and about how their lives, including their perspectives as women, fit into new, web-based entrepreneurial start-ups. Because they received so much assistance through collegial collaboration, Vollmerhausen and Fuller say they are happy to pay it forward at this stage and offer advice to others who are entering this virtual playing field. Among their primary pieces of advice:

- Find an organization or company that can help you work out all the details you need to consider before you start, from ideation to launch, from your business plan to your revenue sources. Because start-ups are usually a leap of faith, this kind of information provides an essential road map that confirms you have an original, interesting, and viable idea for a service or product.
- Developing an online business takes much longer than you think it will. Both women stress the importance of acknowledging the best of intentions and the firmest of schedules still encounter roadblocks, in part because of the steep learning curve related to working online. That curve includes navigating a mind-jolting array of software choices, computer coding and trying to figure out online payment systems with a range of small vendors. Another challenge they faced was in offering a service rather than a prod-

uct. "How do you get people to touch and feel it? It's kind of virtual until you actually have something in your hand that you can hand out," says Fuller. Until their website went live and potential vendors could see how SMAKK was taking shape, Fuller says the process of education and relationship building resembled the "three cups of tea" referred to in a Balti proverb and the book by the same name about development assistance projects in Pakistan and Afghanistan. The idea is that it takes three cups of tea, or at least three meetings, to establish trust and clarity among participants.

- Try things out in small pieces. For example, when trying to find someone who does website development or graphic design, give him or her one project to determine the quality of their work, their communication style, and how it meshes with the way you want to do business. Vollmerhausen and Fuller like working by sharing screens, but they discovered that's not necessarily how other professionals want to operate in such a dynamic, responsive and real-time way.

- Try to find mentors within your own social network. Think about friends and colleagues in different ways so that you can tap into their knowledge and experience. Vollmerhausen says that you can't be shy about asking questions and seeking advice, both from people you're already acquainted with, as well as making new connections through current friends and colleagues. According to researchers such as Rainie and Wellman (2012), the most accurate way to describe the way people communicate, including their use of online social media, is through the metaphor and infrastructure of networks. At its best, these relations resemble a giant, informal system of bartering or leveraging of ideas and services so that, in the end, no one feels taken advantage of and everyone benefits.

Above all, Vollmerhausen credits their young company's progress so far to the realization there are many others out there also trying to make a go of it, each within a unique or creative niche. Out of this diversity and willingness to take risks there is often a spirit of collegiality that sees people exchanging skills and insights. From this experience she says, above all, "the first thing that comes to mind for me is: find a hub."

REFERENCES

Baym, Nancy K. 2010. *Personal Connections in the Digital Age*. Cambridge: Polity.

Edmiston, Alix. 2012. "Wanted: Young Women to Work in High-Tech Sector." *Financial Post*, December 2.

Kitchin, Rob, and Martin Dodge. 2011. *Code Space: Software and Everyday Life*. Cambridge, MA: MIT Press.

Miller, Claire Cain, and Catherine Rampell. 2013. "Yahoo Orders Home Workers Back to the Office." *New York Times*, February 25.

Parks, Malcolm R. 2011. "Social Network Sites as Virtual Communities." In *A Networked Self: Identity, Community and Culture on Social Sites*, ed. Zizi Papacharissi (ed.), 105–23. New York: Routledge.

Rainie, Lee, and Barry Wellman. 2012. *Networked: The New Social Operating System*. Cambridge, MA: MIT Press.

Chapter Six

Keeping My Place at the Table

Growing with a Business

Liz Webler Rowell

When I was pregnant with my first son, I had a great role working with dedicated, talented people. I was helping to shape the future for my business group and it was exciting. I had spent close to a decade carefully cultivating a reputation as a colleague who could be trusted. It wasn't perfect though. Like many corporate jobs, some days my projects moved at a glacial pace. Politics interfered. My commute was exhausting. I never seemed to turn off. Some days I wondered if I was doing the right thing. But the influence I had was satisfying enough to stick it out for the eight plus years I stayed.

But what to do once my baby was born? I wasn't sure. No one around me had carved a path that I wanted to follow: every mom who had achieved a leadership position had a stay-at-home husband or a nanny. If I continued to work in a large office that valued face time, I'd sacrifice my chance to raise my boy. I was scared but I pulled the plug.

I went through what most first moms go through: a radical altering of perspective. I adored my baby. I felt inept and bored. I mournfully replayed the career cliff dive I'd chosen to take.

Close to my boy's first birthday, the regular catch-up calls with an old colleague started to feel like a job offer. Pretty quickly, I'd agreed to ten hours of work with Jennifer Benz, then a solo proprietor of a small and quickly growing business. Since then, I've grown with the business into a role that is better than my old one—I have two sons now and I'm doing work that's more strategic and has a broader impact. Why? Well, this is a book about women thriving in the digital age. My own career and the growth of our company have similar trajectories thanks to free and inexpensive technology and a cultural shift that acknowledges business can happen without face time.

A SMALL COMPANY, GROWING QUICKLY

We're a team of twenty-seven (and hiring!) but Benz Communications started as a one-woman shop back in 2006 of just our founder, Jennifer Benz. Our revenue has grown so quickly in recent years that we landed on the 2012 *Inc.* 5,000 list of the fastest-growing private companies in the United States—number 534 to be specific. We like to call ourselves a "small giant" in a very niche space that is dominated by global consulting and outsourcing firms like Aon Hewitt, Towers Watson and Mercer. Clients include *Fortune* 100 Best Companies to Work For and *Fortune* 500 companies. And, we're a women-owned company.

So what do we do? At Benz Communications, we help companies of all sizes educate employees and their families about some of the most important topics in our times—health care and retirement. In industry terms, we are an HR and benefits communication strategy consulting firm. We are passionate about helping companies motivate their employees to improve their health and plan for a happier and more financially secure future. Nearly 60 percent of working Americans under the age of sixty-five have employer-provided health benefits, and 75 percent of employees look to their employer for health information. This puts employers—and employee benefits communication—in a singularly powerful position to make a tremendous impact. We take this really seriously.

Tell you more about our growth? As an individual contributor and as a company, success required hurdling several of the same obstacles.

1. Infrastructure—We needed the look and feel of a classy black pant-suit, with the affordability and ease of jeans and T-shirt.
2. Credibility—We needed brand recognition or a national sales team to rope in prospects quickly. And, an R&D team tinkering with industry issues and generating perspectives that were meaningful for our clients.
3. Purpose—We wanted to work hard with a team and for clients who mirrored our core values.

Three rather big challenges for a plucky little company and a new mom on a part-time schedule, but certainly not unique. But it was a good time for a fresh start in our industry. The U.S. corporate environment was finding new ways to cut costs as software companies innovated. It's not a new idea to say that the mouse is more nimble than the elephant. Guess who's the mouse?

Wait: Reframe!

One quick way to find a way through any of these mazes—as a business or an individual contributor—is to focus on the client perspective. After all, without paying clients, we're not getting paid. By shifting the focus ever so slightly, it was a lot easier to move quickly and deliberately.

Okay, now onto some tips on our three biggest client questions and how the Internet helped us catapult into growth and profitability.

#1 CLIENT QUESTION: DO YOU WORK OUT OF YOUR BASEMENT?

Clients don't want to pay for overhead, but they also don't want a partner who isn't serious enough to invest a little in the business. No matter if you're selling vintage aprons, physical therapy sessions, or legal representation, clients aren't willing to risk their time or money on a business that isn't "legit." Your need for infrastructure depends on your business—but your customer needs to feel like you have the basics to function properly. And you might even need to offer some luxury items—whatever that means for your industry.

When we were just starting out, we were the equivalent of an online shop. In fact, we were operating out of the individual home offices of our scattered team. But we made smart, free, or inexpensive virtual investments that might help you get started too. We'll rank order these investments based on our own experience, but you may find reshuffling them makes more sense for yours. For instance, if you're in retail, a tracking system is likely much higher on your list.

We Needed Some First-in-Class Infrastructure

As a communication firm, we needed to have a knockout website. Five star. What better way to showcase our skills creating websites for our clients? And, while we don't create brands for our clients, our logo and branding standards needed to be top-notch too.

> *A website.* You don't need to be a communication business to need a website. There isn't an industry we can think of that won't benefit from owning the domain name of their company and have a one-page site. Bare minimum. Why? Unless you're operating a speakeasy, you'd never consider not listing your company in the Yellow Pages or putting your name outside your front door. The Internet is a virtual space, sure, but it is a congested highway where new customers are trying to find you. Give them a hand. Plus, in this virtual world, a website with just the right information puts you on equal footing with

competitors—even more established competitors—and gives you a leg up if the competition isn't taking their web presence seriously.

Your www name. Starting out, you need to invest in a domain name that will last, but the rest can be bare bones. (Newbies: A "domain name" or "URL" are technical terms for the word or letter combination that goes after the www. and before the .com.) A quick Google search yields several companies who can help you establish your URL and own it for the future. And, be sure to stay on top of annual fees. If you don't, it can get snagged out from under you.

Business basics. You need a way for new clients to reach you. As you grow, you can invest in rich content, intuitive site organization (architecture) and functionality. Functionality needs to match your business—a few examples that work across industries include a simple contact form, a blog, and a Twitter feed. Everyone appreciates a generous business—in our industry, fresh perspectives are currency. Using Twitter and our blog, we had a platform to quickly offer up our perspective on industry trends, share interesting articles, and connect our clients to regulatory updates. (More on this later.)

Custom e-mail. Having a number to give out to clients is pretty straightforward. But maybe you've shied away from a professional e-mail? In today's environment, you can easily shift from a personal e-mail account to a professional one. When you establish your domain name, you are likely to find an affordable package that links your e-mail to your domain name. For us, all our e-mail addresses end in our business name. I'mliz@benzcommunications.com. Your e-mail account is a de facto filing system of transactions, vendor negotiations, and evolving relationships.

And We Needed Some Other Systems That Were Just Okay—to Start Out

Tracking systems. Whether you need to track inventory, file documents, or record medical notes, cloud-based systems give you big-business functionality without the IT staff expense. We needed to have functional, but not best-in-class tracking systems, as we launched our business. Our computers offered a sufficient filing system, but as our team grew and we needed to collaborate on documents, we saw a need to upgrade. In fact, we've upgraded several times. We've learned that staying lean means staying plugged in to the ever-changing variety of tools we can purchase or get for free—to help us accomplish project-related work as well as business tracking work.

Flexible working offices. Your best talent doesn't always live a five-minute walk from your office. If you have a low-skill business, you can probably build a good team from local candidates. However, if you need to fill positions requiring technical skills, you may have to cast a wider geographical net. That was us to a T. Not only that, we had a vision for a unique culture and we needed just the right people to make up our team. At a different time in history, we couldn't have made a go of our business. Knowledge workers need to collaborate. But flexible offices are now possible, common, and for many workers, a perk of working at our company. And having kids in the background on company calls is not uncommon or frowned upon.

Team collaboration for a dispersed workforce. Even for a team that's scattered across the country, working side by side will always be important. So we needed systems that allowed our team to (a) conference with many teammates, (b) let each other see our work in progress, (c) video conference, and (d) allow coworkers to collaborate on files. We found a ton of free resources through Google, Skype, BigFileSwapper, and a few others with nominal costs.

#2 CLIENT QUESTION: SHOULD I TRUST YOU?

In professional services industries, sales teams and thought leaders help clients get to "yes." Meaning: I trust you, I will link my success with yours. Establishing credibility isn't easy. Gaining the ear of a new client and colleagues takes a thoughtful approach, good ideas, and the right level of persistence.

As a growing business competing against established firms, we needed a nontraditional way to accomplish this. We didn't have a national sales team and didn't envision one. Nor did we want any client—we wanted the right clients. We want to make an impact on our industry, not just sell our services. We needed a forum to develop and vet ideas among peers and potential clients. Not a soapbox per se, but social media platforms serve as handy microphones.

As with any conversation in life, you can lecture or you can dialogue. You can gather a community and listen to them; you can pepper them with small witticisms and hope they laugh. There isn't a right answer here. What would best serve your business? How about your own career? Social media is no fad; it's part of sales strategy that produces results. Think about it carefully and develop your strategy toward social media: which platforms, what kind of interaction, and what kind of content. All aiming toward a client that trusts you and wants to do business with you. Pick the right channel for you and your industry—for us, Twitter, a blog, and LinkedIn make the most sense.

Our Blog, Our Front Door

We have total freedom on our blog—to express our deepest-held beliefs, to share silly team photos, to acknowledge others in our industry we admire. We are ourselves. To be trustworthy, we need to be transparent—our founder as well as our full team.

Case in point: when health care reform passed in the spring of 2010, we published a blog article titled "What to tell your employees about health care reform," including a free template for our clients and prospects to use at their organizations. We did it on Sunday, because the law passed on Saturday and we knew that the interesting clients, the ones we wanted to work with, were up and thinking about it too. While we don't have a way to measure exactly how many companies used it, we did see some hard metrics that let us know our strategy was working. First, our website traffic spiked in a way we've never seen before. Invitations to speak at conferences and association meetings spiked too. Clearly we were someone worth trusting.

Four Ps to Structure Your Blog

We've refined our approach over time. These four principles have guided us to our current market leadership position:

1. Persistent. Blogging regularly is critical to making real inroads to your audience's psyche. You don't have to have an epiphany every time you post, but your post should be fresh, connecting your key messages to current trends.
2. Prove it. By linking your messages to recent editorials, new research or business case studies, you link your ideas to other established minds. Surprising links—across disciplines—show you think creatively, not just parrot the ideas of others.
3. Personal. Write in a tone that matches your personality. Show your humanity and your soul. People want to hire other people, not vacant sales pitches. Even if your business is a commodity, set your product apart by bringing in quirky, original, imperfect you.
4. Pound cake. Whenever you can, give something immediately useable away for free. Isn't that how you make friends with the new neighbors? What makes sense in your community makes sense at home.

The Pixie Dust of the Micro-Blog

Facebook, Twitter, and LinkedIn all have different personalities, but they serve the same function: cultivate an audience through cocktail-sized conversations. You let your ideas influence others and in turn become influenced by others. Through micro-blogging, you become part of the ecosystem—of ideas, talent, and solutions.

Both individuals and businesses can use the micro-blog format to establish a voice that is unique and distinct. I get excited when I latch on to a new idea, and it comes across in my posts. As a senior independent contributor, I need to keep my ear to the ground for industry trends. While I trust my gut, my ideas become stronger and richer through dialogue. I also benefit tremendously as my network of former trusted colleagues expands their skills and expertise.

While it can be intimidating to start or keep up with micro-blogging, I personally get a lot of satisfaction out of it. I love to meet industry trendsetters that Jen has cultivated Twitter relationships with—she really does have fans; in a field as unsexy as ours, that's pretty marvelous. And I love the iterative nature of micro-blogging—say something, say it again with a slight twist. Blogging and micro-blogging has been the most free I've ever been with my own writing because the conversation moves so quickly:

- No toe dipping. Dive in and participate with ideas and opinions.
- Greet social media contacts with the same respect as in-person contacts.
- Go ahead, introduce yourself. Direct message or "friend" acquaintances.
- Flatter someone. Retweet or "like" often.
- Delineate personal and private. Adjust account settings or establish different accounts.

Get Invited Over

Your own audience will always be important. Expanding your reach not only yields new audience members but it signals to all that your ideas warrant being heard. Ask for an invitation to be an expert. No matter what your field, someone is always new to it and appreciates the perspective of someone seasoned to the potential pitfalls.

Guest contributor, editor-at-large. Find out which industry publications accept articles. Many editors work with a pool of freelance writers—but they have to pay them. Would it be a fair trade to have them publish your article for free in order to reach a broader audience? You can tweak an existing blog to make it fresh for their market. In retail business, you might find a way to be a guest writer for a few blogs where your potential customers go.

Community gatherings. In a knowledge business, speaking engagements have long been an important tactic to reach new customers. The down side? Time away from your team, "wasted time" in transit, and the inherent risk—will you walk away with qualified leads? Webinars, an event that happens in real time with you presenting material to an

audience viewing your materials online, eliminates some of the down-
sides of in-person events.

Hire a PR company. As a small business, it's not easy to invest in professional services—especially something as potentially immeasurable as
public relations. Being a believer in the power of communication, we
hired one of the best professionals in our industry. Through her established contacts, we gained exposure to new audiences, publishing
opinion pieces in more prestigious industry journals and being quoted
in mainstream media outlets.

#3 CLIENT QUESTION: DO I WANT TO TRUST YOU?

Our competition is good. Former colleagues deliver great results for firms
big and small. Why trust us?

I like to think I earned the respect of my peers by leaving my big corporate job—to carve out some new ruts wide enough to allow me to bring my
family along. I think of myself as a woman with integrity. Sometimes that
means quitting. A measure of fearlessness can be an attractive quality in a
potential coworker or client—if you need critical thinking, an analytical
mind or strategy to make the business equation work.

What else matters? What will set you apart from the competition—and
attract the clients or customers you want?

Weaving a Culture

Our business is all about helping regular employees prepare for the health
and financial challenges of life. It makes sense then we'd want to structure
our business operations to support that broad mission.

In service of others. Our clients are employees and family members of
large U.S. employers. But all Americans could benefit from the messages we deliver. That's why we've participated in several pro bono
projects that leverage our unique industry expertise, including the re-
lease of the free Text4baby Toolkit for Employers to promote the free,
bilingual health education text messaging service for pregnant women
and new moms from text4baby.

Vacation—take some! We love our work, but we love our lives. And we
can't live them well without time away from work. Over time, we've
found that company shut downs work better than really generous vacation time. Simply, it means that when a teammate is out, someone
else isn't doing double duty to cover for them. It's a very public
company value, because we tell our clients we're unreachable unless
there's an emergency. Jen recommends we all change our out-of-

office message to say, "We are recharging." Smart phones and tablets allow a few key people to remain reachable if necessary, but honestly, our clients have never sounded a false alarm. Is it a sign of trust that our clients let us take a break, knowing we will indeed deliver on our promised value?

Save more trees. We tell all our clients to have a benefits website. Most American businesses send reams of paper to each employee, annually. Surely you've received a two-pound envelope in one of your jobs—likely describing health benefits in legal jargon. Did you throw it away? Most people do. Clearly better to have a virtual place where people can learn about their benefits! But it's no coincidence that this strategy also has the effect of eliminating a whole lot of paper. And we tell our clients too.

Hire female talent. Not only was it important to be a women-owned business, we wanted our senior team leaders to be women. Working parents bring unique challenges to the office, and we've solved many of them just by opening the doors to the presence of children. Kids and babies routinely join our team video calls and group retreats, helping moms juggle both roles they play (or at least two of the roles!) in life. Our virtual offices and flexible working hours allow parents to do more for everyone.

Chapter Seven

KHORAI

Promoting Reproductive and Maternal Mental Health through an Innovative Web Presence

Marie Hansen, Tasha Muresan, and Aurélie Athan

From the emotional shifts of menopause and menstruation to the subjectivity of women as they make the transition to motherhood, women's bodies have strong relationships to their inner worlds. In the field of psychology, women are frequently the site of mystery and confusion, particularly around issues related to living within a reproductive body. As far back as the early 1900s Freud famously proclaimed women to be "the dark continent" of psychological understanding. Today, despite the growing numbers of women entering into the mental health professions, there is a dearth of current research about the psycho-physiology of women. Just recently, the American Psychological Association's blog released a post titled "There Are No Words: Postpartum Mood Disorders and Miriam Carey's Death" (Karraa 2013). The post expressed the inability to articulate and discuss women's postpartum mood disorders specifically because the field has not yet given a name to these experiences. This characteristic confusion about women's maternal and reproductive mental health from within the field of psychology then trickles down into a bewildered public.

KHORAI, a website devoted to exploring these subjects, seeks to shed light on this "terra incognita" by translating scholarly and scientific articles for a general public and by providing reflective thinking on the psychological study of women's bodies and minds. Developed by women from within the field of clinical psychology, the website seeks to increase the status of women by providing a language with which to express their interiority and giving voice to their subjective experiences. As far as we are aware, the development of websites for the general public by academic laboratories are rare, with many keeping their research very much ensconced within the "ivory tower." Furthermore, the websites that do exist on these topics are often written by journalists and web writers who are far from informed and are paid to incite reactionary comments from their audience.

TWO LITERACIES: THE PHILOSOPHICAL ORIGINS OF KHORAI

KHORAI developed out of two overlapping domains: body literacy and psychological literacy. The second wave of feminism saw an increasing desire to understand the female body. Many women felt alienated from their bodies by a male-dominated medical establishment that ignored their requests for technical understanding of their fertility and reproductive capacities. In early documents, such as the Boston Women's Health Collective [BWHC]'s "Women and Their Bodies: A Course," women describe this feeling of alienation as stemming from the exclusionary medical jargon used by doctors and the objectifying of women's bodies as "scientific projects" in medical discourse and practice (BWHC 1970). This corporeal alienation and lack of practical language with which to discuss the body led many women to feel psychological alienation from their own bodies, resulting in the inability to openly discuss with other women and doctors issues such as sexual and reproductive difficulties. Second-wave feminism saw a return to the body, as many women gathered and shared what information they could about their fertility, including pregnancy and birth control options. This bodily information was frequently shared in tandem with explorations of emotions: what does it feel like to be living in a female body within a society that does not value breastfeeding, birthing, or menstruation, but yet wishes to regulate it?

The Internet, much like the women's health collectives of the 1960s and 1970s, has "leveled the playing field" by providing space for women to communally gather to discuss and learn about "bodies of knowledge" otherwise out of their reach. Whereas women once met in each other's living rooms with speculums and mirrors, women now browse websites such as The Beautiful Cervix within the comfort of their own homes. Unsatisfied with popular discourses they might have learned in high school sex education classrooms, these women seek alternative narratives with which to understand their physiologies and their mind-sets. Unlike the body literacy of the 1960s and 1970s, women's health websites today often do not include the psychological study of women and their reproductive lives or help midwife a growing *relationship* with women's bodies that is healthful, holistic, and most of all, *informed.*

In 2008 the American Psychological Association released a statement stressing the need to increase psychological literacy in the average American citizen (Belar 2008). The article connected "psychological literacy" to the ability to think critically, and both globally and ethically. Since the publication of the article, the study of psychological literacy has grown into a global discipline, with publications and an international conference. However, much of the movement toward promoting psychological literacy focuses its attention on undergraduate psychology students, neglecting the need for this type of literacy in the general public. For example, most major texts on psychological literacy appear to be targeted toward enhancing the quality and depth of *Psych 101* courses (for examples see Halpern 2010; Cranney and Dunn 2011). This suggests a need for the further development of methods and practice for psychological literacy for *all* citizens, including those who have not attended higher education.

Citing an original work by McGovern and colleagues, Cranney and Dunn (2011) list the key concepts of "psychological literacy" as:

- having a well-defined vocabulary and basic knowledge of the subject matter of psychology
- valuing the intellectual challenges required to use scientific thinking and the disciplined analysis of information to evaluate alternative courses of action
- taking a creative and amiable approach to problem solving
- applying psychological principles to personal, social, and organizational issues in work, relationships, and the broader community
- acting ethically
- being competent in using and evaluating information and technology
- communicating effectively in different modes and with different audiences
- recognizing, understanding, and fostering respect for diversity
- being insightful and reflective about one's own and other's behavior and mental processes" (p. 4)

For women's reproductive and maternal mental health, these nine facets of psychological literacy are of great importance, and we can see each one as having particular relevance for women.

The first concept very much harkens back to the early demands of body literacy. Without the proper language and knowledge to explain psychological experiences, people often feel frightened, confused, and alone. Here we are thinking of the mothers who may come to us as clinicians feeling unhappy after the birth of their child—is it the "baby blues"? Or is it something more? What is it? Together with the value of "being insightful about one's own behavior and mental processes," scholarly knowledge of maternal mental health may help women as they transition to motherhood to gain a better understanding of the complicated emotions they may be experiencing. Similarly, a basic understanding of scientific thinking and evaluation is very important for women as they navigate the often-labyrinthine reproductive and mental health medical systems. A strong competence in using information, evaluating information, and finding information is critical. Finally, we find the concept of "recognizing, respecting, and fostering respect for diversity" to be crucial, particularly in respect of mothers. Mothers are frequently the site of great scrutiny and judgment. From debates about bottle-feeding vs. breastfeeding, to co-sleeping and attachment parenting, mothers are constantly under the microscope, and often feel unable to make a decision for themselves. At KHORAI, we feel it is important to embrace all types of mothers, whether we personally agree with their practices or not, and to provide them with fact-based information to support their process. We see this respect for the diversity of mothers as possible through fostering an active engagement in understanding of the psychology of mothers by providing information about what it feels like to *be* a mother. In many ways this is also a form of activism, though one that is on a quieter front. KHORAI's content hopes to create an inner shift of perspective within the women who read it—one that awakens them to compassionate action for their *own* experience by sharing in the experience of others.

WOMEN AND THE WEB: WOMEN'S INFORMATION-SEEKING BEHAVIORS

As psychological and bodily literacy shows, information can have a profound effect on one's sense of self and their understanding of the world. It is well known that in contemporary Western society we are continuously flooded with information pertaining to our health and well-being on a regular basis. This information is of varying qualities and it is often very difficult to separate the wheat from the chaff, particularly in the case of the Internet. And yet women are searching, and they are searching more than ever. In a study on the information-seeking behaviors of undergraduate students, Percheski and Hargittai (2011) found women more likely than men to use the Internet to seek out information related to health. This high use of the Internet seems to continue into adulthood as women become mothers. In a survey of 303 midwives, Lagan, Sinclair, and Kernohan (2011) found that 86 percent had the experience of a pregnant patient bringing them information they had found on the Internet. Midwives found the information that their patients found on the Internet to have strong impacts on the treatments and services their patients choose. Interestingly, despite the fact that 98 percent of midwives noted analyzing for the quality of the Internet information they were given by pregnant patients, only 15 percent of them were able to name at least one quality indicator they used to evaluate online sources. This is a startling indicator of the "dark continent" even from within the field of women's health. Studies have also shown women's Internet searching to increase with ambiguous news coverage of health information. For example, Weeks et al. (2012) found an increase in the volume of Google searches for information about mammographies after controversial news stories regarding the practice appeared on television. This increase in Internet searching indicates the desire of women to gain a hold of their own understanding of medical practices and to develop their beliefs based on various information sources.

On the mental health side, women experiencing psychological distress often turn to the Internet for answers. Maloni, Przeworski, and Damato (2013) found 69 percent of the women they surveyed used the Internet to search for information regarding their symptoms of postpartum depression, and 90 percent of their sample reported that they would use the Internet to learn about ways to obtain help for postpartum mood disorders. These findings suggest how important a tool the Internet can be to women struggling with maternal and reproductive mental health issues.

FROM THE LAB TO THE WEB: THE DEVELOPMENT OF KHORAI

KHORAI is a production of the Maternal Psychology Laboratory at Teachers College, Columbia University. The lab explores motherhood and reproductive mental health through multiple domains, from the psychological experience of the mothers themselves to the curious lack of psychological research devoted to mothers. To this end, the lab has conducted research in such diverse topics as motherhood and spirituality, motherhood and anxiety, motherhood as a developmental stage, postpartum hallucinations, and even the frequency of motherhood as a topic of psychological journal articles.

KHORAI developed after an especially animated and impassioned group discussion at the lab. Excited about our research on such an unacknowledged group as mothers, it clicked: "What we have here is *good*— let's spread the wealth. We need to find a way to engage others in this conversation." For the next several months, our lab became a think tank as we dreamed up ideas for an online magazine where we could share with the layperson the fascinating research and literature we were uncovering as we studied the maternal mind. A prototype was established, a mission statement recorded, and KHORAI was born. The words "open access" flashed in our minds like a neon sign: this would be an opportunity to blow down the walls between the scientist and the layperson, taking information sharing between the two to a new level. We could inform women about our research and in turn, they could respond to us via online comments, allowing us to then be informed by them. It has required a dedicated, nurturing spirit from its most infantile stages, but we are dedicated to promoting psychological literacy for women navigating the feminine experience. Since its conception, however, the response has been moving in its depth and breadth. We have had thousands of hits from across the globe. While our most concentrated readers are from the United States and other Western or English-speaking nations, we have also been privileged with visits as far off as Laos, El Salvador, Chile, and Zaire, among others. A Google Analytics world map of site "hits" reveals that there are few places KHORAI has yet to reach.

WHAT IS KHORAI?

The name "KHORAI" is a product of the following equation: KHÔRA + KORAI = KHORAI. *Khôra* is a philosophical term used to describe the space and place from which all things originate. Frequently likened to the womb, khôra is a feminine, primordial arena that gives birth to ideas. *Korai* is the ancient Greek word for daughters. The singular form is *kore*, used to evoke the female form in all its life phases, (e.g., maiden, mother, and crone). Kore is also the diminutive name for Persephone, the Greek goddess of the underworld and regeneration, who ate the multifaceted pomegranate and thus became a woman. From this myth we have adopted as our logo the archetypal symbol for the mysteries of femininity, the pomegranate. Thus, KHORAI is multiple spaces for defining the experience of women as they mature— nature's many daughters from whom infinite possibilities spring forth, and the uncharted territory of female development waiting to be known.

At its core, KHORAI is an online magazine about reproductive and maternal mental health, but its topical range includes a multitude of issues related to women's general well-being. It is designed to stimulate discussion related to women's emotional, physical, and spiritual formation throughout the lifespan—tracing women's passage through adolescence, potential motherhood ("matrescence"), and menopause—as well as more abstract notions of the maternal or feminine within nature. KHORAI was established to become a trustworthy public forum to thoughtfully collect, interpret, and disseminate information regarding women's development—particularly at the intersection of psychological and reproductive health.

KHORAI is vastly different than what is normally represented in women's magazines. Recognizing the tendency in new media to reduce, and therefore misrepresent, academic research, KHORAI writers understand that they are accountable for the content they are creating. Hence, KHORAI posts are reflective, employing deep analysis and trusting the intellectual capability of the audience. In essence, we are telling our readers, "We know you can read this, we know you are smart." The biggest challenge has been to learn and foster the art of translating this (sometimes) lofty material chock-full of academic jargon into concise, compelling prose. It is a delicate balance that requires thoughtful contemplation and the will to perpetually curate. When a lab member "translates" a journal article on our website, the post goes through a process similar to the peer-review process of major journals. Three lab members read the original journal article with the newly written post to check for both accuracy and clarity.

KHORAI also wishes to garner dialogue with our readers. The editors and contributors critically reflect upon the relevant topics at hand and actively encourage readers to take similar ownership of their individual and collective wellness through the power of education; many posts end with questions directly posed at the audience, which spurs a fruitful discussion among passionate, opinionated readers. In fact, KHORAI makes it a priority to employ an inquiry-based perspective, asking questions and examining the claims of empirical science and mass media.

In addition to the written word, KHORAI uses imagery to inspire, recognizing the power of aesthetic beauty in moving an audience. In popular women's magazines, image often promotes anxiety and frustration as women are forced to constantly compare themselves to unattainable ideals. In many ways, images in the popular media are used to dictate to women *how they should be*. At KHORAI, we seek to find images that speak to the individuality of women, allowing them to express or explore *who they are* and to use image as a healing resource for mirroring, rather than for harming. A recurring category on KHORAI is "Artwatch," which spotlights compelling artistic endeavors that draw attention to women's experiences. For example, we recently featured a series of whimsical short films by actress Isabella Rossellini entitled "Mammas," which explores the conceptualization of "maternal instinct" across species by donning the costumes of various animals and role-playing their maternal behaviors to better understand "the essence of femininity." Through aesthetics, art such as Rossellini's piece allows women to explore their own psychology as it relates to the not-so-comforting reproductive realities alive in the animal kingdom. In addition to "Artwatch," KHORAI is deeply aware of the imagery chosen for our website. For each KHORAI post, whether it is a "translation" of a scientific journal article or a piece about body literacy, we strive to pair with it an image that will invoke in the reader the reflective thinking that comes with artistic viewing, deepening their understanding of the textual information given.

PROVIDING A LANGUAGE WITH WHICH TO SPEAK

Reflecting on our own conversations with acquaintances not so deeply immersed in academia as ourselves, our laboratory members have come to identify a sort of *craving* that exists for language to describe different facets of the human experience. This, we observe, is why such media outlets as pop-psychology magazines continue to exist—people want to educate them-selves, to become participants in the conversations about mental health and well-being. KHORAI provides this knowledge and vocabulary in various ways. When we translate academic articles into accessible, shorter-form pieces we take care to highlight official terms that our audience may wish to incorporate into their own vocabulary. One example of this is "empathic abandonment," a term we found in a recent journal article on teen mothers, which was used to describe the feelings of disruption in a relationship be-tween a pregnant adolescent and her closest family members. Another is a "Body Literacy" post about "mittelschmerz," or the dull pain frequently ex-perienced during ovulation. Often our audience responds to these posts with statements such as, "I never knew there was a word for this," indicating an excitement found from the new ability to articulate these experiences.

RESPECTING DIVERSITY

KHORAI seeks to bridge the gap between clinical science, mass media, and the personal experiences of contemporary women. Our writing represents a desire to interpret public health information in a manner that is both rigorous and empathic of women's unique status, makeup, and subjectivity. The idea of highlighting and honoring a woman's "subjective experience" in research is a theme of the laboratory that has seeped into KHORAI's own distinctive goals as a journalistic outlet. It is a deep-rooted hope that the writing we produce inspires our readers such that they develop a heightened sense of interpersonal awareness, that is, a woman reading about the experiences of black mothers recovering from the loss of a child to gun violence might read news reports a little differently. By prioritizing "compassion raising," we acknowledge the ways in which women have historically been misrepresent-ed, misevaluated, misperceived, and simply *misunderstood*. We hope to chal-lenge our readers to resist deviant or negative descriptions of women's expe-riences that are so commonly portrayed in mass media and the sciences alike. In contrast, KHORAI celebrates women's maturation processes as distinc-tive, and seeks to conceptualize alternate models of growth that optimize their well-being. Additionally, while it is popular for female writers from such a standpoint to use language that supports the feminist power agenda, KHORAI instead honors multiple viewpoints and empowers women to voice their own informed perspectives on complex subjects. Recognizing that while conversations about power within feminist discourse are absolutely crucial, this bent has overpowered other items on the feminist agenda that are equally vital and might forge a more inviting and inclusive atmosphere, awakening a rich discussion replete with new perspective. In light of this, KHORAI seeks to remain transparent about its agenda to highlight the subjective experiences of women, whether their voices go with or against the grain of the larger discourse. By maintaining this stance as our utmost responsibility, our writers provide thoughtful, often open-ended contributions to this conversation.

KHORAI AS CASE STUDY

For those of us working at the Maternal Psychology Laboratory, KHORAI has served as a quasi-experiment. When we first developed KHORAI, we questioned: Is it possible to bridge the gap between academic researchers and the populations they study through using the Internet? Are women interested in reading about their bodies and minds without the sensationalism of mass media? Can we carve out our own little piece of the web in order to add to the conversation? Since the creation of our website in 2012, our readers have answered these questions for us with a resounding "Yes!" Through our work with KHORAI, we wish to inspire not only women with questions about their bodies and minds, but also researchers from other academic disciplines, in hope that they may also use the Internet to bring knowledge back into the community. Like *khôra*, the Internet suggests the possibility of a birthing space. What will women make of this opening?

REFERENCES

Belar, C. 2008. "Increasing Psychological Literacy." *Monitor on Psychology* 39(10): 56.

Boston Women's Health Collective. 1970. *Women and Their Bodies: A Course*. Boston: Author.

Cranney, J., and D. S. Dunn. 2011. *The Psychologically Literate Citizen*. New York: Oxford University Press.

Halpern, D. F. 2010. *Undergraduate Education in Psychology: A Blueprint for the Future of the Discipline*. Washington, D.C.: American Psychological Association.

Karraa, Walker. 2013. "There Are No Words: Postpartum Mood Disorders and Miriam Carey's Death." *Psychology Benefits Society*. Retrieved from: http://psychologybenefits.org/2013/10/15/postpartum-mood-disorders/ .

Lagan, B. M., M. Sinclair, and W. G. Kernohan. 2011. "A Web-Based Survey of Midwives' Perceptions of Women Using the Internet in Pregnancy: A Global Phenomenon." *Midwifery* 27: 273–81.

Maloni, J. A., A. Przeworski, and E. G. Damato. 2013. "Web Recruitment and Internet Use and Preferences Reported by Women with Postpartum Depression after Pregnancy Complications." *Archives of Psychiatric Nursing* 27: 90–95.

Percheski, C., and E. Hargittai. 2011. "Health-Information Seeking in the Digital Age." *Journal of American College Health* 59(5): 380–86.

Chapter Eight

Leveraging the Power of the Web for Work

Female Veterans' Online Efforts to Combat Unemployment

D. Alexis Hart and Mariana Grohowski

A 2012 Gallup poll found: "Female veterans of the U.S. military have a much better outlook on their lives than male veterans do [and are] far more likely to rate their lives as 'thriving' (54%) than their male counterparts (44%)" (Myers and Liu 2013). This positive outlook is somewhat surprising in light of another recent study, this one by the Institute for Veterans and Military Families (2013), which found, "the rate of unemployment for young female veterans remains close to double the rate of non-veteran females ages 20–24 (12.1%)," and that the unemployment rate of female veterans ages 25–39 rose between 2011 and 2012. These numbers are certainly concerning, and while "[n]o one can pinpoint exactly why the transition to the civilian workplace seems tougher for female veterans," one likely factor is "a civilian sector that may not fully understand the role of women in the military" (Thiruvengadam 2011). Another contributing factor lies with the female veterans, who, due to "family expectations and societal stereotypes . . . often end up downplaying their skills and values. 'They learn that people don't get what they've done in the military, and over time, they stop telling their military service story'" (Ledford 2013). In combination, the lack of understanding on the part of civilian employers and the reluctance or inability on the part of many female veterans to capitalize on their military experiences and training often results in confusion and frustration when these women veterans begin to seek jobs in the civilian sector.

The U.S. military does offer some job transition training to members separating from the active service through Transition Assistance Program (TAP) workshops. At TAP, attendees ostensibly "learn about job searches, career decision-making, current occupational and labor market conditions, and resume and cover letter preparation and interviewing techniques" and are "provided with an evaluation of their employability relative to the job market" ("Transition" 2013). However, these government transition programs tend to be "severely out-dated" and may be less helpful to female veterans because most of the training materials were developed in "the era before there were high numbers of women in the military" (Quast 2011). As a result, many women who have separated from the military may feel inadequately prepared to begin their civilian job searches, and may have limited ideas of where to turn for additional help. Fortunately, the web is increasingly becoming a viable resource for female veterans seeking assistance with their career transitions. As D. Alexis Hart (2011) has noted in her article "Inquiring Communally, Acting Collaboratively: The Community Literacy of the Academy Women eMentor Portal and Facebook Group," Web 2.0 and social networking sites afford current and former female military-service personnel opportunities to make professional and personal connections and gain access to contacts and information about career changes that they might not otherwise—practically or geographically—have access to.

For example, in a recent article on the ClearanceJobs website, two female veterans and founders of organizations that help women veterans personally and professionally—Kimberly Olson, CEO of Grace After Fire, and Celia Szelwach, CEO of Women Veterans Network (WOVEN)—discussed how women veterans have begun to create "their own solutions to success" (Ledford 2013). Olson has found that "when women are active in peer support groups, they increase their opportunities to move forward, both in life and in the job hunt. They meet others with whom they can relate, and learn more about how to best present themselves to prospective employers and how to tailor their interests to the job search" (Ledford 2013). Because women veterans have been found to be more hesitant to seek out resources (Hickey 2011; Bhagwati 2012), leveraging the power of the web may offer a more appealing and/or accessible means for female veterans to seek guidance and to acquire job resources to facilitate their transitions.

In what follows, we provide an overview of several groups on LinkedIn and Facebook, as well as some stand-alone websites aimed at helping female veterans who are shifting their professional focus from military service to civilian careers. We describe what each site offers as well as some of the benefits and constraints of each.

LINKEDIN GROUPS

LinkedIn is a social networking platform for professionals. A LinkedIn profile allows a user to share her education and work-related experiences and expertise, and to connect with others in related fields. Users who connect to each other can also add skills endorsement tags (e.g., "leadership," "product development," "project planning") and post brief statements of recommendation. A 2012 survey reports "93 percent of job recruiters" use LinkedIn "to find qualified candidates" (Whitney 2012). Although the report notes the use of Facebook and Twitter for similar purposes, it credits LinkedIn with "lead[ing] the list as the top social media site scoured by professional recruiters to track down job applicants" (Whitney 2012).

Project Transition USA

How to join: Create or sign in to a LinkedIn account; this is an open group.

What is offered: As a recent article by Bobbie O'Brien (2013) noted, veterans transitioning back into the civilian workforce are finding guidance and success through LinkedIn. O'Brien's article features the newly established nonprofit Project Transition USA's LinkedIn group. The president and founder of Project Transition, Nancy Laine, conducts in-person workshops locally on and off MacDill Air Force Base in Tampa, Florida. Laine uses LinkedIn to promote her workshops as well as to post relevant information to assist veterans and military-service personnel with the types of skills, experiences, and language use civilian business professionals are expecting from potential applicants, but military-service personnel may not be familiar with.

Benefits: Those residing in and around Tampa, Florida benefit by finding information about upcoming job expositions, job postings, and workshops.

Constraints: Those not residing near Tampa, Florida, will miss out on the various in-person workshops and expositions the group hosts or co-hosts.

American Women Veterans

How to join: Send a request to the group facilitator; this is a closed group.

What is offered: The members of this group post links to job-search-related items for veterans and transitioning military members such as tools to help translate military skills to civilian terms or to format resumes as well as announcements about opportunities nationwide to meet with recruiters or to attend job fairs. The group also provides links to resources for aspiring female veteran entrepreneurs such as advice on working for oneself and a list of veteran-owned women's small businesses. In addition to job search and career advice, the members of this group offer each other tips on obtaining educational and health benefits and post discussion topics and links to articles targeted at other, non-job-related challenges faced by women veterans, such as caring for children, aging parents, or injured spouses.

Benefits: The group has more than six hundred members and therefore provides a high degree of potential networking opportunities for job seekers. The group members also seem willing to provide emotional and psychological support to others living in similar circumstances or with similar backgrounds and interests. E-mail updates are sent to members' e-mail accounts, allowing them to click on links of interest without having to log on to the LinkedIn site to check for the latest postings.

Constraints: The "Jobs" tab for this group lists no jobs, and only two discussion threads are explicitly labeled as "job discussions."

Military Women

How to join: Join via LinkedIn groups; this is an open group.

What is offered: The postings on this group include announcements about programming on "Veterans Helping Veterans TV," such as "Find a career, not just a job." Other posts are directed specifically at helping women veterans to transition, such as links to programs to teach female veterans how to "make it in civilian life," to other women veterans with "entrepreneurial passion" who have started their own businesses, and to career coaches. This group, too, expands its scope beyond job advice to include discussion threads on military women and suicide; homelessness among female veterans; VA health and educational benefits; and opportunities to engage in community service.

Benefits: At just over 100 members, this group is smaller than the American Women Veterans LinkedIn group, which may afford the opportunity for individual members to establish closer connections to other group members.

Constraints: Most discussion topics and links are posted by the group's manager with limited response or interaction by other group members.

Women Veterans Empowerment Network: WoVEN

How to join: Send a request to the group facilitator; this is a closed group.

What is offered: WoVEN's stated mission is "To provide dynamic social networking and career resource venues to empower and encourage women, from all U.S. Military Service Branches, to gain and maintain meaningful, well-paying civilian jobs." Not surprisingly, given its more explicit mission statement, the discussion threads in this group tend to focus most often on job-related topics such as transitioning from military to civilian careers, business networking, getting referrals, start-ups and women entrepreneurs, and avoiding job scams, although some of the posts are aimed at creating a social network of military women, such as announcements about women veterans' conferences and events at the Women in Military Service Memorial.

Benefits: The manager of this group, a corporate recruiter herself, is highly motivated and, in addition to posting helpful links, she frequently encourages the members of the group to communicate more frequently with each other in an effort to create a "tightly-knit sisterhood of U.S. Military women sharing knowledge, challenges, possibilities & pride."

Constraints: Despite the group manager's best efforts, few other members of the group actively post announcements or comments or otherwise engage in discussions, and a stand-alone website for the group has become inactive as a result of limited engagement and support.

Lady Vets

How to join: Send a request to the group facilitator; this is a closed group.

What is offered: Of the LinkedIn groups featured here, Lady Vets may have the most diverse postings, from "great advice for everyone at any point in their career" and "link to 100,000 jobs for vets" to announcements about Ms. Veteran America, the Army testing female-specific body armor, homelessness, and coping with deployments.

Benefits: The more diverse nature of the postings seems also to have led to more direct requests for assistance and advice from its members.

Constraints: If a new member has to scroll through a number of non-job-related posts before seeing any job-related links, she may question whether the group will be valuable to her in her job search.

FACEBOOK GROUPS

During a recent Senate Subcommittee Hearing (*Hearing to Receive Testimony on Sexual Assaults in the Military*, 112th Cong. 35 [2013]), U.S. Army veteran and social media expert BriGette McCoy reported that Facebook has been crucial for uniting veterans because Facebook groups provide a way for veterans to share advice and to offer helpful programs aimed at professional development (Burke 2011). With "1.11 billion people using the site each month" (Associated Press 2013), Facebook has the advantage of volume and is likely to be a site on which many female veterans already have accounts and on which they may already be connecting with other veterans and therefore can see what groups their peers are joining and following.

Women Military Aviators, Inc.

How to join: Request to join via Facebook or be invited by an existing member.

What is offered: As stated on the "About" page for the group, "WMA was established to promote and preserve for historical, educational and literary purposes the role of women pilots, navigators, and aircrew members in the service of their country during times of war and peace. It offers networking, scholarships, biennial conventions, and links to additional information on women aviators. Membership is open to all female aviators and flight crew members from all services and nations as well as people who support women in military aviation."

Benefits: Group members post job opportunities in aviation-related fields and share current events about aviation in general and about women in the military in particular.

Constraints: Group members rarely initiate discussion threads in which others can ask questions or offer personal support to one another.

AcademyWomen

How to join: Send a request to one of the group administrators.

What is offered: AcademyWomen is "a non-profit organization which supports the personal and professional growth of current, former and future women military officers. It is [their] belief that every woman who chooses to serve her country should be fully prepared to do so. [AcademyWomen] stand[s] behind this belief by providing programs that support and enable women to reach their full potential as leaders." The AcademyWomen Facebook group, while not specifically aimed at offering career advice, does include occasional job-related posts on topics such as at-home work and the Teach for America Veterans' Initiative. Members of the group also promote their own businesses, books they have published, events they are sponsoring, etc. Many posts are driven by current events related to women in the military service, such as the removal of the ban on women in combat, sexual assault in the military, etc. Members also post comments related to the service academies, such as sporting events or featured public speeches.

Benefits: Most members of this group share a bond of having graduated from one of the federal service academies and having served as officers on active duty. A friendly rivalry among the services branches is present, as is a sense of community involvement and engagement for those still in the active service and those who have separated or retired from the service.

Constraints: The group is currently limited to female officers.

STAND-ALONE WEBSITES

A seasoned scholar of the World Wide Web, Jay David Bolter (2001) has noted just how accommodating the web is for "even the tiniest political organization or interest group" (207). While somewhat less visible than LinkedIn or Facebook groups, stand-alone websites can offer their managers more versatility and control over the design and content. In this last section, we feature three stand-alone websites for female veterans looking to harness the web for work.

eMentor

Website: http://ementorprogram.org/about
   How to join: Send a request to the group facilitator.
   What is offered: eMentor is "a cutting-edge online mentoring program for military personnel, veterans, and DoD civilians. eMentor connects individuals for dynamic mentoring experiences that powerfully move them forward in their personal and professional lives." The eMentor program is divided into a number of groups, each of which is targeted to specific demographics. Below are two:

The OfficerWomen eMentor Program

This program is "open to ALL women officers, officers-in-training, officer reservists and officer veterans of the U.S. military services: Air Force, Army Coast Guard, Marine Corps, merchant Marine and Navy. Commissioned men in leadership positions and GS15 and above Civil Service professionals may also participate as mentors only." Common postings among this group include advice on work/life balance, ways to improve/boost your resume, ways to be smart about managing your money, links to virtual career fairs and to conferences such as the Women Veteran Entrepreneur Corps conference. The site also includes links to articles with job advice (e.g., the "top 5 jobs military veterans should consider," telecommuting/working from home, "working women know your value").
   Benefits: The group offers female military officers, cadets, and midshipmen a space in which to receive mentorship and job advice both while on active duty and after separating from the military. With almost double the number of mentors as compared to protégés, those seeking advice are likely to be able to connect fairly easily with more than one mentor.
   Constraints: Both mentors and protégés may find themselves waiting for the other party to reach out and make the first connection, causing mentors to wonder why they have not been contacted by any protégés, and vice versa. Protégés may initially feel uncomfortable contacting a higher-ranking officer, despite that officer's clear willingness to serve as a mentor.

The Veteran eMentor Program

An outgrowth of the Officer Women eMentor Program, the Veteran eMentor Program, which is available to female and male veterans, officer and enlisted personnel, "leverages the internet to create a dynamic information sharing, learning and support community that extends far beyond the veteran's current network. Protégés can receive personalized career guidance, advice, support and inspiration from more experienced veterans, career mentors and veteran-friendly employers." Common postings in this group include links to resources such as Hiring Our Heroes, virtual job fairs, and a veteran-owned business directory, as well as advice on making the transition from military to civilian life, getting college classes/credits, and accessing veterans' health benefits. The site also provides links to career coaches and career counselors who can help members match their skills and education to civilian careers.

Benefits: The Veteran eMentor Program has partnered with a number of corporations and businesses such as the Better Business Bureau, Capital One, Lowe's, and Toyota, as well as job consulting agencies such as InQuest Consulting, Elite Personnel, and Talent Curve and military-specific job agencies such as Hiring Our Heroes, Military One-Click, and Military Transition Services to provide additional resources for its members.

Constraints: The openness of the group may create some barriers to mentorship given differences in rank and gender.

VetNet

Website: http://www.vetnethq.com/

How to join: To gain access and make use of all of VetNet's resources, users need to sign in, or sign up for a Google+ (GooglePlus) account. VetNet's website offers a brief "New to Google+" tutorial (a PDF with images) for setting up a Google+ account.

What is offered: A very helpful video, "How to Get Started with Vet Net" walks users through the involvement process in a step-by-step manner. The video begins by establishing empathy with viewers (veterans transitioning into the civilian workforce). It then guides users through a simple, two-step process of signing up to access VetNet's resources and online courses.

VetNet offers three content tracks:

1. Basic Training: Resume writing workshops, interviewing tips, help searching the online database of "over 100 million veteran-specific jobs" (video).
2. Career Connections: Helps users identify which fields or careers are most suitable for their experiences and skills. This track allows users to participate in mentoring and to receive civilian career advice via video chats with career experts and other veterans.
3. Entrepreneur Track: Focuses on those users who are interested in beginning their own businesses.

Benefits: If a user can't be present during the "live" Google Hangouts, these sessions are recorded and shared on the group's Google+ page.

Constraints: Due to the flexibility and synchronous nature of this platform, it may be difficult for most participants to meet "live." Therefore, opportunities to network with other veterans may be limited, but participants will receive one-on-one attention from trained professionals.

The Veteran's Coach

Website: deannawharwood.com/blog/

How to join: The option for this site is not "to join" as much as to follow "The Veteran's Coach," Deanna Wharwood, on one or more social networking sites (e.g., Facebook, Twitter, LinkedIn, and Pinterest). Interested followers can also sign up to receive a newsletter.

What is offered: Wharwood, The Veteran's Coach, is a Navy veteran and trained job coach who posts a number of free resources to help veterans transition from the military into the civilian workforce (e.g., information about possible jobs, pragmatic tips such as highlighting the differences between military networking and civilian networking, and mentorship through her online posts). Wharwood is particularly interested in small business ownership for veterans. Her tagline is "Get free tips to win in business and in life."

Benefits: The Veteran's Coach offers a significant amount of resources for veterans, posting multiple times a day on various social media platforms and offering psychological and professional support. This emotional, psychological support and the sharing of resources and information that female veterans might not otherwise encounter is one benefit of using social networking delivery platforms.

Constraints: Following The Veteran's Coach on multiple social media platforms is dizzying, and those who follow Wharwood on more than one platform may receive either repeated information or feel a sense of information overload.

CONCLUSION

At a time in which unemployment numbers nationwide are high and the opportunities for advancement and retention within the military are decreasing, female veterans, in particular, are feeling the pinch. Often constrained by caregiver obligations and geographical limitations, these women have begun to leverage the power of the web to create powerful social networks to share their experiences and advice with other women transitioning out of active military service. As Sallie Krawcheck, former chief of Sanford C. Bernstein and Citi Global Wealth Management recently noted, social networks "enable their members to contribute to, and pull from, the network to accomplish more than the sum of the parts would indicate" and therefore, "increase professional success" by acting as "platforms for the exchange and promotion of information and ideas, [thereby] accelerating [members'] acquisition of skills and knowledge" (Krawcheck 2013). Groups on LinkedIn and Facebook, along with stand-alone websites created and maintained by female veterans, are fostering and sustaining networks for women who have served in the military and are now seeking to establish professional success in the civilian marketplace. By not only providing spaces for sharing information and ideas about improving resumes and translating military experience to civilian skills, but also by offering opportunities for female veterans to discuss other issues of importance in their lives—from caregiving to combat—these web-based sites have the potential to make a positive difference in the working status and personal lives of their female veteran participants.

REFERENCES

Associated Press. 2013. "Number of Active Users at Facebook over the Years." *Yahoo! News* , May 1. Accessed May 22, 2013. http://news.yahoo.com/number-active-users-facebook-over-230449748.html .

Bhagwati, Anuradha K. 2012. "Military Women at Risk for Suicide." *New York Times: Room for Debate*, March 20. Accessed May 21, 2013. http://www.nytimes.com/roomfordebate/2011/11/20/how-can-we-prevent-military-suicides/military-women-at-risk-for-suicide .

Bolter, Jay David. 2001. *Writing Space: Computers, Hypertext, and the Remediation of Print.* Mahwah, NJ: Lawrence Erlbaum Associates.

Burke, Matthew M. 2011. "Social Media Bridging Gap between Troubled Vets and Treatment." *Stars and Stripes*, September 23. Accessed May 22, 2013. http://www.stripes.com/social-media-bridging-gap-between-troubled-vets-and-treatment-1.155937 .

Hart, D. Alexis. 2011. "Inquiring Communally, Acting Collaboratively: The Community Literacy of the Academy Women eMentor Portal and Facebook Group." *Community Literacy Journal* 6(1): 79–90.

Hickey, Allison A. 2011. "Honoring Women Veterans: A Message from Under Secretary Allison Hickey." *The White House Blog: Council on Women and Girls*, 11 Nov. Accessed May 21, 2013.

Institute for Veterans and Military Families. 2013. *The Annual Employment Situation of Veterans (2012).* http://vets.syr.edu/wp-content/uploads/2013/03/Annual-Employment-Report2012.pdf .

Krawcheck, Sallie. 2013. "Why a Woman's Network? Why Now?" *Forbes*, May 16. Accessed May 21, 2013. http://www.forbes.com/sites/85broads/2013/05/16/why-a-womans-network-why-now/?ss=forbeswoman .

Ledford, Tranette. 2013. "Women Veterans: Creating Their Own Solutions for Success." *ClearanceJobs*, May 8. http://news.clearancejobs.com/2013/05/08/women-veterans-creating-their-own-solutions-for-success/ .

Myers, Robin, and Diana Liu. 2013. "In U.S., Women Veterans Rate Lives Better Than Men: Women Veterans' Positivity about Future Boosts Their Overall Life Ratings." *Gallup*, April 25. Accessed May 21, 2013. http://www.gallup.com/poll/162035/women-veterans-rate-lives-better-men.aspx .

O'Brien, Bobbie. 2013. "LinkedIn Connects Transitioning Military to Civilian Careers." *Off The Base*, May 3. Accessed May 21, 2013. http://offthebase.wordpress.com/2013/05/03/linkedin-connects-transitioning-military-to-civilian-careers/#more-9264 .

Quast, Lisa. 2011. "The Struggle for Female Veterans to Transition into Civilian Jobs." *ForbesWoman*, April 11. Accessed May 20, 2013. http://www.forbes.com/sites/lisaquast/2011/04/11/the-struggle-for-female-veterans-to-transition-into-civilian-jobs/.

Thiruvengadam, Meena. 2011. "Job Market Leaves Female Vets Behind." *USA Today*, March 19. Accessed May 21, 2013. http://usatoday30.usatoday.com/printedition/money/20110217/womenvets17_st.art.htm .

"Transition Assistance Program (TAP)." 2013. *Transition Assistance Online*, January. Accessed May 21, 2013. http://www.taonline.com/TAPOffice/ .

Whitney, Lance. 2012. "Heads up, LinkedIn Users: 93 Percent of Recruiters Are Looking at You." *CNet*, July 10. Accessed May 21, 2003. http://news.cnet.com/8301-1023_3-57469282-93/heads-up-linkedin-users-93-of-recruiters-are-looking-at-you/ .

Chapter Nine

Tips for Starting Your Own Dream Business on eBay and Etsy in Thirty Days or Less

Kathleen Clauson

Millions of women are leaving the traditional workplace for a variety of reasons: to follow their dreams of owning their own businesses, to spend more time with their families, to set their own schedules, to use their creativity and artistic talents, or to embark on a new after-retirement career. Whether it is to moonlight a few nights a week or work full-time, online businesses offer the most flexibility and start-up has never been easier. Online shops can easily be operated out of the home, started up without breaking the bank, and sellers can start earning profits right away.

With the click of a mouse, a storefront can be set up in a few hours. Online U.S. retail sales reached $169 billion in 2010, an increase of 16.3 percent in one year. Online sales for the electronic shopping and mail-order accounted for 51 percent of total sales in 2012 (U.S. Census Bureau 2012). E-commerce platforms or marketplaces, such as eBay and Etsy have made starting an online storefront as easy as pie without having to hire a web designer. Both eBay and Etsy have strong web presences and whenever you search for an item, the first hits you'll see are usually listings on eBay and Etsy. Sellers on eBay and Etsy enjoy a built-in customer base of millions of registered buyers. Etsy's sales continue to skyrocket. In December 2012 sales were up 73 percent, compared to December 2011 (Steiner 2013). For the fourth quarter of 2012, eBay showed the largest growth it has reported since 2011 (Stambor 2013). In customer satisfaction, eBay remains one of the top five of the major leaders of e-commerce (Dusto 2013).

Women are creating new businesses at a higher rate than ever before and changing the dynamics of the workplace. The number of women-owned businesses increased twice as fast as men-owned businesses in the last decade and employment at women-owned companies continues to increase, while employment in men-owned firms has shown declines (National Women's Business Council 2012, 22). One of every eleven adult women is an entrepreneur. *Forbes* is calling entrepreneurship, the "new women's movement" (MacNeil 2012). It is expected of the 9.72 million new businesses on the horizon by 2018, women will start-up half of them (MacNeil 2012). From a global perspective, one-third of all entrepreneurs are women.

WOMEN ENTREPRENEURS WHO MADE THEIR DREAMS COME TRUE

Greta Andersen, with sweet recollections of candy sprinkles and fun cake-top decorations at her parents' bakery, searched for baking supplies of her own a few years after her parents sold their business and she became a mother, only to discover these types of items were not readily available to non-professional retail customers. Greta launched the Layer Cake Shop on the Etsy marketplace with a few items, investing less than $100. She designed a baking supply storefront with a vintage look and it was a big hit. A year later, she recruited the help of another mom, her friend Kristen Nevill, and they launched their own website (*Country Living* 2011, 20). LayerCakeShop.com offers a variety of unique baking cups, cake toppers, cupcake picks, and sprinkles in every color of the rainbow for any occasion. They operate their business out of Kristen's home and sales continue to increase. Greta and Kristen are enjoying sweet success, make a comfortable living, and have plenty of time with their kids.

Tara Agacayak probably didn't expect she would have a successful career in IT, meet the man of her dreams, and move to Turkey. She met her husband while working for the Department of Defense. When he was offered a job back home in Turkey, they relocated. Living in a foreign country with a new culture and language was exciting, but also overwhelming, plus Tara found no promising career prospects. Inspired by an article about a woman who made a living on eBay, she bought handcrafted cashmere shawls and scarves from local artisans in Istanbul and resold them on eBay. She could set her own schedule and could still run her business if she went back to California for a visit to her family. Tara found her calling at a seminar about globally responsible entrepreneurship and realized she could help Turkish women make better livings by teaching them how to sell their own items online (Sisson 2010.) Today, Tara and her business partner Anastasia Ashman operate GlobalNiche.net, a small business training program serving women from fifty-five countries.

PLANNING YOUR DREAM BUSINESS

Making plans for your dream business is really an exercise in self-discovery. Becoming an entrepreneur is not just about making a living; it is about creating something that provides meaning and satisfaction in your life. Identifying a passion that pulls at your heartstrings is important because if you love what you are doing, you will put your heart and soul into it. To find your passion, sit down in a quiet place for about an hour with a notebook and jot down your thoughts on the following ways to find your passion (McClelland and Padilla 2011, 23–40.)

What do you love doing? Are you inspired by an entrepreneur who is doing what you would love doing? Who is it? What do they sell? What are the things that attract you to that business?

Are you an expert in something? Is there something you could teach others? Is there something you can tell someone about, down to the last detail?

Whenever you web surf, where does it take you? What kinds of things do you look for? What kinds of information do you find? Can you identify a pattern in your web browsing?

What are the things you have in your home that have special meaning and most reveal something about who you are and what you like? What things do you love most? Which ones inspire you?

What skills do you have that could help you translate your passions into a career? Which ones are your strengths? Your weaknesses? Your favorites?

After identifying your passions, which can become an online business? How do you envision your business? What kinds of items will you sell? Where will you find the items you plan to sell? If you plan to make the items yourself, what will you need to make each item? What will make your business different from those selling similar products? Who will be your customers? One of the best ways to decide what kind of business you want is to find out what's out there. "Watching" the sales of items similar to your own will help you in your own pricing.

DOING YOUR HOMEWORK

I recommend searching on eBay and Etsy for items similar to the ones you are interested in selling. This will give you an opportunity to see how others sellers operate firsthand and at the same time it will give you more insight as to how eBay and Etsy work. Before you start researching other buyers on eBay, I recommend setting up separate accounts for buying and selling. Both buyers and sellers can leave feedback. On Etsy your purchases are private. On eBay, unless auctions are set as private, anyone who wants to look at your "buyer feedback" can see what you bought, the seller's user name, and how much you paid for any purchases you made in the last ninety days. If you buy and sell using the same eBay account and you buy something on eBay and decide to resell that same item on eBay a month later, your potential buyers will be able to see what you paid for the item you are selling if they take the time to look. By setting up separate buyer and seller accounts, not only does it make your bookkeeping easier, it eliminates the possibility your buyer will see your actual cost for something you are trying to sell.

To be successful in venues like eBay or Etsy, it is important to find a way to stand out, by doing something unique or different to create a customer following, something that can become your signature feature. What makes you different isn't just what you do, what you sell, or what you make—your customer service can set you apart from the sea of other sellers, just as much as your product.

After ordering a few things, take a few moments to evaluate your buying experience with each seller. I keep track of my experiences with buyers on index cards and include the following information: seller's user name or website; contact information; item purchased, date of purchase, and price; and information about speed of delivery; opinion about item, price, packaging, and customer service; and notes about any special touches you liked that could be adapted for your own business.

NAMING YOUR BUSINESS

The name of your business is as important as the types of items you sell and the special touches that differentiate you from other sellers. The name of your business should be easy to say, easy to spell, and easy to remember. If your business is going to be identified by your user name only, then the same rules apply. The easier you make it for your customers to find you, remember you, or refer you to their friends, the better, make sure the name you choose is not already trademarked by another business or organization (Ilasco and Seto 2012, 138–39).

SORRY FOLKS, YOU HAVE TO PAY TAXES ON PROFITS

Before we go any further, let's clear up one issue. If you are selling online "you have to pay taxes on every penny of profit you make, even if you make just one dollar" (Ennico 2007, 4). You are running a retail business if you are buying and selling things online and making a profit. This means you must comply with the same laws and regulations as brick-and-mortar businesses and you are subject to the same federal, state, and local taxes.

Many sellers believe if they treat their business as a hobby they won't have to pay taxes. That is incorrect. You still have to report your profits as income on your personal income tax. If you made profits in three of the last five years (including the current year) you will be considered to be in business by the IRS. If you are a business you are eligible for a number of deductions. No matter what you call your selling, it is imperative that you keep accurate and proper records of your income and expenses (Ennico 2007, 18–19). I strongly recommend that you make an appointment with your tax accountant before you start your online business.

CHOOSING YOUR MARKETPLACE: EBAY OR ETSY?

After you have an idea what you want to sell, the next step is to choose a platform. Before setting up your store, go online and carefully read the policies for sellers, including information on listing fees, and items that can be sold. On eBay you can sell just about anything under the sun as long as it's legal. Etsy is a specialized marketplace designed to bring artists, crafters, and collectors together. The only kinds of items you can sell are handmade items, vintage items twenty years old or more, and items that can be categorized as supplies.

On eBay you can sell your items by auction or at a fixed price. If you auction your items you can choose any starting price you like. Another option is to set a "reserve price" so your item will not sell below your chosen price. For eBay auctions, sometimes the hardest part is deciding what your starting price will be. Although I have seen sellers start their auctions at 99 cents and still earn hundreds of dollars for single items, there is more risk associated with auctions. For example, if you have a vintage ring worth $500 and you start your listing at a low price, with no reserve price, it is entirely feasible that you could lose money if you paid more than it sells for and there are few bidders.

The biggest difference between eBay and Etsy is the fee structure for listing your items for sale and the percentage you will pay after your item is sold. Both eBay and Etsy charge an "insertion fee" also known as a "listing fee" per item. On eBay the listing fees for auctions are different from fixed price listing fees. For auction items, the listing fee also differs according to the starting price. Optional listing upgrades are also available on eBay but for every upgrade you are charged a fee per listing ranging from 10 cents to $4.00. This tiered fee structure is the one of the most difficult things for new sellers to understand. On Etsy there is a flat listing fee of 20 cents per item.

In addition to listing fees, sellers are also charged final value fees which are a percentage of the selling price. On eBay this final value fee varies according to type of listing (auction or fixed price) and final selling price. For auction items, eBay charges the sellers 9 percent of the final selling price for auctions (with a maximum fee of $250) and for fixed price items the final value depends on the category and the selling price, ranging between 7 percent and 11 percent. For items sold in Etsy, the final fee structure is much simpler—3.5 percent of the final price. You will also be charged a minimal PayPal fee for processing payments from buyers. Keep in mind that all fees you pay are direct costs that must be considered in your pricing. If you have items that can be sold on either eBay or Etsy, perhaps you will want to compare fees before deciding where to list it.

PRICING YOUR ITEMS

How do you know how much something is worth? Several factors come into play. For vintage and antique collectibles, it is imperative to know what you are selling. How many identical or similar items were produced by the manufacturer? Was it a limited production? Are the items signed or numbered? What is the average selling price for these items in traditional auctions, online auctions, retail shops, or online shops? How much did you pay for it? Just because you saw someone on television appraise a vase, just like one belonging to your great-grandmother for $3,000, it doesn't mean you can *sell* it for that much.

Auctions are based on the premise that bidders will drive up the price by competing for items. Online auctions are very similar to traditional auctions, except there is no auctioneer to keep up with and the other bidders are invisible. In many ways, it is easier to get caught up in the frenzy of an online auction, especially if the buyer is prepared to pay whatever it takes to own an item. It is not uncommon for something that appears to be an ordinary item to sell for an outrageous amount of money. On eBay the last few seconds are the most exciting for buyers and sellers. The downside of this splendor for sellers is that sometimes the items don't bring an amount even close to what they are worth. If you are trying to price an item you want to sell on an eBay auction, you can start the bidding at any price. Some sellers are confident about starting all their auctions at 99 cents even though it's a gamble. Many, particularly those who can buy items for low wholesale prices, establish lucrative businesses, but some sellers don't get to see the kinds of bidding wars that usually generate dream prices. Some end up losing money. There is an option on eBay to set a reserve price (which costs an additional fee) but sometimes that immediately turns off potential buyers. Setting starting prices for your auction items requires a little experimentation to find a practice you are comfortable with.

If you are trying to set a fixed price for an item, the traditional pricing model calls for a 100 percent markup. If you bought an item for $50, you must add direct costs (such as shipping boxes, shipping costs, packing supplies, fees you pay to eBay, Etsy, and, PayPal, and factor in indirect or overhead costs (such as Internet expenses, office supplies, equipment, advertising expenses, etc.). Let's say the direct costs are $10 and your estimated overhead is $5. If you up the 100 percent markup model your total cost would be $65 and your selling price would be $130 (Strine and Shoup 2011, 118). There is no magical pricing formula that will be perfect in all instances. By knowing what similar items sell for in the stores of other sellers, it will be easier for you to set a price that is competitive.

If you are making the item yourself, it is important that you keep records of the costs of raw materials you use in the making of your products, as well as direct costs and indirect or overhead costs. While it is a good practice to keep track of how long it takes you to make an item, you cannot deduct hourly wages as an expense. The length of time it takes to produce your product will be most useful for planning when you have orders to fill. Again, there is no formula set in stone, but knowing your target market and the asking prices of other sellers will help guide you as you price your items (Malinak 2013, 72–78).

LAUNCHING YOUR BUSINESS

After deciding what kind of business you want to start, collecting the items you want to sell, and choosing your business name, it's time to draft a basic business plan that will become the "roadmap" to your dream business (Monosoff 2007, 48–52).Sometimes when budding entrepreneurs hear the words "business plan" they go into shock because they don't like to write. Some consider forgetting the whole thing and talk themselves out of even starting a business. But hey, you've come this far.

Here's an easy way to write a simple business plan. Take blank piece of paper, leave three equally-sized spaces on the back and front, and write the following six headings: my vision, my mission, my goals, my strategies, my plan, and my dream. Here's an example. Let's imagine your dream business is to sell homemade ragdolls inspired by an old ragdoll that was made by your great-grandmother in France. You have been collecting vintage fabric and trim that you will use to make the dresses. You made one design that you will use for all your dolls. By dressing them in different colors, with different hair, and so on, they will become one-of-a-kind. You have already made and sold several of these dolls. You know you can easily make twenty-five dolls on your own each month, and for twenty-five it costs about $500 or $20 each. You plan to sell them for $40–$60 each.

Your vision could be something like this: "Build a successful online shop that specializes in handcrafted ragdolls, specifically designed with a vintage Old World style for girls of all ages." Sweet and simple. You can always revise or refine it later. Your mission could be: "Fulfill growing demand for handcrafted dolls by developing affordable beautiful one-of-a-kind dolls that can be passed down through the generations." Your goals can be simple. If you can make twenty-five dolls per month and you would like to make $500, your goal for the first year is "to sell three hundred dolls" and in your second year you would like "to sell six hundred dolls." Your strategies will reveal how you plan to grow your business over time and they could look like this: "One strategy I plan to employ is starting a blog about dolls, the history of doll-making, celebrity dolls, and more with a link to my store. I also plan to donate some dolls for underprivileged girls at Christmastime and ask the local newspaper to do a story." You can add more to your strategies as you go along. Your plan can be specific with deadlines. "Five months before the holidays I plan to have three hundred basic dolls ready to dress. By the end of September my special holiday dolls will be ready to sell." The "why you want to do this' part should be the easiest: "Growing up, my ragdolls were my favorite toys to play with and I want to create a similar experience for my own daughter and other girls. I also hope to rekindle the art of doll-making, using vintage fabrics and garments that pull at the heartstrings." And there you have it—in just a few words, you have a basic business plan to get you started.

It's time to set up your storefront, and organize the items you plan to list. When writing the descriptions of your items, don't over-embellish. Keep your descriptions detailed but factual. Sellers who exaggerate can easily find themselves in hot water with buyers who perceive what was written in a different way. Include all pertinent information, color, size, condition, and origin if you know for sure. Online photos truly are worth a thousand words. I recommend taking as many photos of your items as you are allowed, from all angles. If your item is flawed or scratched, make sure you show that clearly in a photo and indicate that in your description. Using a digital camera with close-up capabilities is a must. Items should be photographed on simple backgrounds that don't distract from the item. Also included should be your policies for accepting payments, shipping, and returns.

Your store is ready to launch. Your listings are finished, your photos are uploaded. As soon as you post your items, make a habit of checking your e-mail at regular intervals in case customers have questions. As soon as your item sells and you have received your payment, pack your item carefully and ship it out immediately. I recommend sending everything with delivery confirmation so you have proof you item was delivered. Take the extra time to follow up with your buyer after the sale. If you make it a pleasant memorable buying experience, the word will spread, and you will be on your way to owning your own successful dream business.

REFERENCES

Country Living. 2011. "Making a Country Living; How Two Moms Launched an Online Baking-Supplies Shop from Home," February.

Dusto, Amy. 2013. "E-Retailers Beat Stores in Customer Satisfaction," *Internet Retailer,* February 26. http://www.internetretailer.com/2013/02/26/e-retailers-beat-stores-customer-satisfaction.

Ennico, Cliff. 2007. *The eBay Seller's Tax and Legal Answer Book.* New York: American Management Association.

Ilasco, Meg Mateo, and Cat Seto. 2012. *Mom, Inc.: The Essential Guide to Running a Successful Business from Home.* San Francisco, CA: Chronicle Books.

MacNeil, Natalie. 2012. "Entrepreneurship is the New Women's Movement," *Forbes*, June 8. http://www.forbes.com/sites/work-in-progress/2012/06/08/entrepreneurship-is-the-new-womens-movement/.

Malinak, Jason. 2013. *Etsy-Preneurship: Everything You Need to Know to Turn Your Handmade Hobby into a Thriving Business*. Hoboken, NJ: Wiley.

McClelland, Audrey, and Colleen Padilla. 2011. *The Digital Mom Handbook.* New York: Harper.

Monosoff, Tamara. 2007. *Secrets of Millionaire Moms.* New York: McGraw-Hill.

National Women's Business Council. 2012. "Women-Owned firms in the U.S." January. http://www.nwbc.gov/sites/default/files/NWBC%20Final%20Narrative%20Report.pdf.

Sisson, Natalie. 2010. "How Creative Entrepreneur Tara Agacayak Used a Turkish Bazaar, eBay, and Social Media to Create a Life of Freedom," *The Suitcase Entrepreneur*, September 9. http://suitcaseentrepreneur.com/entrepreneurs/how-creative-entrepreneur-tara-agacayak-used-a-turkish-bazaar-ebay-and-social-media-to-create-a-life-of-freedom/.

Stambor, Zak. 2013. "U.S. Sales on eBay Jump 19% in Q4," *Internet Retailer*, January 16. http://www.internetretailer.com/2013/01/16/us-sales-ebay-jump-19-q4.

Steiner, Ina. 2013. "Etsy Sales Up 73 Percent in December 2012." *E-Commerce Bytes*, January 22. http://www.ecommercebytes.com/cab/abn/y13/m01/i22/s03.

U.S. Census Bureau. 2012. "E-Stats." May 10. http://www.census.gov/econ/estats/2010/2010reportfinal.pdf.

Part II

Running a Business

Chapter Ten

Plus-Size Fashion Blogging for a "Size" of Our Own

Jill Andrew and Aisha Fairclough

In 1929 Virginia Woolf published *A Room of One's Own* in which she argued that "a woman must have money and a room of her own if she is to write fiction" (Woolf 1957, 4). Woolf audaciously advocated for and professed that, in a world defined by patriarchy, the enthralling prose of William Shakespeare and the like, it was crucial that women's literary prowess not be ignored but acknowledged and celebrated within the literary canon. Today, Woolf's demand for our "own room" is an inspirational metaphor for us as we navigate through the often unforgiving world of women's apparel as two fashionable fatshionista "plus size" fashion bloggers.

Regardless of the euphemism you choose, "voluptuous," "misses," "above average," "curvy," or our personal favorite, *fat*, women's apparel above a size 14, otherwise referred to in the fashion world as "plus size," has been traditionally ignored as "the ugly cousin" of the industry (Ellison 2013; Scaraboto and Fischer 2012; Snider 2012). Plus-size fashion has typically been defined as clothing that is sized 14 to as large as 72 (Winn 2004). In 2011, Canada's women's apparel industry was valued at approximately CDN$13.2 billion with the plus-size segment worth a "whopping" CDN$1.9 billion (Fortune 2013). In 2012 United States figures were approximately US$42billion with the plus segment valued at US$7.5 billion (Binns 2013). Clearly, plus-size fashion apparel isn't seen as a significant market to satisfy and the thin body "straight-size" ideal continues to reign as the muse for most retailers and designers. So what are the consequences of all of this to us plus-size shoppers, and how can plus fashion blogging be a game changer? Before we answer this, let's first discuss just how significant clothing is to our self-esteem and to the way in which we present ourselves publically.

THE SIGNIFICANCE OF CLOTHING

Clothing is a "second skin" that helps project our sense of self to loved ones and strangers alike. Our clothing choices can be linked to our best memories and life experiences in that we are likely to wear, more often than others, items we've had great experiences and social interactions in (Woodward 2007). They aren't "just" clothes. Our clothing choices are symbols of who we are, who we think we are, and who we aspire to be (Entwistle 2001). As such, *variety* truly is the spice of life. Just as that perfect outfit helps you shimmy your way into a crowded room beaming confidently like a Best Actress Oscar winner, so can an ill-fitting or matronly styled plus garment make you feel out of place and invisible—especially if it's that same blazer or dress you end up wearing repeatedly due to limited options. Our self-esteem and our public persona are deeply wrapped and in projected through our dress.

These are some of the consequences of a fashion industry that routinely gives larger women the shorter end of the *rack*—and these merely scrape the surface:

- Limited plus-size options are often more expensive than "straight" size clothing (clothing under a size 14).
- Plus size clothes are usually "sized up" from straight sizes and therefore do not fit the curves of a larger body, which make us often look like "shapeless boxes"
- Contrary to popular belief, using idealized so-called "perfect" models that reinforce unrealistic Western beauty ideals actually leaves female shoppers feeling unmotivated to shop because we do not identify with these models and are increasingly aware of the fallacy of so-called "perfection" (Barry 2013).
- Plus styles are often not as "cutting edge" and high fashion as straight sizes (unless you have the finances to afford exclusive "specialty" plus-size designer threads!).
- Conservative styles seem to imply that fat bodies should be covered up in loose-fitting fabrics, matronly draping, and more basic color palettes (Andrew 2013).
- Plus-size clothing areas in department stores are often located near the luggage, children's wear, or the chinaware, once again suggesting that plus-size women are an afterthought (Andrew 2013).
- Plus merchandising (i.e., the styling of mannequins and/or other print and in-person advertising strategies) is often underwhelming and "thrown together," therefore plus women don't get the same opportunity as straight-size women to see a complete stylized image, for our bodies, we can truly aspire toward.

FASHION BLOGGING

Plus-size fashion blogs have consistently built momentum since the mid- to late 2000s. Internationally recognized plus fashion blogs like U.S.-based *GabiFresh,* formerly *Young, Fat and Fabulous* (created in 2008), Marie Denee (*CurvyFashionista,* created in 2008), and *Nicolette Mason* (created in 2006) are notable examples of highly successful, monetized blogs with tens of thousands of followers—everyday plus-fashion consumers and exclusive industry leaders. These fatshionista bloggers not only review plus clothing and recommend fashion stores/designers to plus women but they have turned their personal blogs into full-fledged careers. These and many other plus fashion blogs are striking lucrative partnerships with fashion brands and selling products via their blogs. Some fatshion bloggers have been hired as columnists for national fashion magazines, spokespersons of plus fashion lines, and some have become plus-fashion designers and plus-fashion store owners themselves.

Canadian plus-fashion blogger Karen Ward (*CurvyCanadian,* created in 2010) opened one of Toronto's newest plus-fashion stores, Your Big Sisters Closet, in 2012 following the positive response to her plus-fashion blog. According to Ward, whose store tagline is "Plus Size Clothing for the Uncompromising Woman," her store name was inspired by her own envy of her big sisters' "straight-sized" closets she could never fit into. Like many plus-fashion bloggers, Ward wants every plus woman to have access to fashion at any size. Fellow Canadian Karen Johnson (*KillerKurves,* created in 2011) was approached by Canadian fashion retailer Addition Elle and became one of the most recognizable faces of the brand. Johnson also starred in the retailer's "Be a Showstopper" advertising campaign. These and other Canadian plus-fashion bloggers have been featured in national newspapers, radio, and television such as *The Toronto Star*, the *Marilyn Dennis Show,* and *News Talk Radio.*

Our blog *FatinTheCity* was created in 2013. Since its inception some of our partnerships have included Old Navy, Wet Seal and *Huffington Post Canada.* In addition to promoting plus fashion and body positivity awareness through countless speaking and hosting engagements we've been commissioned for, we also created Body Confidence Canada Awards and A Toast to Curves: Celebrating Size in Film, Fashion and Television which takes place during the Toronto International Film Festival (TIFF) season. In 2012 plus-fashion blogger Tanesha Awasthi (*GirlwithCurves,* created in 2011) won the Navabi Curvy Fashion Blog of the Year Award. She was flown to England where she was featured in Britain's Plus Fashion Week. *FatintheCity* was nominated in 2013. In many regards, plus-fashion bloggers have become "stars" in their own right, advocating for accessible fashion choices and for better treatment, and acknowledgment of bodies of all sizes.

PLUS-FASHION BLOG: GETTING STARTED

Here is what you will need:

- Access to a computer and experience navigating the Internet.
- A great wardrobe for your pictures. In the beginning don't be discouraged if your items are from previous seasons. Source your favorite wardrobe items and these will make the basis of your first blog outfit posts. Your three-year old Jones New York blazer paired with a great pair of jeans and your favorite stilettos can still make an eye catching post!
- Domain/Host: an Internet hosting service that hosts your site (e.g., Word-Press, Tumblr, Blogger).
- Digital Camera: Good-quality pictures help to show readers and brands that you are invested in your blog. Remember, first impressions go a long way.
- Blog Title: A blog title immediately tells the reader who you are and what type of blog they are reading. Keep it memorable and short! Remember the blog title is the first thing that the reader sees so make sure it's a title you want to keep.
- Logo: A logo represents your brand so take the time to create one that readers will remember. A logo can be an image or words. Think about famous logos that are memorable such as Nike or the McDonalds logo.
- Unique Content and Voice: There are thousands of blogs worldwide; ensure that you have a unique voice and stick to your vision.
- Passion for Fashion: Fashion trends are constantly changing and it's important to stay abreast of new trends. Read fashion magazines, know fashion brands and attend events.
- Blogging Schedule: It's critical to decide how many posts you will post a month (e.g., one to four). The more your audience sees your posts on a consistent schedule, the more they get familiar with your blog. The more brands see your work, the more likely they are to contact you for partnership.
- Social Media: Ensure you are on at least three of these social media platforms: Facebook, Twitter, Tumblr, Instagram, and Pinterest. If you don't know how to use these platforms, there are simple instructions on each of their websites. Social media platforms are used to drive your readers to your blog.

Equipment for Self-Portraits

- Camera with a self-timer
- Remote control
- Tripod

Taking Self-Portraits

- Select a shoot location.
- Set up the camera where you want to take the photo.
- Figure out where to frame your shot by using a marker (a rock, chalk) or anything that is around to mark the spot where you want to take the photo.
- Take a test shot by standing at the spot you marked.
- Ensure that your photo is clear and in focus.
- You can now begin taking blog photos.

YOUR FASHION BLOG

Here are some tips for writing your blog:

- Your blog is written primarily in the first person. However when you are providing general tips or fashion reviews you may switch to third person.
- Choose a post title: The post title tells the reader what your post is about (e.g., Winter White for the Holidays).
- Decide what type of post you are writing (current trends, general fashion tips, or personal story on a favorite clothing item). A fashion brand shout-out may be a single mention of a plus fashion brand such as ASOS or Lane Bryant. You may also be hired to create an exclusive blog post on a particular fashion brand. In a general fashion brand review you may be providing a more general review of a variety of fashion lines.
- Length of post: be concise (i.e., four hundred words or less).
- Why are you writing this post? (Is it to gain brand recognition and to solidify yourself as a fashion "expert," or are you writing posts to share about your personal journey with fashion?)
- Be honest with your readers: Ensure that readers are learning something new about your fashion sense every time you write a post.
- Read your post out loud to ensure that there are no grammar and spelling errors.

We are providing a general overview to help you make income off of your plus-fashion blog. There are many online professional associations that can help you with this in more depth. One of our favorites is *The Independent Fashion Bloggers*, www.heartifb.com.

Before you work with fashion brands, ask yourself the following questions:

- What are your goals? What type of blogger are you? What are your goals for the blog? Do you want to get free products and review them, or do you also want to generate income from your blog? It's important to know your personal motivations for your blog before approaching or accepting offers from external fashion brands.

- Research fashion brands you are interested in partnering with and see if they have a history of working with bloggers.
- As a plus-fashion blogger you should always have an arsenal of "story pitches" (i.e., ideas you can blog about that may be of interest to potential fashion brands seeking partnership).
- Ensure you have a media kit to help promote yourself to potential partners.
- Insiders tip: Before approaching a brand, blog about one of their clothing items. It shows companies that you are familiar with their brand.

Visit seasoned blogs to see how much they charge for partnerships with fashion brands or to have fashion brands advertise on their blogs. We cannot stress how important it is to communicate with other fashion bloggers, especially when you are a newbie. Most blogs have media kits that are available online. Reading their rates can give you an estimate of how much you should be charging. Your rates are often determined by your page views and number of followers you have. If you are putting in eight hours of work to write a sponsored post, don't undercharge. Remember your time is money! If you have approximately five thousand views per month you might start at a rate of $100 per post. Some well-known fatshion bloggers with tens of thousands of blog followers and monthly views can command thousands of dollars for their partnerships. When you are about to monetize your blog, ensure that you have communicated with the brand your rate and your expectations. Maintain copies of all signed contracts and e-mail communications.

TOOTING YOUR OWN HORN: PROMOTE YOUR BLOG

Use a media kit and networking to promote your blog. A media kit is the most important tool that a blogger needs to approach brands for partnerships. A media kit shows professionalism and gives brands your advertising rate and social media outreach (statistics about your followers/views).

Creating a Media Kit

- Know your statistics: Your blog statistics tracks visitors, demographics, page views and most popular posts. It's important to use a reputable tracking platform like Google Analytics. Google analytics is easily downloadable to your site. Presenting your stats is an essential part of your media kit.

- Advertising: If you are contacted by a third party to post plus-fashion advertising on your blog, you need to decide on an ad rate.
- Search Engine Optimization (SEO) makes your blog searchable on the web. There are plenty of SEO tips on the web, simply Google SEO and you will find several SEO tutorials.

Networking Tips

Networking with other bloggers is another way to promote your blog.

- Visit many blogs. The best way to become familiar with fashion blogging is to read them.
- Be an active part of social media. Comment regularly on other blogs and form relationships with other bloggers.
- Pitch yourself as a guest blogger on other fashion blogs and websites to get your name out there.
- Introduce yourself to local and national media. As you build your blog brand you may be contacted as a plus-fashion "expert" based on the success of your blog.
- Join the Independent Fashion Bloggers www.heartifb.com. This free online resource provides support for fashion bloggers.

PLUS SIZE FASHION BLOGGING, BODY POSITIVITY, AND ACTIVISM

As proponents of Health at Every Size (Bacon 2010) and what we've coined Fashion at Every Size (HAES/FAES) we want our blog *fatinthecity* to be socially responsible. As such we try to incorporate body positivity to ensure all our blog visitors feel welcome. We created a Body Equity Checklist for Plus Fashion Blogs as a tool for helping new blog creators evaluate whether their blogs are body positive or not. Here are some of our checklist items that may help you:

- Reviewing a diverse range of fashion sizes promotes body diversity.
- Refrain from negative body talk on your blog (this includes "fat talk" such as promoting weight-loss strategies or suggesting that certain styles makes bodies look better by making them appear "thinner").
- When partnering with fashion brands and designers, never lose sight of your blog vision. If their vision conflicts with your core principles for your blog, kindly decline; there will be others (Perkins 2012).
- If anti-fat or otherwise body negative comments are made on your blog posts, don't ignore them. By addressing them head-on you illustrate to

your followers that you are passionate about both plus fashion and promoting positive body acceptance.

CONCLUSION

Plus-size fashion or "fatshion" blogging is exploding online. Not only is
fatshion blogging helping to provide representation, visibility, community,
and a size-acceptance platform for plus-size women, but it is also making
plus-fashion bloggers celebrities and entrepreneurs in their own right. Full-
Figured Fashion Weeks are popping up all over the world from Canada to
Africa. Twelve of the most popular plus-fashion bloggers from across the
world were flown to Milan, Italy, in 2013 by renowned, high-end plus fashion designer Marina Rinaldi to collaborate on her "Women Are Back" campaign. In 2013 *GabiFresh*'s capsule plus-size swimsuit collection with retailer Swimsuits for All sold out in a matter of days. Canadian plus-fashion
blogger Franceta Johnson was one of five plus-fashion bloggers commissioned to co-create designer leather jackets alongside MYNT1792. She has
also been featured in *Teen Vogue* and most recently *Seventeen Magazine*.

Plus-fashion bloggers have become sought-after style experts and featured columnists in U.S. publications such as *InStyle, Redbook, Marie Claire*,
Canada's *Chatelaine* and *LouLou Magazine*, and in such international publications as *Italian Vogue* just to name a few. Fatshion bloggers from around
the world, often referred to as "fatshionistas," have become plus-size style
authorities and have gone on to collaborate with mid- to high-end design
houses; large-scale retailers; and print, on-air, and online magazines. All of
this has resulted in additional revenue and "plus power" for many plus fashion bloggers. This is not to suggest that the plus-fashion market is thriving,
because, in relation to "straight-size" markets, there is still plenty of work to
do to ensure we have equal access to fashionable threads. However, the plus-
fashion blogging movement has certainly placed a new face and a new medium on the way plus women, fat women, and all euphemisms in between,
shop, swap fashion likes/dislikes, and in essence create their body image and
fashion identities.

REFERENCES

Andrew, Jill. 2013. "'Plus Size' Fashion Blogging: Fat Activism or Fat Consumerism (in
    Sheep's Clothing) and Shades of Grey in Between." NAAFA Annual Convention & Expo
    Conference.
Bacon, Linda. 2010. *Health at Every Size: The Surprising Truth about Your Weight*. Dallas:
    Benbella Books.
Barry, Ben. 2013. "'Does My Bottom Line Look Big in This?' Strategic Model Selection to
    Attract North American and Chinese Women." *Strategic Direction* 29(1): 3–5.
Binns, Jessica. 2013. "Full Figures: Front and Center." *Apparel*, January 20, 8.

Ellison, Jenny. 2013. "Weighing In: The 'Evidence of Experience' and Canadian Fat Women's Activism." *CBMH/BCHM* 30(1): 55–75.

Entwistle, Joanne. 2001. "The Dressed Body." In *Body Dressing (Dress, Body, Culture)*, ed. Joanne Entwistle and Elizabeth B. Wilson, 33–58. Oxford: Berg.

Fortune, Carley. 2013. "The Bigger Picture." *The Grid*, March 23. http://www.thegridto.com/life/fashion/the-bigger-picture/.

Perkins, Natalie. 2012. "When Activism Gives Way to Advertising: How Fat Girl Blogging Ate Itself." *XOJane*, November 28. http://www.xojane.com/fashion/fatshion-blogging-ate-itself-natalie-perkins.

Scaraboto, Diane, and Eileen Fischer. 2012. "Frustrated Fatshionistas: An Institutional Theory Perspective on Consumer Quests for Greater Choice in Mainstream Markets." *Journal of Consumer Research* 39: 1–24.

Snider, Stefanie. 2012. "Fatness and Visual Culture: A Brief Look at Some Contemporary Projects." *Fat Studies* 1(1–2): 13–31.

Winn, Jane. 2004. "Making It Big." *Entrepreneurship Theory and Practice* 28(5): 487–500.

Woodward, Sophie. 2007. *Why Women Wear What They Wear*. Oxford: Berg.

Woolf, Virginia. 1929/1957. *A Room of One's Own*. New York: Harcourt, Brace & World.

Chapter Eleven

Leveraging the Linky Party

Knowledge Sharing in the Blogosphere

Jennifer Russum

WHAT IS A LINKY PARTY?

As the blogosphere has expanded over the past decade, blogs written by women for women have emerged rapidly, where bloggers share expertise on a wide range of topics, including entrepreneurship, writing and publishing, life in the home, parenting, fashion, design, and crafting. In fact, female bloggers now outnumber their male counterparts (Nielsen Media Research 2011). A significant number of these women are "do it yourself" (DIY) bloggers who promote the ethic of self-sufficiency by conducting their own repairs and projects around the home instead of paying for someone else's labor. As blogging websites and social media have emerged and transformed, DIY bloggers have developed complex practices to solicit, share, and gain knowledge over the World Wide Web. One of these knowledge sharing practices is the "linky party" or "blog hop," which is an online social event commonly hosted by niche bloggers who write about craft and design, food, or fashion.

Linky parties are an example of what Henry Jenkins (2013) calls "collective intelligence," which describes the ability of virtual communities to leverage the combined expertise of its members. During a blog hop, a blogger will host a party, where she will invite other bloggers to link up to her website with their own posts sharing a recent DIY project. These DIY projects might be anything creative made by these other bloggers, such as a refurbished piece of furniture, handmade holiday décor, or a homemade recipe. Each blogger creates and shares the handmade project through text and pictures in a blog post, along with instructions so other bloggers can recreate the same product. The host will announce in advance what day the party will take place and will invite other bloggers to come "link up" their posts. When the party goes live, the host will publish her own post regarding the topic (for example, she might post her own recipe) and at the bottom of her post, she will include a widget where other bloggers can copy and paste a URL to their own blog posts that feature a recipe. A small text link or picture will appear at the bottom of the host's blog post for each URL that is linked up, and a visitor to the party can "hop" from blog to blog to read and collect new recipes. For example, Heather, the blogger behind *WhipperBerry*, hosts a party every Friday called "Friday Flair." She shares an idea for a project she would like to create in the future, usually citing another blogger for the idea and sharing the original designer's photographs and blog links. Heather then opens up her party for bloggers to post any kind of creative project, whether a craft, furniture refurbishing project, or a recipe. On a typical week, two hundred to three hundred other bloggers will link their own posts to her blog and each post will be represented by a small square graphic picture of the linking blogger's project with a text hyperlink that will lead away from the *WhipperBerry* site to the contributing blogger's website when clicked.

There are certain expectations for participants in any linky party. If a blogger links up, she is supposed to include a hyperlink to the host's blog on her own post, to give credit (and traffic) to the blogger taking time to throw the party. Also, many hosts will include "rules" for the party, which often remind bloggers to only post blog entries that match the theme or purpose of the party, as some bloggers will try to post giveaways or other off-topic posts to gain free exposure to their own blogs. The host might also remind participants to "hop around" and visit a few new blogs each week. Heather of *WhipperBerry* states the same rules each week:

- Please Link up only YOUR OWN projects. As much as I love your round-ups, giveaways, Etsy shops and such, please refrain from linking them here.
- Please link back to *WhipperBerry* in your post with a text link. I am currently working on a new blog button, but I don't have anything ready at this time, so a text link will be GREAT!!
- Stay and mingle {remember, this is a party!}. Leave a couple of comments for other guests who have inspired you!

Often these rules are not enforced, but sometimes the host will take the time to remove posts that do not match the theme of the party. In general, it is considered blog etiquette to follow these basic guidelines when joining any blog hop, whether or not any explicit guidelines are stated by the host.

The most successful linky parties will drive significant new traffic to each of the blogs that link up and will often become weekly events where bloggers are constantly refreshing the host's webpage vying for the top spot at the party when the post goes live, usually at a set time each week. The links appear in chronological order as to when they are uploaded and the earliest links always stay at the top of the link list, which usually results in maximum traffic to one's blog.

The posts that participants link up are usually tutorials, which means they give step-by-step written and visual instructions to readers, so that others can recreate the project or recipe posted. For a DIY tutorial, for example, a blogger might start her post with a well-lit and edited photo of the final result of her DIY project, along with a narrative about why she did the project or how happy she was with the outcome. Then she might list the materials needed for the project, sometimes with accompanying photographs. Next, she will give step-by-step written instructions for making the product, usually accompanied by high-quality pictures so the reader can visualize each step. At the end of the post, she might again post a different picture of the final product and then list the blogs to which she is "linking up." She might list anywhere from one to twenty or more blog parties where she is linking her post, although one to five is a common amount. Women who link to too many parties are often seen as desperate or attention-hungry by other bloggers. The blogger will then link the URL to this specific post to the parties she lists and watch as traffic increases to her blog. New readers might introduce themselves in the comments, compliment her project, ask her a question about the creation process, or even pin her link to a board on Pinterest. A well-written tutorial can earn quite a bit of attention in this social network. Also, it is common for the host of the party to choose a few of her favorite links for the week and feature these projects in separate blog post after the party ends. For example, the hosting blogger might choose her five favorite DIY tutorials posted by other bloggers and write a whole blog post about them, in which she shares pictures of the projects with links to the creators' posts. This is called being "featured" and is another way bloggers receive attention, acclaim, and traffic in the blogosphere.

The result of the linky party is a rich remixing culture (Jessell 2013; Jenkins et al. 2013). As these bloggers read about and see each other's projects online, they often save the links to recreate the product later. However, bloggers will often modify a craft or a recipe to represent their own unique tastes and preferences. If this new blogger decides to blog about her re-mixed project, she will cite the original blogger with a hyperlink to the creator's blog and then explain how she changed the project to make it distinct. If one were to follow an original project through all its iterations on Pinterest and various blogs, the path would be a tangled and rich web of modifications and creativity.

WHY LINK UP?

While linky parties are social events that celebrate creativity and foster networking, they are also an important component to blogging entrepreneurship. Since participating in busy and well-attended blog hops can result in hundreds of new visitors to one's blog, linky parties are an important business component for women trying to run a business online, especially for those who use their blog as a marketing platform for their business. Women who participate in linky parties while also running a related business online (a monetized food blog, a handmade shop, a photography business) must carefully decide what expertise they should give away for free in a linky party in order to gain more traffic to their blogs, which can result in increased readership, more clicks on affiliate advertisements, or more sales to one's online shop.

As any business person knows, sometimes giving away a product or idea for free (or at a nominal price) can actually result in more sales in the long run. This is the philosophy behind door buster sales on Black Friday. Linky parties are one way to get readers through the virtual "door" of one's blog or business. Once a new reader clicks to a new blog in a linky party, the blogger then has the opportunity to engage potential clients with her voice, branding, personal narratives, stunning photography, or unique products. The key is deciding what products, knowledge, and ideas can be given away for free. If a blogger receives profit through affiliate advertising on her blog and increased readership will result in increased revenue, then sharing any post that relates to the blog's core content (a DIY tutorial if one is a craft blogger, for example) will bring appropriate new readers to one's site. Bloggers must just be careful not to give away for free what they are also trying to sell. If one is a blog designer, it might be appropriate to give away pieces of information about how readers can make custom changes on their own blogs. Perhaps a designer will "give" away a tutorial about how to make a moving picture or a hyperlinked graphic to help amateur bloggers. But this same blogger must also withhold some information, in order to preserve her business. If she teaches everyone how to customize their own blog, she will no longer have a product to sell. The linky party is a very useful tool for online entrepreneurs, but bloggers must engage with caution, protecting the knowledge and products that make them experts in certain niches of the marketplace and knowing that the web is vast land of imitating, remixing, and stealing, where copyright laws are ambiguous.

BUILDING YOUR POST

With a few exceptions, the most appropriate type of post to link to a blog hop is a tutorial post, where the blogger teaches readers how to do or make a product using photographs and written instructions. (Exceptions include fashion posts, where bloggers share pictures of their outfits or networking blog hops, where participants simply share links to blogs and social media sites—such as a Twitter hop—and there is no set theme or topic for the party.) In general, these tutorial posts should be as brief as possible while still giving adequate instructions so readers can remake the project being shared. Pictures, especially well-lit, detailed, high-quality photographs are appreciated, if not expected, by readers. When creating a tutorial post, here are some general guidelines to keep in mind:

1. Introduce your project with a brief, engaging narrative. Did you make these paper princess crowns for your daughter's birthday party? Share a few sentences about the party and a picture of the young girls wearing their crowns. Is this an old family recipe? Share a short story about rolling out pie dough as a young girl at your grandmother's farmhouse. This narrative should be engaging but short. Ultimately, your readers want to know how to make the product, but feel free to draw them in with a bit of your personality or history.

2. Often it helps to share a picture of the finished product near the top of the post. Readers want to see the result of the project to decide if it's worth reading all the directions on how to recreate it. All pictures should be well lit and high quality. Experienced bloggers will use advanced editing programs such as Adobe Lightroom or Photoshop and create custom backdrops for their photos. Some bloggers will put a watermark on their photos, so they can't be "stolen" by other bloggers. If these skills are beyond your expertise, it's okay. Just make sure you take photos in good light (preferably daylight) and clear clutter from the background. There are free online editing programs, such as PicMonkey and Ribbet, that can help you crop, brighten and resize your photos with ease.

3. You should include clear, written instructions on how to recreate your project. It is helpful to include pictures of the step-by-step process as well.

4. Some bloggers will include a list of necessary ingredients or supplies at the top of the post (figure 11.1). Again, this helps readers quickly assess whether this is a feasible project for their skill level or allows them to use resources they already have on hand.

5. Conclude the post with another clear photo of the finished product, perhaps at a different angle than the first photo at the top.

6. It's common courtesy to "link" to the blog hops you will be joining with your post. This means you include a hyperlink to the host's blog. Many linky party hosts will create "buttons," which are small, hyper-linked graphics that advertise the name of the party and link directly to the host's blog when clicked. You can usually copy the code to this button on the host's site and then paste it into your own blog post. A button leading to the blog party will then show up on your blog. If no button exists or if you are linking to a number of blogs and don't want to clutter the bottom of your post with graphics, you can also include text links to the hosting blogs, where you simply write "Linking to: Blog A, Blog B, Blog C." When you type each blog's name you will hyperlink the text to the blog's website. Figure 11.2 is an example.

HOW TO LINK UP

When a host's party goes live, a post will go up on her site with a widget at the bottom. In that widget, you will copy and paste the URL to your blog post (make sure to add the URL to the direct post and not just the home page of your blog). You will also give your post a title and usually you will be asked to include your e-mail address. Some hosts also require you to give your name. The exact requirements depend on the host's preferences and the linky

SUPPLIES:

Figure 11.1.

software she chooses to use, but expect to give the URL and a title for your post at the very least.

There are two types of link lists: text and photo. If the host is only doing a text link list, after you enter your URL information and click "next" or "done," the title of your link will appear in a list at the bottom of the host's blog post. If I were to click on your title, it would lead me directly to your blog and the specific post you linked to the party.

However, the more common type of linky party includes photo links. After you enter your URL information and click next, you will be transferred to a page where you are asked to choose the thumbnail for your photo. Your thumbnail options will be photos and graphics taken directly from your web-page. Often, the first few on the list will be icons and graphics from your blog branding, which you want to avoid using. Scroll down and you will start to see pictures from the blog post you are linking up (figure 11.3). Choose a clear, engaging picture and push select. You can also crop the thumbnail, but usually this isn't necessary.

When you click "next" or "done" your thumbnail will pop up in the link list on the host's blog. It will look like figure 11.4.

Figure 11.2.

These are the images found at the page you entered
Click the one you want to be used as thumbnail

Please be aware that it may take a couple of minutes
for the thumblink to show up in the collection!!

Figure 11.3.

WHERE TO LINK UP

The best way to decide where to link up is by trying new linky parties each week. Many bloggers share a list of parties on their blogs and if you type "craft linky parties" or "food linky parties" into Google, it's easy to find lots of new parties to join. In general, bigger parties with at least a hundred participants are better for increasing traffic because there are more bloggers hopping around to each other's sites. However, some linky parties get so big (with over five hundred or even a thousand posts each week) that it's easy to get lost in the crowd. Remember, that link lists stay in chronological order, so if you get to a party "late" and your link is number 892 in a list of 900, you will probably not see much new traffic to your blog. However, if you get a

Figure 11.4.

top-row spot in a huge party (i.e., one of the first ten posts), you might receive hundreds of new visitors to your blog. Most parties go "live" at the same exact time each week, often at midnight on the day the party starts. Some bloggers might choose other times, such at 5:00 PM on a Friday for a weekend party or 6:00 AM for a weekday party. Usually, if you keep your eye on a site for a few weeks, you will be able to figure out when a party starts each week. If you aren't sure, feel free to e-mail or tweet the host and ask. Linking up as early as possible in the party gives you the best real estate for new traffic.

Although small parties (with only ten or twenty participants) might seem like a waste of time, sometimes that is not the case. In smaller parties, participants might visit many, if not all of the blogs, on the short list, and might engage more with other bloggers. Also, some hosts are better than others at encouraging participants to hop around and visit new blogs, so traffic will vary significantly just based on the tone of the party and the expectation set in the past for participants to visit new blogs. Again, your best bet is try new parties each week that relate to your niche area or the topic of your tutorials and see which ones are the most active and fun. Do new readers leave comments? Do you get new followers or 100 extra hits to your blog? Those are the parties you might want to start linking up to on a consistent basis.

PROPER ETIQUETTE

Here are a few more general guidelines to follow when linking up to blog hop.

1. Although there is no set number, it is usually considered poor form to link a post to twenty different blog hops. It comes across as desperate for attention. Most bloggers will only link a specific post to no more than five different blogs.
2. Be sure to visit a few new blogs when you link up. If you want people to visit your blog, it's nice to reciprocate and visit theirs as well. Often, if you visit a new blog and leave a comment, that blogger will stop by your site as well. A sale could be made or a friendship could be formed.
3. Make sure you link to the host's site on your own blog post. It's a lot of work to run a party, and while it benefits the host, she is also giving you free advertising in a sense. Don't be rude and link up with her blog without giving her credit on your own webpage.
4. Make sure your post matches the topic of the party. If it's a recipe party, don't share how you reorganized your pantry. There are organization parties out there—find them. And don't post completely unrelated topics like giveaways or shop items, just to steal some free publicity for your blog or business. Share a bit of your knowledge and creativity at a blog hop. If you are as engaging and creative as you think you are, new readers will stop by your site and look around.
5. If you get featured by the host, meaning she chooses your post as one of her favorites of the week and writes about your project in a follow-up post, be sure to thank her, either in the comments on her post or with a personal e-mail.

CONCLUSION

The linky party is a great way to connect with other bloggers and increase traffic to one's blog or shop. In a sense, the host of a blog hop is offering you free advertising for your own product, brand, and voice online. As a participant, one must decide what to give away in exchange for potential new readers and customers, knowing that anything submitted to a linky party might get pinned, shared, copied, and recreated by other artists and entrepreneurs in unforeseen iterations. When linking to a party, follow the "rules" of the site, visit some new blogs, and discover how the linky party might enrich your own business and social network online.

REFERENCES

Jenkins, Henry, Sam Ford, and Joshua Green. 2013. *Spreadable Media: Creating Value and Meaning in a Networked Culture.* New York: New York University Press.

Jessell, Matt. 2013. "Remix Culture: Rethinking What We Call Original Content." *Marketing Land.* Accessed June 4, 2013. http://marketingland.com/remix-culture-rethinking-what-we-call-original-content-41791 .

Nielsen Media Research. 2011. "State of the Media: The Social Media Report." Accessed April 17, 2013. http://cn.nielsen.com/documents/Nielsen-Social-Media-Report_FINAL_090911. pdf .

Chapter Twelve

Looking at the Technology Trends of Life Coaches

Finding and Using Successful Online Business-Building Tools

Melissa Cornwell

The World Wide Web has opened doors all around the world for both male and female entrepreneurs to expand their services and products for a greater client base. The Internet has especially provided entrepreneurial opportunities for women to offer their products and services outside of the traditional "brick-and-mortar" business. I have found that nowhere in the online business world is this more accurate than for women that serve as life coaches and offer their coaching services online. Life and business coaching has become a huge occupation within the Internet world, and while these women certainly work with clients in their areas, most of their business comes from the people that they connect with through the Internet. I have yet to find a profession that is more dependent on the Internet for marketing and networking, and the women that I have surveyed all take advantage of the Internet through different technology trends. In this chapter, I will be focusing on my findings from a survey on the different trends in technology used by women entrepreneurs in building their online businesses.

I surveyed websites of different women who were coaches and who provided some sort of specialized service in life and business coaching. There were a couple of women who provided services that did not fit within the general life and business coaching genre and provided more specific services, but as they used the same technology trends, I decided to include them in the survey. These women entrepreneurs were:

- Jenny Blake of *Life after College*
- Kimberly Wilson of *Tranquility du Jour*
- Laura West of the *Business Fusion Studio*
- Joanna Penn of *Creative Penn*
- Mindy Crary of *Creative Money*
- Ashley Wilhite of *Your Super Awesome Life*
- Courtney Carver of *Be More with Less*
- Amy Deagle and Sarah Von Bargen of *Yes and Yes*
- Stephanie Pollock and Carrie Green of the *Female Entrepreneur Association*

After surveying their websites, I identified trends in technology that I felt were essential for any female entrepreneur to consider for building a foundation for a successful online business. These trends were: websites, blogs, e-mail subscription and RSS feed, social media, advertisements, e-books, e-magazines, e-courses, podcasts, and videos. The first five trends have to do with networking and connecting with potential clients; the latter five address some of the ways to create additional content and services to offer to clients.

WEBSITES

The website is "your business card for the whole world to see" (Wilson 2010). The most obvious and important tool for any online business is the website; it is the bread and butter of any online business. Fortunately, there are many options for building a website but, essentially, the two choices are that you can either start one yourself or pay to have it designed for you. Content management systems such as WordPress and Drupal give you options to build your own websites without needing to learn the coding and programming for the entire site and are relatively inexpensive. These platforms also give you multiple options for themes, and you can pay for your own domain name on an annual basis; "make sure the domain is your business name or something similar enough" (Wilson 2010). If you decide to have the website designed by an outside party, remember that price will play a factor more heavily. You are paying for someone else's time on a project that will take weeks, perhaps months, to complete.

While surveying the websites of the female entrepreneurs I listed above, I did notice that many have had their websites designed professionally. If you go to the websites of any of these entrepreneurs, you can usually see in the footer who designed the layout of the site and, if it was done on a content management system, the theme of that website. In her book, Kimberly Wilson mentions that "to determine your look, review other sites and note the URLs so your designer can get a sense of your style. Be sure to list colors, fonts, images, and overall feel" (Wilson 2010). Overall, "the main components for a website are the homepage and pages for 'About Us,' a list of products or services with pricing, testimonials, a blog, a press section, retailers who sell your products (if applicable), a newsletter sign-up, and 'Contact Us'" (Wilson 2010). You can also add other pages that suit your brand or business.

BLOGS

The first step to consider when starting a blog is to "determine your message" (Wilson 2010); this means that you determine if you want your blog to be professional, personal, or informational, but the goal is to choose one main theme. The second step is to actually set up the blog through a blogging service and set up a name. A couple of the most popular services are Word-Press and Blogger, both of which offer free blogging services. Above all, the first goal for any blogger is to start writing and to keep readers coming back to your blog through daily, or weekly, posts. In all of the websites that I surveyed, there was always a blog to complement the website and services offered from the entrepreneurs. Also, the blog was the central place to announce new products and services and to connect with readers from all around the world.

E-MAIL SUBSCRIPTION AND RSS FEED

Again, the purpose of any blog is to connect to readers and other bloggers. One of the best ways to do this is to set up an RSS feed, which will let your "readers know when you've published a new post" (Wilson 2010). The other option is to set up an e-mail subscription service in which your readers will receive your blog posts directly into their inbox. Depending on the type of subscription service, you can also create your own newsletter format for how your readers will receive whatever updates you want to send to them. The goal of the newsletter is to "create content that entices, informs, and inspires your readers" and have a design that "aligns with your brand" (Wilson 2010). In your newsletter, you should also "feature additional media sources you offer, such as links to videos, blogs, and other locations" (Wilson 2010). Above all, you should make it easy for your readers to subscribe to your newsletter and posts by placing a subscribe button on the home page or anywhere near your blog; if a form has to be filled out then make it as simple as possible. Some of the popular newsletter and RSS feed creators used by the entrepreneurs I surveyed included Google's Feedburner and MailChimp.

SOCIAL MEDIA

The explosion of social media has become extremely important for online entrepreneurs and how they connect to their readers and future clients. You will not find many companies now without at least a Facebook page or a Twitter profile. Not only are many of these social media services free but they are also relatively easy to integrate into your website or blog, and there are many different options to help market your brand and products. A best practice to follow when having a Facebook page and Twitter profile is to avoid using them as platforms "for constant promotion of sales, blog posts, or links to your offerings" (Wilson 2010); your readers will already find most of that on your website and blog. Your social media accounts are a way for you to promote your services but they are also a way for your readers to get to know you as a person; think of them as ways to have small chats with your readers about more than just your business. Another best practice for managing social media accounts is to make sure that you update them all at the same time and to be consistent across all platforms in what you are saying about your business and services.

Among the websites I surveyed, I found that Facebook, Twitter, Instagram, and Pinterest to be the most prevalent of the social media platforms. Instagram and Pinterest offer unique opportunities for connecting to readers as they are visual platforms. Carrie Green of the *Female Entrepreneurship Association* uses these platforms to feature images designed with inspirational quotes and advice on entrepreneurship for women. Another use for Pinterest is to post your blog posts for a wider audience to see and read. Managing social media accounts can consume a lot of time and energy so be sure that you choose social media that you actually want to use and will contribute to your brand and business.

ADVERTISEMENTS

To further market your blog and your products, you can also participate in an online marketing movement that will allow you to expand your client base and reach people that may not otherwise have known about your services. Creating opportunities for advertisement will also allow you to start networking with other entrepreneurs and business starters. Many blog and website designers can create buttons and images that can be posted on other sites, which will increase the traffic for an online business's products and services.

Many of the entrepreneurs I surveyed had their own system for advertisements for other entrepreneurs and their products. Sarah Von Bargen with *Yes and Yes* offers a sponsor program in which you can pay a certain amount and she will sponsor your website on her blog; she offers the space in the sidebar of her blog and she will also feature posts on products for those she sponsors on her blog. The setup benefits both Sarah and those she sponsors; she gets paid for the space on her blog and the entrepreneurs that are sponsored get increased traffic for their blogs and products. You too can set up a system like Sarah's; all you need is a way for payment to be exchanged, which is easily accomplished through PayPal.

E-BOOKS

E-books are a great service to offer because they are so easy to create and publish. Writing an e-book is the same process as writing a print book, except that you will want your e-books to be concise and not necessarily as long; it is the publishing and marketing that differs the most. Amazon is one option for an e-book provider, as they offer a service for creating Kindle e-books. If you want to look outside of Kindle, you can also offer your e-books in a simple PDF format that can be read across multiple devices. There are also online services available that will help you design your e-books if you want more than just text and information; if you have an outside company design your website, ask them if they can also design your e-books so that they match your brand.

Many of the entrepreneurs I surveyed offered free e-books to readers who subscribed to their blogs, and these women offered e-books that contained practical advice in their individual specialities. Courtney Carver of *Be More with Less* offers e-books for sale on her blog that relate to minimalism and de-cluttering your life; she also offers her e-books solely in a PDF format so that they can be read across multiple devices and can be purchased directly from her website. Sarah Von Bargen offers e-books in the form of workbooks on travel and starting a business, where you can print the e-book and actively engage in it. When you sign up for her newsletter, Mindy Crary of *Creative Money* also gives out a free e-book on personal money management that complements her blog and online services. Giving out a free e-book is a great way to gain followers for your blog and your business and writing an e-book is a way for you to show your expertise in an area.

E-MAGAZINES

Digital magazines, or e-zines, have been slowly growing in popularity within the last five years or so. With the print industry for magazines slowing down, entrepreneurs in particular have been using e-zines to broadcast their thoughts and expertise for different subjects. E-zines also present great ways for different entrepreneurs in the same niches to come together to comment and write on the same subject, thus providing networking activities with other entrepreneurs in the same genre. Designing an e-magazine has been made especially easy with the web as there are several different options for design. You can have a blog that is devoted entirely to the e-zine and that features posts from different authors; another option is to design a PDF in a similar layout to a print magazine.

Of the websites I surveyed, three offered a fully designed PDF e-zine for free to their subscribers and readers. Carrie Green of the *Female Entrepreneur Association* offers a monthly e-zine that offers advice to her subscribers and female entrepreneurs on entrepreneurship. The e-zines feature columns and interviews from established female entrepreneurs on topics ranging from starting a business to finding new ideas for your business to avoiding burnout. As a way to expand her business for Women of Possibility, lifestyle design strategist Amy Deagle offers a free e-zine to her subscribers that features articles from twenty different women with small-town roots who created their own lifestyles. Stephanie Pollock, a business coach, not only created the e-zine *Going Pro*, which offers advice to help women turn their passion into a business, but she also offers an e-course on helping other entrepreneurs design their own digital magazines.

E-COURSES

E-courses were perhaps the most common product that I found on all the websites I surveyed, and their designs varied greatly. E-courses allow a reader or a client to interact with a topic more fully than what they may find on the blog or even in an e-book, and thanks to the web, e-courses can include more than a simple PDF workshop. You must also first decide how you want to present the material in your e-course. Would you like your clients to take the course at their own pace (asynchronously) or can they only complete the e-course within a certain amount of time or meeting during a certain time (synchronously)? There are several online platforms available that you could use to build your e-courses and market them, such as Ruzuku and the open-source Moodle, or you could build your e-course through a WordPress blog or website.

Kimberly Wilson of *Tranquility du Jour* offers her asynchronous e-courses as an on-demand service set up through WordPress. She provides podcasts and downloadable PDF worksheets that you can complete throughout the e-course, and with her on-demand service, members have lifetime access to the e-course. Jenny Blake of *Life after College* offers e-courses through the Ruzuku platform and also offers all of her resources in an online toolkit. Laura West of the *Business Fusion Studio* builds her e-courses with videos and recorded desktop presentations that her clients can watch on the Ruzuku platform. Courtney Carver of *Be More with Less* offers e-courses that can be taken at any time but cover only a certain amount of time (i.e., a month) and the entire e-course is offered in a PDF format. Ashley Wilhite of *Your Super Awesome Life* offers e-courses that also include a teleclass once a week. The design of your e-course really knows no boundaries, so you can build them to suit your expertise and your clients' interests and needs.

PODCASTS

Although they can be found as part of an e-course, podcasts can also serve to build your business on their own. What is a podcast? "A podcast is a radio program that people download and listen to at their leisure" (Wilson 2010). You should also be strategic when producing your podcast and ask such questions as: "Who is the audience? Are there enough topics within your genre to keep the show going? How often will you put out new shows? How long will each one be?" (Wilson 2010). You also do not need to buy expensive sound equipment to make podcasts. Most computers come with a built-in microphone to record your podcasts and you can use the free program Audacity to edit them; you can always upgrade to better equipment after you have released several shows. You can then distribute your shows through a podcast feed, iTunes, or Google Play.

Kimberly Wilson of *Tranquility du Jour* records and releases her shows through iTunes. She was able to offer an app to her readers where they could automatically listen to her podcasts without having to download each to a computer; her app is available to both Apple and Android users. Kimberly's podcasts feature interviews with other experts in her chosen genre. Joanna Penn of *The Creative Penn* releases her Creative Penn podcast that covers interviews and information on writing, publishing, and book marketing; her readers can subscribe to her podcasts either through her podcast feed or through iTunes. Podcasts provide another medium for online entrepreneurs to connect with their readers on topics important to them.

VIDEOS

Videos are another way that entrepreneurs can build their online businesses and reach many different groups of subscribers. Videos can allow people to see the person behind the business and to connect with you on a visual level. However, just creating videos is not enough to easily make them accessible to your subscribers. You will need to put all of your videos on a platform that is easily accessible for both you and your subscribers. The most popular platform for many reasons is YouTube, which allows you to create a channel that people can subscribe to for updates and new videos. YouTube videos are also easy to embed in your blog and website if you choose to write a post about it. There are other platforms for storing videos besides YouTube, including Vimeo.

Videos were featured on several of the websites and blogs I surveyed. Carrie Green of the *Female Entrepreneur Association* has a video series for various topics on entrepreneurship for women. Ashley Wilhite of *Your Super Awesome Life* has a video diary series for different topics in designing the life that you want. Laura West of the *Business Fusion Studio* uses videos in all of her e-courses and on her website. Mindy Crary of *Creative Money* offers videos on how to use Mint, the budget management software. All of these women use videos to promote their brand and their expertise in a more visual way than just text and information.

CONCLUSION

In this chapter, I have tried to present some of the technology trends I have seen in online business building. Nowhere have I found a clearer picture of how to build an online business than in the websites, blogs, and services of life and business coaches. The more common technology trends included websites, blogs, e-mail subscription and RSS feed, social media, advertisements, e-books, e-magazines, e-courses, podcasts, and videos. All of these trends can help any entrepreneur build a foundation for an online business as the web presents more and more opportunities for growth and networking.

REFERENCES

Wilson, Kimberly. 2010. *Tranquilista: Mastering the Art of Enlightened Work and Mindful Play.* Novato, CA: New World Library.

Chapter Thirteen

Social, Digital, and Business Entrepreneurship

From Online Community to Business Opportunity

Jennifer Sintime

The Women in Work Boots website, digital magazine, Facebook page and 100 Women Who Work project have all amplified interest in my colleague Jill Drader's mission to attract and retain women to the trades industry (Women in Work Boots n.d.). These four projects are founded with the collective intent of influencing women and minorities to consider a career in the trades as a viable option, highlighting the benefits and wonders of the industry, and forming a supporting community for these individuals. A web-based network, http://womeninworkboots.ca, Women in Work Boots has been enhanced from a means to showcase women in the industry (and showcase the industry to women) to a new business opportunity. Targeting women in the trades who lack the time and, generally, the funds to pursue the higher education that allows them to develop their own entrepreneurial skills, Jill Drader has transformed her online community to a profitable business prospect.

CREATING THE MARKET

With the labor shortages in Alberta having the highest vacancy rate at 3.6 percent in Canada (Alberta Enterprise and Advanced Education 2013), the need for more skilled workers was very evident to Jill Drader. As Working in Canada (2013) highlights, "In Alberta alone, the government has forecast a shortage of 77,000 workers over the coming decade. Since then, that estimate has grown by nearly 50%, to about 114,000 workers." However, women only make up 6.7 percent of those employed in the trades or related occupations (Alberta Enterprise and Advanced Education 2012), which makes it necessary to promote and draw women to an industry with an extremely high level of opportunity. According to Working in Canada,

> Trades affected by the skills shortage in the western provinces are primarily linked to construction infrastructure and the oil and gas sector, and include: Boilermakers, Carpenters, Concrete finishers, Construction managers and estimators, Crane operators, Drillers and blasters, Electricians, Iron workers, Heavy equipment operators and mechanics, Labourers, Plumbers, Steamfitters and pipefitters, Welders and truck drivers. (Working in Canada 2013)

With over a dozen trades that are facing shortages, it's crucial to keep hold of and attract women and minorities to the industry. For this reason, the Women in Work Boots website and related projects aspire to inform, enthuse, and highlight the positive aspects of the skilled trades. The online vehicles have since then obtained and encouraged the target audience, forming a web-based network that expands past the nation's borders.

Nevertheless, what started as a promotion of the trades and an online community has now become a business prospect. Through the venue of the Women in Work Boots website, the target audience has been centralized, so in one virtual location, women and minorities who are interested in the trades or work in the trades can be reached. The target audience has now been molded into the target market.

THE WEB AND ENTREPRENEURSHIP

Undoubtedly, the web offers many women and individuals the ability to take part in activities and ventures they would not normally be able to, opening many doors of opportunity that would have otherwise remained closed. Jill Drader, a public and social entrepreneur, has taken to the web to offer free resources and information to the public in order to serve society. Women in Work Boots, the only online network of women in construction in Canada, has now reached international levels since the launch of the digital magazine this past fall. The magnification of both her brand and audience has allowed Jill to pursue a profitable venture through the online business courses soon to be offered through her website. These courses propose to push trades workers further into entrepreneurship by helping them start their own businesses and make the most out of their careers, ultimately reaping the benefits of an industry that is booming. In this way, the Women in Work Boots brand has proved its ability to reach all realms of entrepreneurship, from public to business.

PUBLIC AND SOCIAL ENTREPRENEURSHIP

Both the magazine and Women in Work Boots website follow the objective of exposing the local community to the benefits of working in the trades industry. Each project successfully focuses on profiling and interviewing women in the field, and providing free educational tools for those who are considering or are in need of more motivation to remain in the trades. Public entrepreneurship, the concept of serving those who desire to learn with free education, is personified through the Women in Work Boots brand, as is social entrepreneurship (defined as a business that is serving the local community and contributing to society). The labor shortages in Western Canada prove that many jobs are available, yet many women are ignorant or unaware that there is a place for them in the construction industry. Information provided to these women through the Women in Work Boots brand encourages them to investigate these alternative career options, ultimately contributing to society by educating many individuals on potential careers and minimizing the labor shortage.

Mainly Internet based, this enterprising network has combined the needs of society with an ease of access, eliminating the difficulties of everyday life intruding on the ability to become informed. Now, those who would like more information about the skilled trades have a free resource available to them through whatever device they see fit.

BUSINESS ENTREPRENEURSHIP

The target audience of the Women in Work Boots audience consists of individuals in the trades who either cannot afford or simply lack the time to pursue higher education. In order to aid those who would like to enhance their business skills, Jill Drader has launched online business courses available through the Women in Work Boots website. The online business courses provide a flexible resource where women and others can be educated as to how to run or grow their own businesses. Consisting of audio files and downloadable worksheets, the courses allow for students to learn at their own pace regardless of their lifestyle. Unlike the digital magazine or the website, which both offer free advice and resources, the online courses are available for purchase.

Still more affordable than third-party business courses and education institutions, the target audience, now target market, for Women in Work Boots courses desires free or low-cost support, advice, and counsel. Available in the one location where the target market has been centralized, this distinct product is easily attainable for those it is intended for. Aiming to deliver the groundwork and beginning steps for new entrepreneurs or to maximize a preexisting business, topics in the courses include, but are not limited to:

- Business profile and summary of service
- SWOT analysis
- Marketing plans, budgets, and analysis
- Guide to investors
- Determining and maximizing assets
- Branding and Internet strategies

The principle behind the online courses is to encourage women (or anyone) to create a greater and more profitable opportunity for themselves within the construction and trade industry. Ultimately, this venture will extend the opportunities the web has offered Jill to her audience and target market.

DIGITAL ENTREPRENEURSHIP

Digital entrepreneurship, a category that Women in Work Boots has obviously mastered, can be presented and analyzed in accordance with each of Jill Drader's projects. In relation to the online business courses, this endeavor will now serve the community by offering education through the web for profit. However, each project uses the web and digital means to serve and provide a distinct service.

The Women in Work Boots website and Facebook page were created to educate, inspire, and attract individuals to the skilled trades. In doing this, both of these projects have centralized accessibility to the target market by creating a network. Through these two modes, the network can be communicated with, sold to, and analyzed. In addition, whereas the cost of publishing and distributing a print magazine would be prohibitive, and reaching an international audience would be very unlikely, the digital magazine has been read all over the world, increasing the audience and enhancing the brand. Though its intent was to also inspire, attract, and educate those in the construction industry, having this information in the form of a downloadable magazine has increased the opportunity for individuals to access and be exposed to Women in Work Boots.

The transition of the free educational resources available through the Women in Work Boots website to a profitable venture offering courses would also be very minimal if not for the advantage of digital communication. Not only is the price point of the courses offered significantly lower than that of an educational institution, the target market and audience are familiar with communicating with the Women in Work Boots brand via digital means. For this reason, as well as the flexibility, the type of education available on the website is deeply rooted in how the information is accessed. Needless to say, like the digital magazine, the courses also work to increase the reputation of the brand and reach a larger audience. Additionally, the online business courses will provide more than just low-cost education, but also create exposure to:

- Career counselors and coaches currently unfamiliar with the diversity of the industry
- Educational institutions that want to hire guest instructors, having Jill consult on design for programs, curriculums, and projects that are in development
- Immigration programs that want to promote entrepreneurs to those looking to immigrate to Canada and are looking for a consultant to coach them.

CONCLUSION

Though there are many not-for-profit organizations that are tied to government-funded agendas in Canada, Women in Work Boots stands alone as a for-profit business, online network for women in construction, and education and resource platform. Jill Drader, social, public, digital, and business entrepreneur, has utilized the benefits of the web and digital tools to not only fulfill her desires of inspiring women to join the construction industry, but to create a profitable business at the same time. From an online community to business opportunity, Drader has unified her audience, set a virtual meeting place where her audience can be centralized, and determined a way to capitalize on the endless possibilities the web has presented her. Nevertheless, the benefit does not remain with her. Through the Women in Work Boots Online Business Courses, free online resources available through the website, and the digital magazine, many doors of opportunity and possibility open up to women and all others who seek to develop their business skills, proving that the opportunities of one can lead to possibilities for another.

REFERENCES

Alberta Enterprise and Advanced Education. 2012. "Alberta Labour Force Profiles: Women 2012." Accessed October 18, 2013. http://eae.alberta.ca/documents/LMI/LMI-LFP-profile-women.pdf.
———. 2013. "Unemployment Rate by Occupational Group." Accessed October 17, 2013.
Women in Work Boots. n.d. "Women In Work Boots: Women Who Work." Accessed October 17, 2013. http://womeninworkboots.ca/.
Working in Canada. "Construction Shortage in Canada's West." Accessed October 19, 2013. http://www.workingin-canada.com/visa/skills-in-demand/construction-shortage#. UmUzpZS8Byc.

Chapter Fourteen

Vodcasting for Profit

Amanda Peach

Amy Mays, the host of the blog and video podcast *The Fat Squirrel Speaks*, took up knitting more than sixteen years ago as a freshman in college. What began as a hobby quickly became a consuming passion, with Amy progressing so rapidly in the craft that she was contracted by the college to teach a knitting class during the winter intersession while she was still an undergrad student there. Despite her obvious knack for the craft, she never gave any serious thought to turning it into a career. Instead, she finished her math degree and then went on to try her hand at a variety of professions, including teaching math at the high school level; baking professionally; and, most recently, data mining in the corporate world. It wasn't until two years after being down-sized during the recession that Amy finally turned her love of knitting into a profitable business via her blog and vodcast.

During the time immediately following her being laid off, it became obvious to Amy that she didn't want to work in the corporate world anymore. She was disappointed to realize she had spent ten years of her life trying to force herself to be something she was not, doing work that she didn't enjoy. She contemplated starting a business making and selling Waldorf dolls and even went far as to begin researching business models at her local library. Not quite ready to take the plunge into online business, though, she sat on the information she had gathered and focused on her responsibilities as a stay-at-home parent to her daughter.

Around Christmas of 2011, Amy decided she wanted to learn how to spin yarn herself. She had purchased a secondhand spinning wheel and instead of attempting to teach herself from a book, as she had when she learned to knit, she turned to YouTube for tutorials. She found one that was put out by The Knit Girllls which, after she had finished it, directed her back to their video blog. Even though she had listened to news and comedy audio podcasts before and enjoyed them, she was unprepared for how much she loved the first knitting vodcasts she found; she was instantly hooked. It was not long, she admits, before "I had a moment where I thought maybe I could do this, too. I was a little bit nervous to put myself out there, wondering whether I would have anything unique to say, whether I could add anything to the conversation." Deciding that trying required minimum risk, she took the plunge.

Amy turned to two books: *The Handmade Marketplace*, and *Craft Inc.* for invaluable advice on using a blog for driving sales. As a result, she created *The Fat Squirrel Speaks* as a written blog first, before realizing that the medium did not provide the creative outlet she craved. Further, she found herself overanalyzing everything she wrote to the point where she was nearly mired in inaction. She chose to switch to vodcasting instead, believing that video was the ideal format for discussing knitting because it is such a visual art form and because the act of knitting it is such a physical process. Once she transitioned to video, it was no longer a struggle for her to produce new content on schedule each week. With the content coming naturally now, Amy focused on developing a fan base before she ever attempted to sell anything on her blog. She believed that once she had a following, it would be much easier to launch her business, and so she waited patiently for almost nine months before opening her online store. Considering how she regularly sells out of merchandise in her store, her gamble seems to have paid off.

THE REQUIRED TOOLS

Amy admits to having initially been afraid of the technical aspect of creating an online business, but says that despite a lack of innate computer know-how, she has been able to do so successfully with very little initial financial investment. Her tools of choice are:

- A blog. Amy uses a free account on the blogging platform WordPress. She pays $18 a year to have a custom domain name, www.thefatsquirrel.com. While a unique domain name is not required, Amy felt the investment was worth it in order to make it easier for her customers to remember her and find her again in the future.
- A video-hosting site. Originally Amy used WordPress's Videopress to store her vodcasts, at a cost of approximately $70 a year, but she eventually migrated to Blip, which currently offers free hosting. WordPress allows her to embed all of her Blip videos on her blog, but the data is stored on Blip.
- An iTunes account. iTunes does not host podcast media files; podcasters must host their own files or contract a third party (such as Blip) to do so.

Instead, the iTunes Store serves as a searchable directory of podcasts. Since iTunes is one of the most popular sources of podcasts on the Internet, and it is free to submit your podcasts to their directory, listing your podcast on iTunes is a marketing necessity.

- An online store. Amy originally considered having a shop on Etsy, one of the largest marketplaces for handmade items online, because the site is so successful at driving people to your shop. The Etsy search engine is sophisticated and egalitarian; whether you have no customers or a hundred, your shop will be treated equally and potential buyers searching for your type of product will find you. The downside, however, is that Etsy requires a flat fee in addition to listing and photograph fees. Unsure if she would do enough business to justify these fees, Amy chose to use Bigcartel instead. Bigcartel is a marketplace for independent artisans, with fees that are currently much less than those on Etsy. The tradeoff for these lower fees is that the site works best for businesses that already have an established audience for their product. Amy's customers find her store by following the link to it embedded in her blog, not by searching Bigcartel the way they might have searched Etsy.
- Video-editing software. While there are a variety of fancier paid editing software programs available, Amy chose to rely on Windows Media Maker, which came freely installed in her laptop.
- A webcam and external microphone. Amy purchased a Logitech HD Pro Webcam C920 (which ranges in price between $75 and $100) with two built-in microphones. It records in high definition (HD) and is of a much higher quality than the camera and microphones built into her laptop.

MAKING MONEY

A hobby, a blog, and a vodcast alone are not a recipe for business success. There are other factors that have helped Amy turn her love of knitting into a paycheck. Among these are:

- An appreciation for, and understanding of, her fan base
- Regularly produced episodes of consistent quality
- Membership in online communities of fellow knitting enthusiasts
- Maintaining minimal stock levels in her store at any given time

Her experience as a fan and viewer of knitting vodcasts prior to producing one of her own has made it clear to Amy the importance of commitment to a consistent production schedule. Occasionally technical issues (such as the Internet crashing) or personal commitments (like a child being sent home sick from school) will interfere with the filming or uploading of an episode. Amy tries her best to minimize such disruptions, however, explaining,

> As a vodcast viewer myself, I have come to expect my favorite vodcasts to be delivered to my inbox on time. For instance, the Knit Girllls better be there on Monday morning. If they're not there, I'm bummed! And I've had that same kind of feedback from my fans. I had a friend, another podcaster, text me and say "I have a flight Monday afternoon and your show is not up! What am I supposed to do?"

The casual, less-polished nature of The Fat Squirrel Speaks also helps Amy to keep to a schedule. Amy does not feel the need to endlessly edit her vodcasts in the way that she did with her written blog. The complicated and time-consuming nature of video editing helps reign in her tendencies to self-correct, as does the positive feedback she has received from her audience, who appreciate the relaxed and conversational feel of her podcasts. More than one viewer has told her that they feel like she is in the same room with them, talking to them over coffee like old friends. Prior to recording an episode, she sometimes makes notes of talking points she hopes to hit, but otherwise refrains from imposing much of a structure on her episodes. Occasionally this result in her rambling or becoming a little too tangential, and so she jokes that her "parentheses have parentheses." Her audience has come to expect and love this quality of hers, though; it is this and her humor that set her vodcast apart from so many others.

The frequent and reliable production of her show does more than just inspire loyalty and goodwill in her listeners—it also provides her a platform for regularly promoting the goods she sells. Many of her customers are fans of her show. People who like her podcast and like her want to support her. Amy explains this phenomenon as a variation on the idea of "buying local." In this case, "local" is not about geographic location and relative closeness, but rather about a sense of community. Feeling a kinship with her based on their shared identity as knitters, many of her customers are willing to pay slightly more in order to support her rather than a large commercial yarn company. As a consumer of knitting and spinning products herself, Amy does the same, trying to support other small, private producers as often as she can. One place where Amy can buy and sell "locally" is through the website Ravelry, which caters to knitters, connecting them via discussion boards and a free searchable database of patterns and products.

The nature of her business guarantees a cap on potential earnings for Amy. She is hand-spinning and then dying yarn, which is a very labor-intensive process, meaning she can only produce so much at any given time. Unlike large commercial yarn retailers, she cannot afford to invest the time or money in a large back stock of product in endless variations of colors or fiber types to satisfy all potential needs or wants of clients. The bulk of her sales are on limited runs of products in colors and fiber types that she enjoys working with. When they are ready for purchase, she announces their arrival in her store via her blog and then once they sell out, that is it until the next batch is available. This can be frustrating for her customers, but it also helps to drive demand and ensure profit for her. She can only ever earn as much as she is able to produce, but she is satisfied with this level of financial success. She never sought to earn a grand fortune, but instead only hoped to replace her lost income, and she has done that. Vodcasting for profit has allowed Amy to earn as much as she once did in the corporate world, while doing something she loves and making new friends along the way.

BIBLIOGRAPHY

Chapin, Kari, Emily Winfield Martin, and Jen Skelley. *The handmade marketplace*. North Adams, MA: Storey, 2010.

Ilasco, Meg Mateo. *Craft Inc.: Turn Your Creative Hobby into a Business*. San Francisco: Chronicle Books, 2007.

Chapter Fifteen

Women in Work Boots

A Website Profiling Women in the Trades

Jennifer Sintime

Commonly known to be an industry that is male dominated, the skilled trades is a field that possesses many career opportunities for women. My colleague, Jill Drader, founder of Women in Work Boots, has taken advantage of the infinite possibilities of the web to bring women in the trades closer together and to inspire those who are interested in the industry. A stage that hosts several of Jill's projects, the Women in Work Boots website, http:// womeninworkboots.ca, supports the 100 Women Who Work project, presents the Women in Work Boots online business courses, and creates a platform in which women in the industry can unite and become a part of a network (Women in Work Boots n.d.).

Finding that there was a severe need for information and resources for women in the skilled trades industry, Drader also aimed to motivate and educate women on opportunities. In fear of becoming another statistic in the industry, she wanted to retain a connection to the trades. Kate Braid (2013), the first female Red Seal Carpenter in the industry, noted that women are still a very small minority in the industry at only 2–3 percent. Thirty years later the percentage of women in the trades was still 2–3 percent, proving that the issue was that the industry was not retaining women.

The creation of Women in Work Boots was founded upon a few simple desires:

- Create literature and more resources for women in the trades
- Attract women to the trades and retain them to the industry
- Form a community for tradeswomen

- Stay connected and a part of the industry despite the inability to work during maternity leave

Though dealing with a very busy schedule with two small children in tow, Jill managed to begin her digital entrepreneurial journey during her consecutive maternity leaves from 2009 to 2010, embracing all of her goals and raising her personal income from $30,000 in 2007 to over $70,000 as of 2012.

A devoted mother with a high priority in family, Jill's schedule, as seen in table 15.1, allows roughly four hours to be dedicated to work each day. These minimal hours eliminate most conventional careers, which call for eight-hour workdays or longer. With the convenience of the web-based programs, schedule conflicts between dropping her son to preschool, family meals, and conducting seminars and other occasional duties have not hindered her ability to become a digital and public entrepreneur. The capability to reach the public from her desktop creates a flexible and manageable schedule, allowing her to create her online business.

Table 15.1. Jill's schedule

Beginning date: September 2013

End date: December 2013

Week	Item	Mon	Tue	Wed	Thu	Fri	Sat	Sun
1	Jake's Preschool	12:30–3:30		12:30–3:30		12:30–3:30		Sunday School
	Family Together Time	7–9am, 6–9pm	7–9am, 6–9pm	7–9am, 6–9pm	7–9am, 6–9pm	7–9am, 6–9pm	All Day	All
	Kids to Drader's				8–4			
2	Women in Work Boots	3–4 hours	8–4	3–4 hours	8–4	3–4 hours		
	Meetings		8–4					
	Jill work in an office or library	10–12, 1–3		10–12, 1–3		10–12, 1–3		
3	CEO Day (Strategy Planning)				8–4			
	Exercise	7–9am	7–9am	7–9am	7–9am	7–9am	7–9am	7
	Dinner	4–6pm	4–6pm	4–6pm	4–6pm	4–6pm	4–6pm	4
4	Coaching							
	Selena / Chris	morning		morning				
	Beth				2–4pm			

Nonnegotiable

1. Family together time—fun
2. Breakfast/Dinner time together, at the table, sitting
3. Exercise, bike ride, walk to parks, play ball sports, alone and as a family
4. Time spent working, focused, quiet, task and goal driven, writing
5. Social media is marketing, but being distracted at home with the family and kids by the smartphone is not focused time

Bringing together women in the skilled trades industry and creating a support network among them to eliminate the sense of isolation often found by females in the industry, the Women in Work Boots website bridges Jill Drader to her target audience. Due to the nature of skilled trades, tradeswomen operate under very complex schedules. With many women being mothers, working in Northern Canada for weeks at a time, or running a trade-based business, having a platform that could be accessed by everyone was necessary. Thus, the Women in Work Boots network is web based, allowing for all women to find support and resources regardless of their lifestyles.

THE COMPONENTS OF WOMEN IN WORK BOOTS

The first step toward forming a support network for tradeswomen was gathering information about what her target audience wanted. After hosting a barbecue to gather information about what women in the trades industry needed and wanted and what they had experienced, Drader soon realized that the way the industry was marketed to women was deplorable and she wanted to see if there was a way to change the way women thought about the industry. Likewise, the severe deficiency in easy-to-understand guidelines for those who were interested in pursuing a career in the trades formed the desire to also cater to those who want to learn more about the trades or are curious as to how to get started. The website and its components tackle all of these issues:

- For those who seek a career in the skilled trades, the site has uncomplicated advice available along the bottom of the homepage: Get Started, Get Skilled, and Get Apprenticed. Each of these respective links directs the viewer to simple and easy-to-understand tips. For example, the Get Apprenticed page lists seven links to resources from occupational profiles to apprenticeship testimonials.
- In order to change the tone in which many women discuss the trades, the 100 Women Who Work project features one hundred women who share their stories in the trades, and what they love about their jobs.
- To create a support system for women to connect and interact, the Women in Work Boots Facebook page works as a meeting place for women to do so.
- The digital magazine that's available for download is an archived source of writings targeted toward tradeswomen and aspiring tradeswomen that is full of resources, stories, and advice.

Women in Work Boots Facebook Page

Marketing for Women in Work Boots has many outlets. Due to the popularity of the project, many public speaking opportunities at trades institutes, as well as media exposure in local newspapers and so on, have served as advertising and have increased the brand value. Through promoted Facebook posts, Women in Work Boots has been publicized and marketed further. With each promoted post, which costs roughly $20–$30, fifty or more followers are obtained, as well as access to each of their Facebook friends' network.

However, the promotion of the Women in Work Boots project is not the only benefit of the Facebook outlet. The Women in Work Boots Facebook page, which currently has more than eight hundred followers, also supports the web-based network by forming an online meeting place for its members. Patrons of the network are now able to communicate; stay regularly informed and updated with fellow women in the trades and with opportunities; and, most importantly, access the Women in Work Boots website right through their news feed.

100 Women Who Work

The complexity of the Women in Work Boots concept is that within the brand are several other projects and ventures. One of the projects hosted on the Women in Work Boots website is the 100 Women Who Work Project. Showcasing one hundred women in the trades working in or around the Calgary, Alberta, area, the project profiles real women in the industry via the Women in Work Boots website. Aiding in Jill's attempt to expose tradeswomen to each other, and allowing their stories and experiences to be shared, the 100 Women Who Work project is a virtual space where other women's encounters inspire and motivate others to do the same type of work, or share their own stories. Through the art of storytelling, the goal to retain and draw women into the industry is brought to life through the project.

Each profile contains a photo of the woman showcased, her personal story, and advice she may have for women who are currently in the industry or considering it. Aside from the educational aspect of this project, it also aids in the promotion of the website. As each woman is profiled and showcased on the website, word of mouth and the inevitable pride of being featured online draws in a large amount of traffic directed by the woman featured.

Women in Work Boots Digital Magazine

The concept of featuring and informing women of the industry has been enhanced further through the downloadable digital magazine. This project has drawn in a significant amount of exposure to Women in Work Boots and was published this fall. The extension of the Women in Work Boots brand and audience was founded in the creation and publication of a thirty-four-page downloadable magazine. Within the pages of the magazine are features on tradeswomen and businesses, tips and advice on taxes, physical fitness, and lists of education institutes. Through this piece of archived literature, the Women in Work Boots audience has now expanded past Canada, to the United States, the United Kingdom, and Australia, boosting the Women in Work Boots brand and producing even more exposure for the project. Several investors, publications and government programs have taken an interest in the Women in Work Boots movement, ultimately creating a larger network and opening many doors of opportunity for Jill. Public speaking engagements at local conferences and educational institutes, teaching courses at many local institutes such as Bow Valley College in Calgary, Alberta, and the creation and facilitation of the Women and Leadership Seminar are just some of the opportunities that have revealed themselves since the creation of Women in Work Boots. Recently, Drader has also taken on an opportunity to work on a new venture that aspires to create a program for women and children. In collaboration with a Northern Alberta–based carpenter (a First Nation woman called Horse Lake) who owns her own business, this new project will be a tool for First Nations women and others to work together.

OPERATION AND ORGANIZATION

However, the creation and operation of Women in Work Boots relies heavily on web-based tools and programs. With roughly four hours to dedicate to her projects a day, each hour and all resources need to be utilized to their highest degree. Web-based programs such as Basecamp, an online project management tool, and e-mail have allowed Jill to employ and communicate with members of her team, regardless of their geographical location, acting as a virtual meeting place or office. Essential to the operation of her projects, the delegation of tasks allows Jill to tackle all of her goals and projects easily. The capability to communicate and work with members of her team via web-based programs has enabled the publication of the digital magazine to go smoothly, regardless of schedule conflicts or geographical locations. Through the project management tool, Jill is able to upload audio files from Calgary, Alberta, which are then downloaded in Toronto, Ontario, by her employee; transcribed; formed into articles; and then uploaded back to the Basecamp website, where Jill can then download and publish them.

CONCLUSION

The centralization of her target market has created a venue in which Jill Drader's several other projects can be exposed. Through this connection, the four desires she wished to fulfill through her entrepreneurial venture have been reached. The flexibility and ease of a virtual workspace, the benefit of having a platform that can be accessed from any location at any time, and the ability to increase her audience to an international level have allowed Jill Drader to become a respected entrepreneur. Within the projects hosted and presented through Women in Work Boots, Drader has created a business that serves the local community and contributes to society, proving her to be a social entrepreneur, and she also serves those who want to learn with free education, which highlights her public entrepreneurship. Moreover, Jill's roles as a social and public entrepreneur have recently been enhanced by the addition of online business courses now available via the Women in Work Boots website. Through the network Jill has created and by unifying and supporting women in the trades, Jill has created a centralized location where her target audience can be reached and has now become her established and target market.

REFERENCES

Braid, Kate. 2013. "Trade Up!" (Keynote speech, Women in Trades Conference). Kelowna, BC, July 6.
Women in Work Boots. n.d. "Women in Work Boots: Women Who Work." Accessed October 15, 2013. http://womeninworkboots.ca/.

Part III

Educational Applications

Chapter Sixteen

Entrepreneurship Research

Using the Tools at Your Local Library

Lura Sanborn

The web is awesome; there's no doubt that Google will turn up great content on entrepreneurship and business-related topics. But what about digital content that Google doesn't see? It's true. There is digital content that is simply not retrievable, not findable, using Google. Just as your local library contains books/ebooks that are beyond what is on your personal bookshelf/iReading device, your local library purchases digital content beyond what is available in Google. These digital collections are paid for by the library, and as such live behind a paywall impenetrable by Google. Good to know about. Similarly, the local library likely still has a print collection that will probably contain print books relevant to your business and entrepreneurship research. This chapter will identify sources and search strategies, as well as library services that pertain to researching entrepreneurship at a local library. Strategies for acquiring (in a policy-adhering manner) access at additional libraries and utilization of publicly available sources are woven throughout. Additionally, the chapter will identify how to identify and utilize available expert advice from business school research librarians. Finally, in an effort to keep the chapter as helpful as possible and to acknowledge the deep importance of freely available collections, several free digital research collections are mentioned as accompaniments to library digital holdings.

BOOKS, EBOOKS, AND SUBJECT HEADINGS

Let's start with what libraries are most traditionally known for: books. How do you find library books related to entrepreneurship? The first step is to locate, on your local library's website, the library's catalog. The catalog (and every library should have one) is essentially a big, long list of all the print and eBooks owned by the library. Most local libraries will have their catalog available online, so this step can be comfortably conducted from home, or anywhere with an Internet connection. How then, to retrieve only the books that are relevant to you/your area of research? If you have a title in mind, searching by book title (or author) will be quite quick. More likely, though, you will not have a specific title, but rather a broad subject in mind. The key, then, is to identify the relevant subject headings associated with your area of need/interest.

Subject headings? Subject headings are basically library-assigned tags associated with each book. In this sense, libraries have been tagging books since the 1800s. To keep things consistent for researchers, from library to library, most U.S.-based libraries use an agreed-upon master list of tags. These are known as the Library of Congress subject headings. Determining which Library of Congress subject headings represent the content you are interested in will unlock the library's e/book collection to you!

The Library of Congress itself creates and updates these subject headings. The subject headings are published annually in what are known to by librarians as "the big red books." The LOC subject headings are also available online at: http://id.loc.gov/authorities/subjects.html. Much like the German language, LOC subject headings can be built upon and built upon, so one may find oneself utilizing a subject search such as the following: Small business—Employees—Insurance requirements—United States.

Some suggested subject headings that could be useful starting points:

- Business planning
- Electronic commerce, United States
- Entrepreneurship
- Entrepreneurship, United States
- Home-based businesses
- Minority business enterprises, United States
- New business enterprises
- Success in business
- Success in business, Psychological aspects
- Success in business, United States
- Self-employed women
- Small business
- Small business, United States, Finance
- Small business, United States, Management
- Self-employed
- Strategic planning
- Women-owned business enterprises

- Work and family, United States

If, while searching the local library's online catalog, a particular title appears exceptionally useful, take a look at the subject headings as listed in the catalog. Usually, subject headings within library catalogs are hyperlinks, and clicking one will then generate a clean list of *all* the books the library's collection that contain that same subject heading. Similarly, if you find a subject heading that really represents the content you are looking for, try searching that same subject in the catalog of other libraries you have access to (if you do have access to more than one library; more on this below). Because these subject headings are so universally used by U.S. libraries, a relevant subject search in one library will likely be a relevant subject search in another library.

Found a helpful print book but a little unsure as to where to find it? In looking at the catalog record for this book, there should be a number associated with the title. This number is referred to as the call number of the book, and essentially provides us, the researcher, with the street address of the book as found within the library. Just as most libraries in the United States use the Library of Congress subject headings, most public libraries will then use the Dewey Decimal system when assigning shelf location to their print collections. Why does this matter? Well, if you were in a physical library and simply wanted to browse the library's collection of print books you might visit the Dewey Decimal–assigned areas related to business. Similarly, if you find one great book on the shelf, that same area should house titles with the same/associated subject(s). Business titles generally can be found shelved at the Dewey number 650, with more specific areas found below.

- 338.7—Business enterprises
- 650—Business
- 650.1—Personal success in business
- 651—Business communication
- 658—Starting a business, entrepreneurs
- 658.1141—Business in the home
- 658.1522—Business plans

A Word on eBooks and Their Advantages

A library catalog can search by author, title, and subject and typically also offers a combined search of all three (usually referred to as a keyword search or as a words/phrase search). The online catalog does *not* search the text of any of the books in the library. Most ebook collections, particularly scholarly ebook collections, will search the entire text of all the books contained within each collection. Meaning, one can pull up the ebook collection in its entirety, and whatever word(s) the researcher types into the ebook collection's search box, is searched throughout every word, on every page, within every book of the ebook collection. Pretty powerful stuff. This is especially useful when hunting down esoteric terms and industry-specific vocabulary. Digital collections also come with the blessing of remote access, meaning digital research can be completed from home, in line at the bank, or even while waiting for the children at school pickup.

Where

Your local library may have some (or even all if you live in a very large or wealthy municipality) of the content you need. Are you finding that not enough is available at your local library? If you're in the United States, depending upon where you live, you may have access to a county library that provides content beyond what is available at your local library. If you are a current student, faculty member, or staff member at an academic institution, the institutional library will be an incredibly (in)valuable resource. If you are not employed or enrolled in an academic institution, it might be worth contacting area academic libraries. Some are welcoming of visitors for a day and do allow visitors to use the library's digital collections. One suggestion: if your area academic library does allow visitors, do bring your own device. Since most of their business research sources will be available digitally, bring a device that will connect to their wireless and then use this same device to access their relevant digital collections. You may be able to save chapters, articles, and charts from these digital collections. Again, plan on using one device to access, research, and save relevant material, especially if you have made a special trip; it will be best to use the sources and your time as effectively as possible.

Please know, however, that the money being used to purchase and fund these academic libraries is coming from student tuition and other private funding related to the institution. As such, the sources are purchased for and intended for use by the institution's students and faculty and each institution has the right to determine to whom, if anybody, beyond the institution it will grant access to the library and its collections. Also, for the safety of students and employees, private institutions may choose to only offer access to those with an institutional affiliation. For this reason, you may have better luck gaining access to a public academic library. Do contact your area public academic institution(s) (state college, university, community college) as policies vary widely. It may be that state residents are welcome, and/or that state or town residents have the option of obtaining a free or low-cost library card. A card will often provide borrowing privileges to the print collection while use of the digital library collections is restricted to on-site use only.

Another option is to check with your local library regarding a local library consortium. It may be that your library card provides access to all the libraries within a local library consortium. The consortium may include an academic library as well as additional (maybe bigger) public libraries. If your local library is not a part of a local library consortium, but a strong local library consortium is nearby, it may be worth contacting a member(s) library of the consortium to inquire about nonresident library cards. Most public libraries do offer a nonresident library card for a fee. This nonresident card will typically provide access to the library's print collection and may provide access to the digital library collections. If the library is part of a consortium, the nonresident card may (or may not) be accepted at the other member libraries of this same consortium. If the answer here is yes, the nonresident card does provide access to the other consortia libraries, and one or more of the libraries is an academic library, this could very well be worth the nonresident fee.

Only Have Access to a Small Library with Limited Books?

One suggestion would be to use Open Worldcat to study available book titles, using the subject headings recommended (and perhaps discovering a few others, unique to your area!) to survey the landscape of available titles. Open Worldcat is a master library catalog; many to most academic and public libraries in the United States have their book collections listed within Open Worldcat. It gives a researcher a sense of books available in a given subject area beyond what is on the physical and digital shelves of their home library. Researchers can home in on additional titles that are/could be useful. Open Worldcat also lists locations of these books—that is, which library— and also allows for limiting by geographic area. So, if you *do* have access to a public library, a university library, and a community college library, this is one way of discerning what titles are within these collections. You could just use the Library of Congress catalog to generate a useful list of titles. However, the Library of Congress catalog represents what is available at the LOC. The ability to search by geographic area can be quite helpful when accessing multiple collections. Likewise, the Library of Congress may be the only, or one of only a few, collections containing a given title. Searching Open Worldcat will give a sense of how widely a title is held. If a title is held in many (at least a couple dozen) libraries, it is pretty likely your local library can borrow this title using interlibrary loan; a useful service if you only have access to a small library with limited books.

What is interlibrary loan? Many libraries participate in a reciprocal borrowing agreement with other area, county, state, or national libraries. The libraries agreeing to the reciprocal borrowing agreement agree to both borrow and lend out materials from all reciprocal member libraries. How much does it cost? Generally, the service is offered to patrons at no charge or with a minimal charge. It is worth keeping in mind that the general industry-standard cost to the library of processing an interlibrary loan is $30. This can be seen by burrowing around in the public library literature, but perhaps more simply, on the "Library Value Calculator" seen on many public library websites (for example, Kendallville, Rochester, Troy). So, even if you don't have access to many libraries, Open Worldcat can still be your friend. I would recommend searching Open Worldcat, selecting five or six titles that appear most helpful to you and bringing them to your local library. The next step is to inquire about your home library's interlibrary loan policies.

Although the libraries within an interlibrary loan system will all agree on broad policies regarding borrowing and lending, each library still has its own in-house policy. This is what you need to be familiar with. For example, is there a charge for borrowing a book that is only available out-of-state? Is there a limit on the number of interlibrary loan requests a patron may place? Oftentimes libraries are unable to request material that was published within the last six to twelve months. A well-funded public library I once worked for would simply purchase any interlibrary loan requests placed for items published in the last twelve months. Some libraries now purchase requested interlibrary loan titles as e-books. Again, policies vary greatly from library to library, not in the least due to budget constraints and constraints on staff time. At the very least, most public libraries do offer an interlibrary loan system, and even if it comes with restrictive policies, this valuable service could be of use if the only library you have access to does not contain many, or any, needed business titles.

INDUSTRY AND START-UP RESEARCH

Many (but not all) public libraries provide access to a database titled Business Source Premiere. Business Source Premiere is owned by a company called Ebscohost, and is available for an annual purchase to libraries. This database contains over two thousand digitized business periodicals including industry and trade publications. This database can be a very helpful source for locating historical and current articles related to industry trends, company research, and a variety of marketing topics. According to the Ebscohost site the database also contains non-periodical content including "market research reports, industry reports, country reports, company profiles and SWOT analyses." Also from Ebscohost is a product geared toward public libraries (again, not all libraries will have purchased this) titled Small Business Reference Center. This digital reference source is a blend of four hundred business periodicals, five hundred digitized books, an easy-to-read Q&A section, short business/entrepreneurial topic videos, and business plan advice.

Reference USA is another oft-purchased database by public (and academic) libraries. Reference USA provides snapshot information on over fourteen million businesses and can be useful in determining types of businesses, how many businesses are within a specific geographic area, and also who the associated contacts are (if you are interested in marketing to a particular geographic and industry type). Information about specific businesses includes company size, sales volume, and years in business. One may also locate businesses for sale. Curious? Reference USA has two great intro tutorials on their site, created by the University of Texas at Austin library and Texas State University San Marcos library (ReferenceUSA). A similar source that you might see offered at your local library is the Dun & Bradstreet Million Dollar Directory. This source is not unlike Reference USA, but with global coverage, thirty-four million businesses indexed (including private holdings), and offering interesting corporate family trees. Again, a similar product you might see offered is Hoover's online. For a long time, Hoover's was a printed set often kept in many public libraries' reference section. Your public library may still have their print copies on the shelves. The Dun & Bradstreet Million Dollar Directory was also a formerly print-only document, and early editions may too be on the shelves in your library.

For more in-depth views of a company's financials, ValueLine, Standard & Poor's and MorningStar all offer investor reports on U.S. companies. Many public libraries offer at least one of these sources in digital form. While traditionally of great use to stock selectors, any of these sources can give you a thorough sense of industry leaders, current and historical industry trends, major shareholders, competitors for market share, as well as heaps of company-specific financials.

No Ebsco or Business-Specific Digital Content at Your Local Library? A Few Thoughts

If your library has no Ebsco content, it likely has some database containing digitized periodicals. Even if not industry-specific, a generalized database of popular magazines and newspapers could still be helpful. These types of titles may run general interest stories related to your area of business; run articles on starting a business; and contain industry forecasts and stories including statistics of business success, areas of growth, and/or articles related to women-run and women-created business. In short, any digitized collection of periodicals is worth spending a moment with to conduct searches related to your topic(s).

EbscoHost (and other suppliers of digital content such as JSTOR and Project Muse) now offer alumni access programs. This off-campus alumni access is coordinated and arranged by each academic institution. It may be worth calling your undergrad and/or graduate institution alumni office(s) to inquire about alumni access to library-purchased digital research content.

No ValueLine, Standard and Poor's, or MorningStar available at your local library? Two freely available sources, Yahoo Finance and Google Finance offer similar information, although slightly less sleekly and conveniently packaged. These two free sources also offer current news articles related to searched-for stocks/companies as well as the market more generally. In that same freely available vein is Google Scholar. This sub-site of Google searches through scholarly articles, e-books, and documents, some of which are freely available on the web. Although the current Advanced Search feature does not allow one to search by subject, it is possible to limit a search to date range and/or words in a publication title (e.g., *Harvard Business Review*) or words in article title. Again, not all the content indexed within Google Scholar is freely available on the web; however, if you do generate a list of useful-looking articles, these may be available from your area libraries and if not, may be acquirable using interlibrary loan.

BUSINESS SCHOOL RESEARCH LIBRARIANS

Wondering what business school research librarians recommend? Try a Google search for *Business LibGuide*. LibGuide? Just as subject headings can be thought of as tagging, LibGuides can be thought of as (at least a bit like) professional blogging. A LibGuide is a mini website, built by research librarian(s) focused on, and in support of, a particular academic course and/or subject. The research librarian(s) will identify the resources owned by the library that will be most helpful to succeed with a particular assignment and/or subject. The LibGuide may or may not also identify freely available Internet sources. LibGuides are most frequently used by academic librarians, although there are some public libraries that use this web-based research framework too.

How could this be helpful to you? Well the LibGuide itself is freely accessible on the web for all to see, whether one has institutional credentials or not. The content within the guide will likely be restricted to those with institutional credentials. If you do have access to an academic library, a business LibGuide may help you identify library business resources available to you. If you do not have an institutional affiliation, you might then use the LibGuides to generate a list of helpful sources and inquire whether these sources are available at your local library or library consortia. Similarly, if you are planning a special trip to an academic library that does allow for visitors, it could be quite helpful to peruse academic business library LibGuides ahead of time, to identify in advance those sources you wish to spend your time searching within, in order to maximize your time during this special trip.

Finally, if there is content included in the LibGuide that is freely available (e.g., from business organizations or government sources such as the U.S. Small Business Association) this free content can be instantly accessed. For an example of this, check out the excellent Rutgers business school library LibGuides on Small Business and also the Rutgers LibGuide on Financing (Financing, Small Business). If looking at a LibGuide from out of state or out of town that recommends specific agencies (e.g., in D.C. it is recommended to acquire a business license from the District of Columbia Business Resource Center), transfer the concept to your own township agencies and offices, (e.g., local government center, local business resource center, local chamber of commerce). Not sure if such a resource exists in your town/county? Google can probably help, as can the folks at your local town hall, and/or, the research librarians at your state library.

Want to see them all? Currently, the LibGuides software company makes publicly available the full collection of four hundred thousand LibGuides created by sixty-two thousand librarians (at the time of this writing) at the LibGuides Community site. Here, one can search by keyword all of the words within all the Libguides (though not, of course, the content linked to or mentioned within the guide (i.e., Ebsco, Mergent, etc., are separate sites, most of which live behind a paywall). One can also filter by library type using the radio buttons on the top of the screen. In early winter 2013–2014, thirty-one guides are available, written by public librarians, that contain the word *business*, and ninety-five guides have been written by academic librarians that contain the word *business*.

MOOCS and Educational Support

MOOC stands for Massive Open Online Course. These often refer to free classes, delivered entirely digitally, open to an unlimited or near-unlimited amount of registrants. There are many MOOC platforms including the popular iTunes U., Coursera and Edx, offering business and entrepreneurship-related courses. Taking one of these classes may be as simple as listening to lectures from one's living room. In terms of library support, if you need supplemental reading or required reading not provided by the course, or you need to conduct business research for the course, the library is once again going to be very valuable, most likely by using the types of sources and services discussed above.

IN SUM

Your local library will surely have books related to business and entrepreneurship. To refine searching for these titles, consider utilizing headings. Take successful subject headings on the road to any other public or academic library you may have access to, either as an alum, employee, or library consortia member. Conduct further research in business periodicals, such as the business databases created by EbscoHost. Investigate other local businesses using sources such as ReferenceUSA and research a wide range of companies using MorningStar, Standard and Poor's and/or ValueLine. Finally, take advantage of the advice of experts (business school research librarians!) and consult their LibGuides to mine freely available sources and compile lists of resources you may be able to access at a local state university and via your local library.

The library is a wonderful place and has a long history of physically representing democracy, which, here in the United States, has a relationship to our capitalist free market system. I hope the library proves an enlightening, fortifying, fruitful, and productive source of research material for you, as you embark on your journey into the free market.

BIBLIOGRAPHY

Business Source Premier. Accessed November 29, 2013. http://www.ebscohost.com/academic/business-source-premier .

Dewey Decimal Classification Summaries. Accessed December 5, 2013. http://www.oclc.org/dewey/resources/summaries.en.html .

Financing Your Business LibGuide. Accessed November 29, 2013. http://libguides.rutgers.edu/money .

Kendallville Public Library Value Calculator. Accessed November 29, 2013. http://www.kendallvillelibrary.org/calculator.htm .

LibGuides Community. Accessed November 29, 2013. http://libguides.com/community.php .

ReferenceUSA Tutorial Center. Accessed November 29, 2013. http://www.referenceusa.com/Static/VideoTutorials .

Rochester Public Library Value Calculator. Accessed November 29, 2013. http://www.rochesterpubliclibrary.org/info/calculator.html .

Small Business and Entrepreneurship LibGuide. Accessed November 29, 2013. http://libguides.rutgers.edu/small_biz .

Troy Public Library Value Calculator. Accessed November 29, 2013. http://www.troylibrary.info/value_calculator .

Chapter Seventeen

Editing Student Writing

Amy J. Barnickel

In 2010, I was a soon-to-be minted PhD graduate, underemployed working a full-time administrative job in the president's office at the nation's second-largest university, trying to make ends meet and panicking at the prospect of having to begin paying back student loans while completing coursework and dissertation hours for my degree.

An e-mail came that a company was looking for a graduate student to help learning-disabled college students in the area edit their papers for $20 per hour. So I e-mailed the contact and told her my basic information and qualifications; she responded and requested a phone conversation to seal the deal. No face-to-face meeting would be necessary because the proof would be in the pudding, so to speak, if the students using her service were happy with the results they would be getting on their papers.

Within about one week, I was set up with the company e-mail account to which all the incoming papers would be submitted for editing. And within about a week and a half, I received my first paper. Back then, I made about $20 per hour. Now, I make $30 per hour, and I can bring in up to $1,000 per month in extra income through this editing job.

To give you an idea of what my online editing work entails, I provide intensive and extensive editing for my clients, which includes not only sur-face-level edits like spelling and punctuation, but also content edits, such as pointing out what might be missing or where examples should be included or thoughts continued and completed. My editing also includes structural sug-gestions to make the document flow better—for example, a typical student paper is written in one shot—so the paper tends to have related ideas all over the place in the document. I will make marginal comments as to which ideas fit better in a certain place in the paper, or sometimes I will simply move them myself and track the change so that the student can see where I've moved something and why. Many of these very substantive edits would be worth much more money to me if I were billing these students directly (probably twice the $30 rate I currently get), but there is a lot to be said for being fed a consistent flow of clients as a subcontractor, and the regularity of the work makes up for the lower rate of pay in some ways because the contractor brings in the clients and does the marketing. All I have to do is what I do best: edit. The following are my tips for managing online editing or document consulting work.

1. Get organized and stay organized. Develop a system that makes sense to you. I save all my editing work to a Dropbox folder designated for each client. That way, no matter where I am in the world, I have access to all of my editing files at any time. I don't have to carry around a flash drive, disks, CDs, or external hard drives. I've got everything in the cloud, where I can get at it from sunny Sanibel Island or snowy Milwaukee.
2. Keep jobs and clients in their own discrete files. Don't mix clients. Ever. You will be confused; you might bill the wrong person for something you did for the other; and you will go insane if ever anyone asks you to find something you edited for him three months ago. Keep one client per folder and don't let them date each other. Ever.
3. Save Save Save Save and Save documents. Save them a sixth time just to be sure.
4. Back up. Back up. Back up, and Back up documents again. Back up a fifth time just to be sure. If you don't have an external hard drive or something local to use for your backup, e-mail copies of your documents to yourself. That way, even if your computer crashes and the files cannot be retrieved by some computer geek expert hacker guy, you can, although painfully, recreate your own set of files by retrieving them from your e-mail. Most e-mail clients will allow you to set up a rule that recognizes a particular e-mail address and sends anything from that address directly to a folder. That's one convenient way to back up files.
5. Have a backup computer and backup Internet connection just in case of emergency. Computers crash. They get viruses. Even Macs. Don't operate on just one. Keep a spare. *Always*.
6. Establish a practice for billing, tracking payments, and communicating payment expectations to clients. Do what makes sense to you and *ask* the client or employer what he expects from you in terms of detail. Comply with what he wants. He is paying you, and you want to get paid, so make it easy for him!
7. Bill as soon as you finish each document and include a due date on the bill. The due date on the bill is very important. If your client is a

corporation or a university, for example, their accounts payable team may pay everything that comes in on a "net 30-day" basis, which means your invoice might not get paid for over a month, depending on when you send it in. It's best to find out each client's individual or corporate policy, but if you can't, many times stating "payable upon receipt" is enough to get a check cut sooner. I always include that statement on my invoices, regardless of the client's policy. Some of my clients want a monthly invoice; some will pay per item. Whichever way you get paid, *record* the bill immediately after finishing the editing job. Do not delay. See below for more explanation about this.

8. Know what to do when you don't get paid. There will be a time when you are waiting for a big check in the mail and it never comes. Know the contact e-mails and phone numbers of your clients so that you can contact them when problems arise. In my experience, usually a glitch of some kind has caused the payment to be misdirected or delayed, and once you notify the client, the process gets going again and you get your check pretty quickly. I haven't had too many instances in which someone just refuses to pay a bill. For me, none of these instances have been worth pursuing beyond some phone calls and an insistence on being paid or threatening no future work until it happens. Then, if the payment doesn't come, I move on with my life. People are mostly good, but some are bad and unfair. My time is more valuable than missing out on a $45 fifteen-page edit. You may feel differently, but this tip is just to say that you need to figure out ahead of time where you stand on these matters and have a plan because at some point, this will happen to you, too.

Next are some more nuts and bolts that provide a little more detail with regard to the actual editing of documents that I work on almost daily. With this particular job, I am a subcontractor who receives clients through the company that hired me. I use the company's e-mail server and its e-mail account that is set up only for editing for its clients. The guidelines I go by for conducting this business are fairly simple. I log into the e-mail account once a day at about 4:30 AM to see if there is any editing to be done. These individuals are college students who do everything at the last minute, so our agreement is that if they send editing in by 12:00 midnight, I will edit it by 6:00 AM that same day. If it's submitted later than 4:30 AM, I may not get to it until the following morning when I log in again. Often, I do check the e-mail in-box more than once a day; typically in the evening while my kids are doing homework, and I will do editing if it has been submitted during the day, but I am not required to check it more than once a day at that early morning hour. I always try to turn editing around as quickly as possible—

doing so helps me get good recommendations and testimonials from clients, and it also brings the money in faster!

1. Log into the e-mail account to check for submissions. If there are none, go back to bed. If there are some, get to work. I often do this work literally in bed; I keep my laptop beside the bed at night so I can simply roll over and check the in-box. Most of the time, I stay logged in so that I don't have to remember passwords when I'm bleary-eyed and in the dark.

2. Download the submissions and save them into your designated Dropbox folder for this company and the subfolder for the specific client. Tip: Establish a naming convention for your documents for each client based on the way the client wants you to bill them. In this case, I bill on one spreadsheet workbook that contains a tab for each individual student. Included in the details my employer needs for billing are the date, my initials, a description of the document edited, the rate of pay I'm charging, number of half-hour increments I spent on the document, line totals, and grant total. So, for example, if my student's name is John Smith, and he wrote an economics essay about supply and demand, I name the document SmithSupplyAndDemand2-9-13, and I file it in a subfolder that is strictly for John Smith. You can use whatever naming convention you like, but I recommend beginning to use this style of naming convention because I have it on good authority that this naming convention is the way of the future since web-based programs recognize it better than they do names of files that contain spaces and underscores and such. Web and cloud-based filing systems are going to surpass filing things locally on hard drives very soon, IMHO, so we'd better get used to saving this way now.

3. Turn on the Track Changes feature in Word. Using this feature can be dicey if the client is a really bad writer. You can end up with more "red ink" on the page than original text. But, I also use the comments feature in Word to explain *why* I'm making the significant changes so that if by chance the student actually reads the comments, he or she might learn something about writing, spelling, grammar, or punctuation and not make the same mistake the next time. This technique, for me, has met with only marginal success (wink). But the writing instructor in me cannot resist the teaching moment when it arises.

4. Edit the document. What helps with editing is getting the actual assignment sheet that the professor has used to prompt the writing. With the professor's guidelines in hand, I can tell whether the student is getting close to addressing the topic she's been given, and I can also garner other useful information pertaining to formatting, length, style, genre, and other technical matters that students tend to ignore. Cita-

tions are a *big* issue for me. If I don't know what style of citation the professor expects, it's hard to recommend changes to the way a student has cited her sources. Generally, I know which citation style various disciplines use, but having the information directly from the professor is ideal.

5. *Save* along the way while you're editing. *Do not* edit the entire document without saving it every five to seven minutes! Believe me, you *will* be sorry some day when your computer crashes mid-edit, and you haven't saved the changes you've made to a client's file. *Save. Save. Save.* Just do it. Often. That is all.

6. Return the file to the student writer via reply to the e-mail she used to send it. This way, you won't have any mistakes in the delivery e-mail address, and your client is sure to receive the returned files. In the case of this particular job, I also copy the student's tutor on every returned document because I know the tutor will check her in-box before the student will, thereby getting the document back to the student's attention more quickly. This is strategic, mind you. It is strategic because if the student gets the paper back sooner, she can make the edits I suggested and possibly send it back to editing a second time before it's due. Ladies, that right there means *more money* for me. Sometimes I edit one essay for a student three or four times, depending on the length and sophistication the student is expected to achieve. At $30 per hour, that's when the money really racks up!

7. Bill it. Go directly to your billing spreadsheet, invoice, or wherever you keep your record for billing, and record the work immediately. Do not wait to record the work you've done. By the end of the day, after you've been up since 4:30 AM and it's now 1:00 AM again and you're just getting back to bed because you have three part-time jobs in addition to your full-time day job, raising two kids, volunteering at their schools, baking brownies for parties, and making sure the dog gets out to pee a few times a day, you will not remember to do your billing before going to bed. Just do it right away and you will never miss getting your money at the end of the month. *Save* the invoice or billing spreadsheet. *Save* it again just to be sure. Yes, it's OCD, but this is about money here, so better safe than sorry.

8. Take a shower, feed the kids and the animals, get coffee, and start all over again.

WHAT CAN BE LEARNED FROM THIS EXPERIENCE?

As you can tell from reading my background story, sometimes women, the web, and fate interact in serendipitous ways and produce a lucky circumstance that yields terrific results and lots of extra dough.

But, ladies, I don't want you to think that you can sell yourselves short and wait for opportunities like these to drop in your lap. In fact, looking back on these gigs, I realize that they did *not* just drop in my lap. So you can learn from my story three things:

- Educate yourself in whatever field you have an interest. Do what you love, learn what you desire, feed yourself with knowledge of any kind and in any way that seems right for you and your own circumstances. Just do *something* to make yourself smarter, to learn a new skill, or to become a more knowledgeable person.
- Claim your knowledge, skills, and intellect and don't give them away for free. If someone asks you to paint her child's bedroom because she saw what a great job you did with your little girl's via your Facebook post of all the before and after pics, you might go ahead and do the first one for free or for the cost of materials. But from that point forward, you should begin a portfolio of the painting and murals and begin to charge a fee for the service whenever you do it again. Do not discount your worth. If you do a good job at something and other people like it, then most likely there are additional people out there who will like it, too, and who will pay you to do what you do for them. In addition, getting paid for your work increases client respect for the work you do. For example, I have been getting paid to work on an academic journal for more than six years now (a job that typically goes to a graduate student for substantially less money). I have been asked to continue by three successive senior editors because of the quality of my work and the perception that with more valued work should come a higher rate of pay. Moreover, by doing so well at this job, I have acquired individual client contracts for editing work through word of mouth and for which I can set my own editing rate depending on the level of service the new client wants.
- Be organized, claim the money that is owed you for doing the work that you have done with skill and diligence, and follow up regularly, especially if you haven't received payment. Most people and organizations don't want to offend or forget you; but sometimes they will. Keep after them— you deserve to get the money you've already performed the work for. You have a right to be a bit of a squeaky wheel.
- Be a professional. You will undoubtedly come across some jerks in seeking and finding work via the World Wide Web. But, *you* must maintain your cool, project a professional image, and rise above petty squabbles

and pissing matches. If you are doing the first two items in this list right, you can say with confidence that you have the education, skills, expertise, and experience to do what you do with confidence. Learn to listen to the complaint and offer some type of compromise, but do not give up your ground to bullies who will ridicule you, yell and scream, and call you names even when doing so is completely unfounded. When you behave with dignity, others will see the bullies for what they are and continue to respect you, which is the ultimate reward and the penultimate way of exposing your naysayers as the haters that they are.

Here are some web-based resources for finding flexible writing and editing jobs that you can do from home. I do not endorse, nor have I worked for, most of these, but I have checked them out and tossed them around with friends who do similar work, and they seem to be relatively legitimate and trustworthy.

- FlexJobs—www.flexjobs.com/
- Indeed—www.indeed.com/
- GoFreelance—www.gofreelance.com/
- JuJu—www.job-search-engine.com/
- ELance—www.elance.com/
- LoveToKnow—www.lovetoknow.com/Careers/careers.html

Chapter Eighteen

Online Instructors

The New Face of Education

Judy Donovan, Julie Adkins, and Debbie Carpenter

As technology continues to be an ever-greater presence in society, a shift in how people acquire education is taking place. Students are no longer tied to the four walls of the classroom, as technology has enabled learners to seek degrees through virtual means that may be more conducive to their current lifestyle. In this chapter, we will examine the field of online teaching by providing an understanding of this educational shift into the virtual world, discussing the various types of online teaching positions that are available, the expectations of an online educator, methods in which to obtain an online position, utilizing skills that reflect successful online teaching, and finally, a glimpse into the personal stories of women online educators. It is hoped that this chapter will provide interested educators the knowledge to determine if online teaching is a viable option.

BACKGROUND

There are many kinds of institutions that offer online classes; K–12 schools, community colleges, four-year colleges, special purpose institutions (such as culinary schools) as well as universities that offer graduate degrees. While there are relatively few full-time online teaching positions, there are many more part-time openings, and this chapter will describe both opportunities.

Enrollment in online classes increased by 9.3 percent from 2011 to 2012 (Allen and Seaman 2013). A recent survey of online learning reveals that the number of students taking at least one online course has now surpassed 6.7

million and the proportion of students taking at least one online course was 32 percent of all students (Allen and Seaman 2013).

Predictions show the growth trend will continue, as witnessed by the following statistics from the report, "The US Market for Self-Paced eLearning Products and Services: 2010–2015 Forecast and Analysis."

By 2015:

- 25 million post-secondary students will be taking some of their classes online.
- Students taking classes exclusively online will increase from 1.37 million in 2010 to 3.86 million.
- The number of students taking classes only online will be almost equal to the number taking classes exclusively on a physical campus.
- By 2018, there will be more full-time online students than students that take all their classes in a physical classroom (Adkins 2012; Nagel 2011).

It is expected that fewer full-time tenure-track faculty will be around to support this move to online learning because of a major shift in higher education. Forty years ago almost 80 percent of faculty were full-time tenure or tenure track, and adjuncts made up about 20 percent of the workforce (Flaherty 2012). Today the numbers are nearly the opposite. "Non-tenure-track positions of all types now account for 68 percent of all faculty appointments in American higher education" (American Association of University Professors 2012, 1).

Some definitions of terms are needed. Traditional tenure-track faculty have three ranks; Assistant, Associate and Full Professor. Faculty who are full-time at one institution are often not on the tenure track, but work on one to three year contracts. These personnel have many titles: Fixed-term, Affiliate, Associate, Clinical, Lecturer and Contract faculty. Adjunct faculty, also called part-time faculty, currently comprise over 50 percent of total faculty (American Association of University Professors 2012).

The reduction in full-time positions and corresponding shift to the use of part-time personnel, has been attributed to economic pressures on higher education. Adjuncts do not have benefits, pensions, sabbaticals, offices, or security. They are paid by the class and generally do not have duties apart from teaching. A tenure-track professor has scholarship duties (publishing and presenting research) and service duties (committee work, curriculum development, program revision, accreditation, etc.). When a tenure-track faculty member achieves tenure, his or her position is practically assured for life. An adjunct is not eligible for tenure, and is employed to teach a specific class, with no promise of work when the class ends.

It is easy to see how the shift to using more adjuncts has benefitted institutions, not just economically, but in terms of flexible scheduling for administrators (Rosenblum 2012). Predictions indicate the trend toward hiring part-time faculty will continue. Combine this with the increase in overall opportunities for online professors, full-time and adjunct, and this field looks very promising in terms of increased growth.

TYPES OF TEACHING POSITIONS

A report titled *A Portrait of Part-Time Faculty Members* was published by the Coalition on the Academic Workforce in 2012. Their findings show that most adjunct faculty (38.5 percent) teach at community colleges or other associate degree–granting institutions. These institutions usually require adjuncts to have a master's in the subject area, or a Master's in any subject and eighteen graduate credit hours in the subject. The report also states that 36 percent of adjuncts teach at institutions that grant bachelor's and master's degrees, while 22 percent teach at doctoral granting institutions. Typically graduate-level courses are taught by faculty members with terminal degrees (i.e., PhD, EdD) and undergraduate-level courses are taught by faculty with at least a master's. In general, having a doctorate is a big advantage to any adjunct, in particular because state and regional accreditation agencies are increasingly demanding that online faculty have doctorates, especially if they are teaching students at the master's level. The report reveals that 94 percent of part-time faculty have as their highest degree a master's (47 percent), a doctorate (30 percent), or a professional/terminal degree in their field (17 percent) (The Coalition on the Academic Workforce 2012).

Some adjuncts find employment at special focus institutions, and many are finding opportunities to teach K–12 students online. K–12 online schools require teaching certificates, sometimes from the state in which they are based. Growth is predicted to be strong in the areas of home schools, virtual public and private K–12 schools, and cyber charter schools. "There were over 455,000 full-time online PreK–12 students in the US as of 2011" (Adkins 2012, para.3).

The report also examines the content fields in which adjuncts are employed. The majority of courses taught by online adjuncts were in humanities (44 percent), about 20 percent of the courses taught were in professional fields, 14 percent in sciences, and 14 percent in social sciences (The Coalition on the Academic Workforce 2012).

EXPECTATIONS OF ONLINE TEACHERS

Teaching in the online environment requires organization, planning, and attention to detail. An online instructor must ensure that all important deadlines are met, such as developing and posting lecture materials prior to the start of each week, facilitating asynchronous discussions effectively, grading responses and assignments in an instructive and timely manner, and posting pertinent announcements throughout the course. Daily activities include responding to discussion posts, posing thoughtful follow-up questions to stimulate further discussion, handling student questions and concerns by e-mail, and evaluating student work. One suggestion is to create a course calendar that provides a daily reminder of expectations, both for the student and for the instructor. Especially for new instructors, a course calendar is extremely useful for self-monitoring and meeting deadlines.

Online teaching requires a tremendous amount of written interaction. Despite the increased use of audio and video tools, there is still a significant amount of written communication required. For this reason, online instructors must be well-versed in the conventions of writing and must be experienced in academic writing in order to provide meaningful, instructive feedback to students. When teaching a course for the first time, online instructors may devote hours of preparation time to reading, researching, and developing mini-lectures that align course content to outside research sources and professional expertise. Once a course has been developed, the preparation work is minimized as the instructor might make only small modifications from course to course. The most effective online instructors are those who take time to establish a strong virtual presence through multisensory web tools, and who build rapport with students through meaningful interaction, personalized feedback, and timely evaluation.

COMPENSATION

Full-time online faculty members are typically salaried and their salary is often comparable to their brick-and-mortar counterparts. Compensation for adjunct online instructors may be based on a combination of graduate-level education, prior years teaching in higher education, and professional experience. The institution may simply pay all adjuncts a set amount per course. The range of pay also can differ by institution and level of course (see table 18.1).

Adjunct teaching positions can be particularly attractive to women because of the minimal discrepancy in compensation by gender. In terms of compensation, part-time adjunct faculty surveyed by the Coalition on the Academic Workforce (CAW) indicates only a scant difference in median pay by gender and there is even less variation when institutional type is considered. In the majority of institutions (two-year, master's level, doctoral, research, and special focus institutions) compensation for male and female instructors is identical. The only exception in this study was for baccalaureate institutions, in which women earned more (The Coalition on the Academic Workforce 2012).

When considering delivery mode of part-time faculty, the study indicated that faculty members who teach on campus report earnings of approximately $2,850, while online faculty members report earnings of approximately $2,250. Part-time faculty taught over 15,000 courses on-site and about 1,660 online (The Coalition on the Academic Workforce 2012). For many, the difference in pay between on-site and online teaching is offset by the greater amount of flexibility one has in working remotely, as well as the ability to teach more courses, as travel time and schedule conflicts are nonissues.

Because compensation and requirements vary from institution to institution, it is advisable for candidates to explore the websites for multiple institutions or contact the talent acquisition/recruitment department for the institution. Often qualified faculty are teaching as adjunct faculty for several different institutions, and may teach pre-developed, standardized courses. The Adjunct Project website allows potential adjuncts to research compensation structure throughout the country. It includes information such as working conditions, opportunities to be included in governance, and availability of health and/or retirement benefits (June and Newman 2013). As additional universities implement online modalities of instruction, opportunities for adjunct faculty to teach online full-time are likely to increase.

Table 18.1. Median Pay per Course, by Institutional Type and Gender

Institutional Type	Female		Male	
	Median Pay per Course	Number of Courses	Median Pay per Course	Number of Courses
Associate's	$2,200	3,609	$2,200	2,141
Baccalaureate	$2,800	711	$2,700	432
Master's	$3,000	2,794	$3,000	1,775
Doctoral and research	$3,493	2,147	$3,500	1,347
Special focus	$3,000	319	$3,000	176
Not available	$3,000	246	$2,500	134
All courses	$2,700	9,826	$2,780	6,005
Pay not specified in response		1,478		780
Total courses		11,304		6,785

BREAKING INTO THE FIELD OF ONLINE TEACHING

There are a number of ways to locate a position teaching online. A university's website serves as a great entry point to accessing potential teaching positions. This information is most commonly located within the Human Resource tab found on the website. If this information is not readily available, there are outside resources that can provide employment opportunities in online higher education.

One of those excellent outside resources is HigherEdJobs, which features job listings in higher education. Here the candidate can create a jobseeker account and select certain criteria tailored to a type of position, institution and content area. This serves as a headhunter or Job Agent, where weekly e-mails are sent to the account holder regarding new teaching opportunities that are available. Additional features allow you to save positions, submit applications, and track their status. The candidate can also post resumes that are visible to prospective employers.

A majority of instructors begin their online teaching part-time. It is important to remain visible and vigilant regarding the expectations a university holds for its instructors. Attend webinars for professional development and program meetings even though attendance is voluntary for adjunct faculty. Many times institutions have internal hiring for full-time positions, and if the university has seen a high level of performance that includes quality instruction and high engagement, they will be more likely to notice when a full-time position becomes available.

ONLINE TEACHING SUCCESS

Many have a preconceived notion that online teaching is "easy." This couldn't be further from the truth. Instructors must be committed to their practice through distinguished preparation and continual support for their students. The following is a reflection of best practices for successful online teaching:

1. Cultivate relationships. Try to take the "distance" out of online learning by engaging in meaningful conversations with students and showing interest in their lives. Use a digital video tool to introduce yourself to the class. This is effective because it gives a face and voice to the instructor. It also doesn't hurt to include a little humor every now and then.

2. Have an active presence in your course. This means engaging students in thought-provoking ideas and asking questions about the content through ongoing discussions.

3. Be sure to provide students with detailed instructor feedback through the use of rubrics and embedded comments. Make sure you provide students with the guidance they need to improve upon their learning and writing skills.
4. Set high expectations for all students. Be sure to inform students of the expectations for the course that will challenge them and guide them toward achieving their academic potential. In addition, serve as a model for those expectations as well.
5. Use digital tools in the course. There are a plethora of digital tools available to make learning in the online classroom more engaging and appealing while also addressing various student learning styles. Some of these digital tools are Jing, Animoto, Voicethread, and Glogster.

These are just a few suggested best practices that will lay the foundation toward becoming a successful online instructor.

PERSONAL STORIES FROM ONLINE INSTRUCTORS

Julie N. Adkins, PhD

Having served as an elementary school teacher for seven years, I knew during my experience that I eventually wanted to share my practices as an educator with future teacher candidates in hopes of adequately preparing quality educators for our students. While working full-time in the public schools, I was able to obtain my doctorate online because of the great flexibility that online learning offered to people like me. It was also during this time that my husband and I expanded our family to four. Having a passion for both my career as an educator and my two little angels, I wanted to find balance between pursuing my career goals and simply put, being a good mom. I knew that teaching online would afford me the flexibility I was looking for that allowed me to spend quality time with my children while simultaneously growing as a professional educator. This is when I began working part-time for several online universities while concurrently maintaining my position as an elementary school teacher. After three years as an adjunct online faculty member, I was then hired as a full-time remote (online) assistant professor.

I love being able to work from anyplace and anytime as long as there is an Internet connection (thank goodness for WiFi!). I also emphatically love the idea of teaching people from all across the world. The Internet has definitely made the classroom more global, as I have taught students living in Japan, Thailand, Italy, Germany, and Guam, just to name a few. It is empowering to know that I have a part in providing students with a college education that previously was unattainable due to the restrictions of a brick-and-mortar classroom setting.

I would say that the most difficult thing about online teaching is finding balance. Many of you will start as an adjunct faculty where teaching online will become your "side" job. You will find that you are working longer hours and it is important that you don't compromise the quality of instruction for your online students. In addition, I have found that it can be difficult to guide students toward improving their writing skills especially when they do not respond to your feedback. Don't be afraid to pick up the phone and express your concerns with your students; they will appreciate that you took the time to call and care about their progress.

Leslie Bowman

During my first online graduate class over ten years ago, I knew that I wanted to teach online full time. I enjoyed the convenience of working on my own daily schedule. I especially liked not having to fight the traffic to drive to and from work. Over the years, I have discovered quite a few more benefits of teaching online, primarily being able to travel when and where I please without having to work around vacation time.

Last year, my Christmas present was a used slide-in truck camper, which allowed me to travel by myself without having to tow a trailer. I have loved taking road trips since I was a kid, and in April of this year, I embarked on my first solo road trip, all the way from Virginia to Texas and back. During that three-week trip, I was teaching two online graduate courses and the week I drove back home, I also started two new graduate courses.

Traveling and teaching online work very well together. My daily routine was to get up around 7 AM and work for about an hour, answering e-mails and checking the discussions in my courses. Then I would get on the road for four to six hours, stopping mid-afternoon to set up camp, fix supper, and work for a few more hours. Any grading I needed to do was done in the late afternoons or early evenings. Some days in the online classes are very slow and others are very busy. Generally weekends are slow, Mondays and Tuesdays are busy with grading, and Wednesdays through Fridays require a couple of hours each facilitating discussions.

I average about 15 hours a week teaching two to four classes online. This works out nicely with traveling because I can fit in those hours throughout the week and never have to spend more than two to three hours working in any given day. Sometimes I teach more classes and since that takes more time each day, I am careful not to plan any travel during those times. It is wonderful being able to travel without worrying about taking vacation and being away from the workplace. Sometimes I wish I didn't have to work at all while traveling; however, the alternative is far less than desirable. I would much rather travel and teach online than teach on campus and not be able to travel except on vacation breaks.

Debbie Carpenter, MAEd

When I began teaching elementary education in 1996, I had no idea that my education and experience would eventually lead to online teaching. While on maternity leave, I transitioned into higher education and directed several teacher-preparation programs for an on-ground university. Because I wanted to broaden my teaching experience, I elected to complete online teaching certification. During this process I discovered:

1. Online programs are effective when offered through a regionally ac-credited institution.
2. Online education is an ideal choice for instructors who are skilled at communicating in written form.
3. When facilitated effectively, the online classroom is an engaging environment in which students access high-quality materials, learning experiences, and discussions.

In my quest to find work-life balance within university administration, I learned that my educational experience qualified me for additional teaching opportunities. After nearly a decade, I left my administrative post and joined my current institution as a full-time online instructor. I have eliminated morning preparation, commuting, and office distractions from my life. Goals are now accomplished in a timely, flexible manner. As a dedicated professional and mother, I do not sacrifice quality time with my children. Teaching online provides me flexibility to be available because in an asynchronous environment I facilitate discussions and communicate with colleagues flexibly, yet effectively.

Teaching online is challenging due to its time-intensive nature and its student diversity. Courses require significant reading, research, and preparation. I must be actively involved in discussions and provide detailed, individualized feedback on assignments. Students enter the online classroom with varied skills, and therefore I must encourage critical thinking and provide professional expertise and resources to enhance learning. Just like a traditional educator, my work is never done. There are always opportunities to develop professionally and to improve curriculum, strategies, and college initiatives.

Jane Doe (Jane did not wish to include her real name)

When I was in the military, I worked long, odd hours with fluctuating schedules. I knew that there was no way that I could successfully hold down a job with a rigid schedule, not even a part-time one. By chance, I found out about online customer service jobs. Interestingly, despite how easy that job was (as it was very similar to call center work I had done upon graduating high school), they required a four-year degree. That trend—hiring only the seemingly overqualified for online work—has not declined in my humble opinion. I was pursuing my graduate degree at the time and I was interested in teaching so I began to research online teaching and that is what I do today.

In general, I feel that working online has helped me to deal with pain associated with my disability and discrimination based upon my appearance. Driving to and from work, walking between students, and operating equipment all takes a strain on me physically when I am teaching traditionally.

It's sad but I've dealt with a bit of interracial prejudice, as well as people who just think I'm plain weird because of how I look. After a few years of working online, my relative freedom from conforming to societal norms regarding appearance finally hit me and, in celebration, I dyed my hair blue . . . because I could.

CONCLUSION

The growing demand for online education has fostered a significant opportunity for educated women who seek ways in which to remain professionally engaged. As the number of online students increases and as more traditional universities offer online modalities for their learners, the demand for online instructors is rising. The research indicates women in online education have an opportunity to be compensated equally and according to the testimonials, can benefit from the flexibility, anonymity, and freedom that the online modality offers (The Coalition on the Academic Workforce 2012).

It is advised that prospective candidates use the tools and resources provided to initiate a successful job search because compensation varies among institutions. The authors' hope is that this chapter provides the encouragement, expectations, and information necessary to further increase the number of female instructors in the field of online education.

HELPFUL RESOURCES

- Make Money Teaching Online. A listserv for online professors: http://groups.yahoo.com/group/OnlineTeachingJobs/

- A comprehensive listing and ranking of online graduate degree programs: http://www.geteducated.com/
- *U.S. News* ratings of the best online graduate degrees: http://www.usnews.com/education/online-education
- Compares compensation levels at different institutions (type online into the search box) http://adjunct.chronicle.com

JOB HUNTING RESOURCES

- Chronicle of Higher Education Jobs: http://chronicle.com/section/Jobs/61/?eio=1
- HigherEdJobs (there is a separate section for online positions) http://www.higheredjobs.com/default.cfm
- Online Adjunct Jobs: http://onlineadjunctjobs.blogspot.com/

Table 18.2. 2010 Student Enrollment Data for Institutions with Largest Online Enrollment

Institution	# full-time students	Institution	# part-time students
American Public Education	77,700	University of Phoenix Online	362,500
Bridgepoint Education	77,100	State University of New York Learning Network	111,400
UMassOnline	45,800	The Ohio Learning Network	110,400
Walden University	45,600	Kaplan University	75,000
Liberty University	45,000	DeVry	66,500

WHERE THE JOBS ARE (AND WILL BE)

- An article that describes explosive growth in the PreK–12 area: http://thejournal.com/articles/2011/01/20/prek12-dominates-growth-in-e-learning.aspx#v6KUmWP4sdth4wHZ.99
- In the article "5 Ways Technology Will Impact Higher Ed in 2013," Chris Proulz predicts that there will be strong growth in online education in a newer area, among highly selective universities and colleges: http://www.forbes.com/sites/groupthink/2012/12/11/5-ways-technology-will-impact-higher-ed-in-2013/
- This report describes continued strong growth for eLearning: "The US Market for Self-Paced eLearning Products and Services: 2010–2015 Fore-

cast and Analysis." Ambient Insight: http://www.ambientinsight.com/
Resources/Documents/AmbientInsight-2011-2016-NorthAmerica-
SelfPaced-eLearning-Market-Abstract.pdf

REFERENCES

Adkins, Sam S. 2012. "The US Market for Self-Paced eLearning Products and Services: 2010–2015 Forecast and Analysis." *Ambient Insight*. http://www.ambientinsight.com/ Resources/Documents/AmbientInsight-2011-2016-NorthAmerica-SelfPaced-eLearning-Market-Abstract.pdf .

Allen, I. Elaine, and Jeff Seaman. 2013. "Changing Course: Ten Years of Tracking Online Education in the United States." *Babson Survey Research Group and Quahog Research Group, LLC*. http://www.onlinelearningsurvey.com/reports/changingcourse.pdf .

American Association of University Professors. 2012. "Background Facts on Contingent Faculty." http://www.aaup.org/issues/contingency/background-facts .

The Coalition on the Academic Workforce. 2012. *A Portrait of Part-Time Faculty Members: A Summary of Findings on Part-Time Faculty Respondents to the Coalition on the Academic Workforce Survey of Contingent Faculty Members and Instructors*. http://www. academicworkforce.org/survey.html .

Flaherty, Colleen. 2012. "Making the Case for Adjuncts." *Inside Higher Ed*, January 9. http:// www.insidehighered.com/news/2013/01/09/adjunct-leaders-consider-strategies-force-change .

June, Audrey Williams, and Newman, Jonah. 2013. "Adjunct Project Reveals Wide Range in Pay". *Chronicle of Higher Education*, January 4. http://chronicle.com/article/Adjunct_Pay_ Conditions/136439/ .

Nagel, David. 2011. "Online Learning Set for Explosive Growth as Traditional Classrooms Decline." *Campus Technology*, January 26. http://campustechnology.com/articles/2011/01/ 26/online-learning-set-for-explosive-growth-as-traditional-classrooms-decline.aspx .

Rosenblum, Bruce. 2012. "Adjuncts and Online: Intersecting Trends." *Envisioning Online Learning*, November 15. http://onlinelearning.commons.gc.cuny.edu/2012/11/15/adjuncts-and-online-intersecting-trends/ .

Chapter Nineteen

The Six Ps of Editorial Assistantships

How the Web Paid For My Doctoral Education

Jenny Ungbha Korn

Few students have been willing to share their experiences in the role of editorial assistantship (do an online search, and you'll see), but in this chapter, I share how the entirely web-based work of my editorial assistantship helped to fund my doctoral education. My aim is to inform parents, friends, colleagues, professors, and advisors of doctoral students and other PhD students themselves of this important, online-based way for funding. I present the six Ps of editorial assistantships:

- Papers
- Prestige
- Preparation
- Productivity
- Procrastination
- Power

"Congratulations" is a word that is earned from two sides of the publishing process, both the author and the editor. Publications are the currency of research-oriented academia (Frey 2003), and hearing congratulations upon a manuscript's conversion into an actual article is just about always welcome. For graduate students, a research assistantship is one choice for securing data for successful manuscripts that eventually earn congratulations. Indeed, research assistantships often conjure images of graduate students working with faculty to produce publishable work. However, the other half of the publication process, namely the editorial side, is also critical in deciding who receives congratulations. In this chapter, I focus on an under-researched specific type of research assistantship that benefits not just the immediate professor, but also academia as a whole: the research assistantship known as the editorial assistant of scholarly journals.

METHODOLOGY AND LITERATURE REVIEW

Editorial assistants are well-known because most established journals hire graduate students to serve in that role, aiding with the process by which manuscripts (and authors) become published. Editorial assistantships have not been researched widely, and few students have been willing to share their experiences in the role of editorial assistantship. Indeed, only a couple of academic articles have been published on editorial assistantships (Minicucci 2002; Turkiewicz, Kim, Tenzek, and Herrman 2010). Focusing on this influential yet understudied case of editorial assistantship as research assistantship gives a deeper analysis of this particular type of research assistantship, adding to the wider body of literature on research assistants. Unlike past research on editorial assistantships, my work situates the editorial assistantship within research assistantships, delineating similarities and differences between the editorial assistantship and the traditional research assistantship. I conclude my paper with specific advice to professors and students engaged in the editorial process.

I define "research assistant" as a formal title and employment for which a student has been hired. In my experience, because editorial assistants do not exist as a larger category within the pay structure at universities, editorial assistants are labeled as research assistants, as opposed to teaching assistants or even general assistants. I exclude undergraduate students who serve as research assistants (cf. Gueldner, Clayton, Bramlett, and Boettcher 1993) and focus only on graduate students who have been designated as research assistants at a university. Further, I outline the responsibilities of a research assistant (RA) as my institution has: "The duties of a research assistant primarily involve applying and mastering research concepts, practices, or methods of scholarship by such means as conducting experiments, organizing or analyzing data, presenting findings in a publication or dissertation, collaborating with faculty in preparing publications, overseeing work of other R.A.s, and other research activities" (University of Illinois at Chicago n.d.). Past studies on research assistantships have utilized case studies of research assistant participants in Canada (Grundy 2004), Australia (Hobson, Jones, and Deane, 2005), and the United Kingdom (Newbury 1995), among other countries. Like those previous researchers, I also provide a case study of my experience. In addition, I base this study on an analytic autoethnography (Denzin 2006; Anderson 2006) of my editorial assistantship across three years for a journal that focuses on research related to the Internet. Because of my experiences in both a traditional research assistantship and in the lesser-known editorial assistantship, I am in a unique position to compare and contrast these two assistantships.

PAPERS

Editorial assistants are the shepherds for the papers that are submitted to the journal. The entire publishing process is web based, which means that editorial assistants may work from anywhere that provides Internet access. Papers are called manuscripts until they have been accepted officially, which converts the manuscript into an actual article. Once the manuscript is received by a journal, the manuscript may be rejected outright, which occurs if the manuscript is outside of the scope of the journal. For example, rejected papers might include a quantitative paper that is submitted to a qualitative journal, or a paper on furniture that has nothing to do with the Internet that is submitted to a journal focused on research related to online interactivity. Generally, a manuscript will undergo one to three rounds of review by two or more reviewers that are familiar with the topic or method in the paper. Those reviewers are sought by the editorial assistant and may require several requests before two reviewers agree to peruse the manuscript. Among other tasks, the editorial assistant ensures that references to the author have been removed for the process of blind review. My journal utilizes a double-blind process in which the authors do not know the reviewer's identity and each reviewer's identity is kept hidden from the other reviewers and the author. The editorial assistant reminds reviewers to submit their feedback and stays in touch with the author as the manuscript advances through the review process. Finally, the editorial assistant alerts the author of the outcome of the review, which may be acceptance of the manuscript, a request to revise and resubmit the manuscript, or the declining of the manuscript. The editorial assistant also safeguards that the proper documentation has been completed once manuscripts have become articles, including copyright permissions.

PRESTIGE

As has been noted (Minicucci 2002; Turkiewicz, Kim, Tenzek, and Herrman 2010), editorial assistantships carry prestige. Within institutional categories, editorial assistantships qualify as research assistantships because of their connection to current research and the scholars who create such research. Editorial assistants earn social clout from their position due to consistent interaction with scholars seeking publication and with scholars providing reviews. Conferences become a different networking scenario for editorial assistants as people recognize the name of the graduate student and associate the person with a journal. These people include not just authors who would like to be published, but editorial board members who recognize the graduate student's name from frequent e-mails requesting reviews from them. Editorial board members are often research-oriented themselves (Chan, Fung, and Lai 2005), and the opportunity to interact with them helps to establish professional rapport between the editorial assistant and editorial board members. The socialization that occurs on the job as an editorial assistant is immediate entry into the culture of an academic workplace. Such socialization through editorial assistantships is a rare opportunity; professionalization as an institutional priority in general has been found lacking in doctoral programs (Austin 2002; Austin and McDaniels 2006).

PREPARATION

While the interaction with individuals who would like to be published is generally pleasant, the same cannot always be said of faculty whose manuscripts have been deemed wanting. Scholars whose manuscripts are rejected by a journal may react negatively to the editorial assistant, but that is precisely when the "assistant" part becomes key. I am blessed to work with an editor who protects me from undue negativity and who steps in when authors take a journal's declination a little too personally. Working as an editorial assistant inculcates graduate students with the values of developing a thicker skin and also with the appreciation for good research. Reading submitted manuscripts, looking at reviewer feedback, and following the outcome of each submission, editorial assistants gain greater understanding about author mistakes that might lead to rejection, author strengths that might lead to acceptance, and everything in between that leads to the decision to revise and resubmit.

In addition, editorial assistants learn the trends in the field of the journal, including the incredible gatekeeping role that journal editors play. Publications are crucial in a research-oriented academic's career, and understanding which research questions are significant currently and which methodologies are favored in a journal is part of the socialization process (Stegmaier, Palmer, and van Assendelft 2011). The distinction between a good cover letter and bad cover letter becomes more apparent with experience. Differences in how authors address reviewer feedback show up not just in content, but also in style of the document, from authors choosing to utilize spreadsheet columns in their response letter, to authors opting not to address or summarize their revisions in any way.

Editorial assistants also learn how to prepare their own submissions for academic journals, including the protocols for acceptable journal styles and the double-blind process. Anonymizing a manuscript for the double-blind process involves stripping author information from the properties fields in

Microsoft Word (this latter component is often overlooked by authors when they submit to journals, which may result in the journal outright rejecting the manuscript, returning the manuscript to the author to remove all references, or requesting the editorial assistant to remove author-identifying references manually. In general, research assistants work with professors to produce their own research, while research assistants as editorial assistants work with faculty to publish others' research. In fact, graduate students serving as editorial assistants end up with one less option for the future home of a paper, as we are prohibited from submitting our own work to the journal for which we are employed.

PRODUCTIVITY

While traditional research assistants focus on research of their own, editorial assistants learn quickly about time management. The work I do as an editorial assistant benefits the journal first; for me to produce my own research, I must allocate time outside of my editorial duties to pursue studies that will advance my own career. The workload of the editorial assistant is heavy, often worse during summer and winter breaks between terms because those times are the most convenient for academic authors to finish and submit their manuscripts. While the contract rules of my research assistantship limit my weekly workload to under twenty hours, the real responsibilities of the journal override the actual cap in hours invested into the journal. For example, if an influx of manuscripts needs to be processed, then those new manuscripts must be checked for author identity and assigned reviewers. The time of the tasks associated with the new batch of manuscripts is independent of the time necessary for reminding individuals about their pending reviews. The reality of the editorial assistantship is that a student could spend entire days outside of class and research, searching for reviewers and reminding them that their recommendations are due. Surprisingly, the work related to the journal that is readily available sometimes provides a "productive" distraction from other responsibilities.

PROCRASTINATION

Time is my largest concern as a research assistant. I have learned how to multitask requisite coursework, personal research, and editorial duties, but often, it is to easier to prioritize editorial tasks over other responsibilities because I receive financial compensation for those tasks. My employment as an editorial assistant helps to finance my doctoral education, so I tend to place editorial work before classwork and research. Through working for the journal, I have learned that my editorial assistantship responsibilities sometimes become an odd procrastination from my own research. For example, I may spend an entire day working on the journal, which is productive, but it does not advance my own studies necessarily. Like the traditional research assistantship, the editorial assistantship has work that is always available. However, while a singular study for a research assistant will eventually end, the editorial work never ceases: another manuscript may be reviewed, another reviewer may be contacted, another reminder may be sent. Multiple tasks exist that may be executed at any time, including during finals when three papers are due within the same week. Some professors may not value the time of their research assistant, but considerate professors will check in with their students to see if the time of actual work matches the expected hours in the research assistant contract, especially during the predictably stressful times of mid-terms and finals (and yes, I am grateful for collaborating with compassionate faculty). For me, I would argue that traditional research assistantships and editorial assistantships conducted in healthy, mutually satisfying ways have resulted in increased productivity for both the student and the professor. Still, graduate students juggling between completing coursework deadlines and the journal's rolling due dates find themselves asking which should be prioritized: classes or the journal.

POWER

The power dynamic between faculty supervisor and the research assistant is skewed (Aguinis et al. 1996), even more than the usual professor-student relationship, because of the added employment element for research assistantships. Like a typical research assistantship, the potential for exploitation exists between the professor and student in an editorial assistantship (Hobson, Jones, and Deane 2005). Some professors advance their research by building upon the groundwork developed by graduate students without giving credit to their research assistants, in name, title, or spirit. Unlike traditional research assistantships, the name and title of editorial assistants are listed usually in the journal's print and online representations, so graduate students are reassured that their editorial work will be publicized. Nevertheless, the power in creating a supportive ethos falls mostly upon the professor who influences the editorial assistant to spend more time on the journal or classwork, depending upon the faculty's subtle signals.

ADVICE TO PROFESSORS

As editors of a journal, professors should consider hiring two or more editorial assistants concurrently, so that one editorial assistant has experience with which to train the newer editorial assistant. Overlapping tenure helps to ensure smoother facilitation between the outgoing editorial assistant and the incoming editorial assistant. I was trained during the summer before my first-year classes began, and I appreciated several weeks of meetings with my predecessor. She and I kept in touch during the transition and afterward so that I could ask her for advice as new situations arose.

In addition, editors of journals may remember that editorial assistants are graduate students first. Coursework should not suffer due to journal work. While the editorial assistant bears responsibility in voicing concerns about workload, the thoughtful faculty member may remember that frequent communication with the editorial assistant should include queries about classes. Such questions signal to the student that schoolwork is a priority. These regular interactions between the editor and editorial assistant may yield a positive influence in terms of informal mentoring. Research assistantships allow doctoral students to get paid to work closely with professors; ideally, we learn from our faculty, not just about the current state of research in our field, but also how to become successful faculty ourselves, modeling ourselves after our professors. If our professors are exploitative, it is up to us to break that cycle. And if our professors are thoughtful, we are obligated to pay that kindness forward as we take on students of our own. Through electronic messages, the editor of my journal and I connect every day. While our communication is primarily about issues related to the journal, we do interweave personal matters, like school questions, classwork updates, family news, and informal guidance. The editor of the journal for which I work is also my dissertation advisor, and he has provided compassionate mentoring, a lesson in thoughtfulness that I intend to replicate in the future.

ADVICE TO STUDENTS

After reading the above, students should consider strongly whether their personality matches the responsibilities for an editorial assistantship. Specifically, editorial assistants must remain professional and detached during all interactions with authors, particularly those authors whose manuscripts are not accepted. While I expected negativity from rejected authors, I did not anticipate anger from reviewers. Reviewers may react with frustration over deadlines, with surprise over (possible) recognition of the author, or with extreme disdain over the quality (or lack thereof) of the manuscript. Through the many attitudes encountered and the serious time commitment mandated, the editorial assistant must be reliable, proficient, and communicative. These qualities are also the ones necessary for a successful, long-term career in academia, so the editorial assistantship provides practical acculturation in scholarly interactions (Minicucci 2002; Turkiewicz, Kim, Tenzek, and Herrman 2010).

Students may seek editorial assistantship opportunities based on the home institution of the journal editor. Potential editorial assistants may contact the editor to discover when the journal might need a new editorial assistant. Editorial assistantships are more numerous than graduate students may realize. Even if a journal is not housed permanently at a certain institution, many publications rotate their editorships among professors, which means that when a faculty member becomes editor, the opening of an editorial assistantship will materialize. For graduate students, that research assistantship is one way to attach their names to a journal: first, as editorial assistant, and later, as an author (hopefully!).

CONCLUSIONS

I have organized the findings from my analytic autoethnographic study around the six Ps of editorial assistantships: papers, prestige, preparation, productivity, procrastination, and power. In so doing, I have highlighted the advantages and disadvantages of editorial assistantships within the larger set of research assistantships. I highly recommend to any graduate student that, if given the opportunity to choose between a traditional research assistantship and a "journal" assistantship, to choose the latter.

The editorial assistant of a journal does not conduct research in the traditional manner of a research assistantship. Literature reviews by research assistants are solo endeavors requiring multiple hours online and in the library, and success depends on the professor's approval. In contrast, as the journal's editorial assistant, I am privy to current research across my field, especially research that has not been published anywhere yet. I gain insight into the collective topical interests of the smartest minds in my discipline and where hot topics have fallen off now as no longer in vogue. The editorial assistant reads just as much research as a "regular" research assistant (if not more), but the editorial assistant works actively in concert with the authors behind such research, contacting them about editorial decisions and other publication issues, instead of in isolation from other individuals and negotiating only with texts.

The key component that enables my work to be performed is that every part of the editorial process is based online. Through web-based work, my editorial assistantship has helped to fund my doctoral education. Getting my PhD paid through my online editorial assistantship has been rewarding, educational, and worthwhile.

REFERENCES

Aguinis, Herman, Mitchell S. Nesler, Brian M. Quigley, Suk-Jae-Lee, and James T. Tedeschi. 1996. "Power Bases of Faculty Supervisors and Educational Outcomes for Graduate Students." *Journal of Higher Education* 67(3): 267–97.

Anderson, Leon. 2006. "Analytic Autoethnography." *Journal of Contemporary Ethnography* 35(4): 373–95.

Austin, Ann E. 2002. "Preparing the Next Generation of Faculty: Graduate School as Socialization to the Academic Career." *Journal of Higher Education* 73(1): 94–122.

Austin, Ann E., and Melissa McDaniels. 2006. "Preparing the Professoriate of the Future: Graduate Student Socialization for Faculty Roles." *Higher Education: Handbook of Theory and Research* 21: 397–456.

Chan, Kam C., Hung-Gay Fung, and Pikki Lai. 2005. "Membership of Editorial Boards and Rankings of Schools with International Business Orientation." *Journal of International Business Studies* 36(4): 452–69.

Denzin, Norman K. 2006. "Analytic Autoethnography, or Déjà Vu All Over Again." *Journal of Contemporary Ethnography* 35(4): 419–28.

Frey, Bruno S. 2003. "Publishing as Prostitution? Choosing Between One's Own Ideas and Academic Success." *Public Choice* 116(1–2): 205–23.

Grundy, Annabelle. 2004. "Learning Experience and Identity Development as a Research Assistant." Master's thesis, Brock University.

Gueldner, Sarah Hall, Gloria M. Clayton, Martha H. Bramlett, and Janet Hardy Boettcher. 1993. "The Undergraduate Student as Research Assistant: Promoting Scientific Inquiry." *Nurse Educator* 18(3): 18–21.

Hobson, Jane, Gar Jones, and Elizabeth Deane. 2005. "The Research Assistant: Silenced Partner in Australia's Knowledge Production?" *Journal of Higher Education Policy and Management*, 27(3): 357–66.

Minicucci, Daryl Sharp. 2002. "Reflections of an Editorial Assistant." *Research in Nursing & Health*, 25(5): 329–30.

Newbury, Darren. 1995. "A Journey in Research: From Research Assistant to Doctor of Philosophy." *Journal of Graduate Education* 2(5): 53–59.

Stegmaier, Mary, Barbara Palmer, and Laura van Assendelft. 2011. "Getting on the Board: The Presence of Women in Political Science Journal Editorial Positions." *PS: Political Science and Politics* 44(4): 799–804.

Turkiewicz, Katie LaPlant, Jihyun Kim, Kelly E. Tenzek, and Anna R. Herrman. 2010. "Behind the Scenes: Life as an Editorial Assistant." *Communication Monographs* 77(4): 452–59.

University of Illinois at Chicago. n.d. "Research Assistants." http://grad.uic.edu/sites/default/files/legacy/files/Research%20assistantship.shtml .

Chapter Twenty

Teaching Online from Home

Katherine Sanger

I always knew that I wanted to teach. Sure, there was a slight detour when I decided to get a bachelor's degree in IT and when I had my son. But all hope was not lost; I was lucky enough to start teaching developmental (i.e., remedial) English classes at a local community college while I worked on my MA in Liberal Arts, which would give me enough graduate-level hours to teach college English. From there, it was just a matter of hanging on for a somewhat wild ride, and before I knew it, there I was—teaching online full-time, being able to stay home with my son and still earn a living. The chance to teach online means that I can be at home with my son, picking him up from school, taking him to doctor's appointments, and not worrying when he gets sick and needs to stay home. It lets me be more flexible with my days, sometimes working at night and using the day for other tasks.

MY PAST EXPERIENCE

So what made me the lucky one who could get hired for a job teaching college from my home? First, I had experience taking online classes. I had completed a few classes for my associate's degree through an online format, and then I finished my bachelor's degree online. It also helps that my BS degree was in information technology, and I had experience with databases and creating web pages. I also had completed a Distance Education Administrator Certificate while working on my early degree since I had been interested in teaching online. Finally, I completed two master's degrees—one in liberal arts and one in English literature. All those things helped to show that I had both experience in the content area I was going to teach and experience with the format I was going to teach it in.

Now, what helped make it even better was that when I was teaching those developmental classes, the community college I was teaching for was looking for someone who was comfortable working in the online environment because they wanted to offer those classes online but only had a few faculty members who wanted to teach online. Because of my experience with online classes, I offered, and so I got in on the ground floor of their online classes. It never hurts to be first in line!

MY QUALIFICATIONS

At this point, I have been teaching online for over ten years. I began teaching online after having completed an associate's of general studies and a bachelor's of science in information technology. While teaching, I completed an MA in liberal arts, an MA in English literature, and a post-master's certificate in college teaching. I also completed forty-eight hours of doctoral coursework in adult and post-secondary education. At this time, I am almost halfway through a Master of Fine Arts in creative writing. My BS was completed entirely online, as was my MA in English Literature. For my doctoral coursework and my MFA, I attend "residencies" while completing the rest of the work at a distance.

Over the past ten years, I have taught for community colleges, career colleges, and for-profit universities. Classes I've taught range from developmental English to sophomore literature to grant writing to professional communications. I have taught both part-time and full-time, fully online. While I have taught some on-campus classes during the past ten years when the opportunity presented itself, for the past few years, I have only taught online.

JOB REQUIREMENTS

To teach college classes online, the requirements vary by the type of college, the type of classes, and the type of accreditation.

For example, the minimum for a developmental or nontransferrable course is often a bachelor's degree in the subject you want to teach in. However, many colleges will require a master's degree with eighteen hours in the subject being taught. To teach transferrable courses, or courses that are at the college level, the minimum requirement is generally a master's degree with eighteen hours in the subject. To teach graduate-level courses, the minimum requirement is a master's degree with eighteen hours, although many schools will require a terminal degree, such as an MFA (Master of Fine Arts), a PhD (Doctor of Philosophy), or an EdD (Doctor of Education).

Other than having education, many colleges want you to have experience with online education already. You can get this by taking or teaching classes online. They don't always have to be for credit; offering classes through organizations or community groups is another way to get experience teaching online. In some cases, colleges are willing to take teachers who do not have online experience but who do have teaching experience in another format. In that case, you can also look at teaching continuing education classes in your field of expertise.

Many colleges that offer online classes also want their professors to have experience in the field. For example, as an English professor, I am expected to have publications, belong to professional organizations, and attend professional development or teach professional development within the field. Having real-world experience in the field can make the difference when it comes to getting a job teaching online.

A final important requirement for teaching online is the ability to work at a distance. You must be comfortable communicating through e-mail, looking things up on the Internet, and attending phone and web conferences. You must be able to work without having someone looking over your shoulder.

HOW TO FIND ONLINE COLLEGE TEACHING JOBS

Finding a job teaching online can be difficult. Luckily, there are many places to look. *The Chronicle of Higher Education* lists many different teaching jobs. Having a subscription allows quicker access to their job listings, a perk for paying. However, you can still access the job listings through their website once they have been posted publicly.

Another popular website is HigherEdJobs. They actually have a specific section that lists online jobs, and they have more than just teaching positions listed. If you are interested in working a virtual job within the education field, they are a great website to check out.

Believe it or not, even Craigslist can be useful. While you may find virtual tutoring jobs are listed more often than teaching jobs, sometimes online teaching jobs do pop up. The tutoring jobs are a great way to get experience with the online experience, if you don't already have it; it can make you a more viable candidate for an online teaching job.

If you're interested in a pay service, there is Flexjobs. Flexjobs is a subscription-based site that offers job seekers the ability to set up multiple resumes and job searches that will allow you to look for online teaching jobs. They actively search out nontraditional jobs, freelance jobs, and telecommuting jobs so that you don't have to. You can then search their listings. Some jobs can be applied to through Flexjobs directly, while others simply offer links to the original job listings.

Of course, there is also Monster and Career Builder. Both of the websites allow you to list your resume. I have to admit—one of the current colleges I am teaching at actually recruited me from Monster. Their hiring firm found my resume listed and called me one day to find out if I would be interested in teaching for them. While the websites themselves aren't exactly friendly for searching for online positions, they do list some, and getting exposure on them is not a bad idea.

LinkedIn is another option for getting exposure. Again, you can list your resume and your experience. If you know other teachers, they can endorse you for skills, allowing you to try to connect to other teachers who may be hiring for their departments. Be sure to join "groups" that discuss online teaching; networking is your friend when it comes to working online! If you can show that you're comfortable networking online, then it may help show that you're also comfortable teaching online.

Finally, you can also check out the actual college and university websites themselves. If there is a college you want to teach for, go and see what they have listed! Most major colleges and universities have systems where you can save your resume, and you can sometimes even set up job alerts so that if a position opens up in a department you want to teach in, you'll get an e-mail.

WHAT CAN YOU EXPECT WHEN YOU TEACH ONLINE?

While all colleges have their own styles, there are some things that you will want to be prepared for if you want to teach online.

First—who makes the classes? In many larger (and for-profit) colleges, you will not have much, if any, say in the course development. You are often given a premade class, complete with tests, quizzes, discussions, and sample assignments. While this can be a boon—less time spent on the development of the class for you—you will often still need to bring in outside sources from your own experience, and you may not be allowed to change things. This can be difficult, especially if you are used to teaching classes you've created. You may not agree with assignments or how points are awarded. You may feel that a rubric is unfair. Unfortunately, with the premade classes, you often do not have the option to make a change. You can, however, always contact your department chair or supervisor and make suggestions that can be given to the instructional designers and subject matter experts (SMEs) who actually make the classes.

At smaller schools, you will often create the class yourself, but you may be given a "shell" to work with. This shell might include certain components, such as an "Introduction" module or a test/assignment that is required department wide. Another item you may need to use is a predesigned syllabus. While you can create your own assignments, discussion questions, and more, you may need to have them all written up in a certain way, including course outcomes and learning objectives.

Second—what is the class size? Again, this can vary based on the type of class and the type of college you're teaching for. As a general rule, online classes can be smaller than their on-campus counterparts. For example, while I may teach classes as small as six to ten students, they are often not considered "full-size," and so I may be paid on a per-student basis as opposed to a full-class stipend. The majority of English classes that I teach have anywhere from fifteen to thirty students, regardless of the college or the class.

Third—how long do the classes last? This is another time when it really depends on where you teach. Many of the for-profit institutions offer shorter classes that allow students to complete their degrees more quickly, so classes may be anywhere from five to ten weeks. Average college semesters at community colleges and universities tend to last for sixteen weeks or so, but many colleges are now moving to having summer semesters and even "mini-mesters" (mini semesters) online, so even traditional colleges may be offering classes that last only two to three weeks. Of course, an important thing to remember is that the length of the class does not affect what is being taught; a five-week summer course at a community college covers the same work as a sixteen-week fall course. This means that you are doing a lot more per day and per week in order to have the same final outcomes.

Fourth—what is the turnaround on grading and communication within the class? Many schools have very specific requirements on how quickly you as the teacher must respond to students and grade their work. It is not unusual for a school to require an online instructor to log in five or six days a week and respond to student posts and e-mails within twenty-four to forty-eight hours. In addition, having grades due two days to one week after due dates is also normal. Shorter classes generally have quicker deadlines. One school where I currently teach offers five-week classes. Instructors have twenty-four hours to respond to student questions and seventy-two hours to grade student work.

Fifth—what makes up each class? Here's where it can get interesting. There is often a bit of a struggle between asynchronous elements (things that do not have to be done at the same time) and synchronous elements (things that are done at the same time). Some colleges require teachers to host "office hours" where the teachers are available either in a chat room, on the phone, or in a web or phone conference site. Other colleges require an online "class" that might include audio or video. Some require both. The amount of synchronous participation might vary, but the basics for each class, regardless of type, generally include reading that may be in an electronic text or a hardcopy, practice exercises, tests (either proctored or done online and on the honor system), asynchronous discussion through discussion "boards," and assignments such as papers and other written work. Obviously, math classes will have slightly different assignments than English classes, but most online classes do require quite a bit of writing, both of the instructor and the student. The amount of interaction you'll have will depend on the requirements of the institution, and you may be required to "post" in the discussion area once a week, three times a week, five times a week, or not at all. You may need to provide feedback on every assignment, or only on certain assignments.

Sixth—what else is required of an online instructor? Just like teaching on campus, you will probably be required to complete continuing education and attend meetings. Most of the meetings will be virtual, but you may need to travel to some of them. You may also join teaching circles, a faculty senate, and other groups that you would find in on-campus colleges as well. Many schools limit the number of classes a teacher can take on. A standard full-time teaching load can be from four to six classes, and adjuncts (part-time teachers) may only be allowed to have one or two per school per semester, so you may find yourself having to balance multiple schools in order to earn a living wage.

Seventh—how much do you get paid? Salary, like everything else, will vary quite a bit. Part of it depends on the type of college you are teaching for. Community colleges often pay the least because they are often the most strapped for cash. Classes, depending on the requirements and the time involved, generally pay anywhere from $1,200 to $2,000 per class. This is not per month per class, this is per class.

WHAT YOU NEED TO TEACH ONLINE

The two most important things you need to teach online are a reliable computer and a reliable Internet connection. Reliable is key! You can't say, "Gosh, my computer crashed, and so I couldn't do my work." That won't cut it; you are expected to be responsible and to set an example for your students.

I tend to always have two computers: my old one, which functions as a backup, and then my new one, which is what I use on a daily basis. I also have two Internet connections available at all times. I have used both cable and DSL for my Internet, and both were fast enough and reliable enough, but since I believe in having a backup for everything, I also subscribe to a monthly WiFi service through Verizon. This helps me in multiple ways. First, it allows me to know that, even if something happens and my cable gets cuts through no fault of my own, I will still have a way to connect to classes and my students. Second, it allows me to be able to work from anywhere. Since I do teach online and travel, it's good to be able to bring my work with me, whether it's to the airport or a hotel room while I'm attending a residency and working on my MFA.

Another good technology to invest in is an off-site backup service, like Mozy or Carbonite. For a small monthly fee, you can set your computer up so that it will run a backup each day and send work to the cloud. This lets you avoid the dreaded computer crash: as long as you are backing up your work, you will be able to get it back if something goes wrong. I have mine set to back up all my documents once a day. This means that if something happens (and it has happened before), all I need to do is restore my computer and download what I have sitting in the cloud. Admittedly, you will still lose some work, but missing a day is nothing compared to missing a week or a month.

Where you work is another important thing to consider. I have an office in my home that is set up with my computer and a docking station. Since I have a laptop, I enjoy being able to hook it up to a large monitor and a keyboard with a 10-key for quick number entry. But sometimes working from home doesn't cut it; if I really need to focus, it can be easier to go somewhere else where the lure of laundry and dishes won't be as strong. You'd be amazed at how attractive housework can seem when the alternative is grading a virtual stack of essays! When I need to truly focus, I often take my computer and WiFi to a coffee shop or a library. It gives me the chance to toss on my headphones, play some loud music, and really get through my work.

PROBLEMS WITH TEACHING ONLINE

Teaching online has a number of benefits. Being able to schedule my work around my home life and son is wonderful, but there are times when I wish I had a traditional job.

Teaching online means it's hard to take vacations. While many traditional colleges have set vacation times, many of the nontraditional and for-profit schools will have school year round, so you never really get a day off. On top of that, having to check in five or six days a week can mean that you never get a full weekend off, either.

Another issue is convincing other people you're working. Just like any work-at-home job, friends and family may know that you're at home and therefore assume that you're available to sign for packages or pick up and watch kids after school. Be firm when you tell people you need to work. If you must, you can also choose to go work at a coffee shop or library so that the temptation isn't there for other people to contact you.

Many online colleges expect you to train with them before they hire you. This means that you may spend a few weeks in a training course that is unpaid. Whether or not this is a problem is up to you. I enjoy the training period because it gives me a chance to check out the college while they get to check me out. I have turned down teaching positions after going through part of their training due to things I've learned about the company and their expectations.

Weird work hours are another issue. Because you are working around your own schedule and any schedule imposed upon you by the type of class, you may find that you work Sunday through Friday or Thursday through Sunday and Tuesday. You may find yourself up at midnight, trying to finish up grading or responding to student posts. You may also find that you're putting in more hours than you expected, especially the first time you teach a class. As you get more comfortable with the classes you teach, the time will go down, but there are always classes that will have students who require more one-on-one or additional duties that may pop up. Instead of working a forty-hour work week, don't be surprised if you are working fifty or sixty if you have a full-time teaching load.

There is also the issue of weird pay schedules. Community colleges and universities tend to pay their teachers only once per month. So, for example, if you are teaching a standard sixteen-week course and being paid $1,600 for it, then you would be paid for four months, once a month, $400 (minus taxes, etc.) per month. If you do not teach over the summer, you don't get paid. In addition, most community colleges and universities do not pay their part-time teachers in January because of the way the timing works out, so it can make for a very long month after the holiday. Other schools may choose to pay differently; I know of one school that pays two-thirds after the class starts and the final one-third after the class ends. Another school pays the full amount only after the class's final grades have been submitted. These dates can vary widely—for example, if a class starts on April 1, but the cut-off date for payday on April 7 was the March 24, then you won't get paid until the next available pay date. Sounds confusing? It can be! Most of the time, however, you will receive a contract that specifies the pay dates and amounts you can expect. You may find yourself needing to invest in some budgeting software to make it through the month, though!

FINAL ADVICE

Some closing words of wisdom I'd like to share are pretty simple.

First, don't admit to having a life. That might sound silly, but it's true. It's always best to say that you have a "previous engagement" or "previous booking" if you aren't available for a meeting. It sounds much more professional than saying that your son has another doctor's appointment or a play-date. Just don't use it too often—you do need to be available!

Second, remember that if you need to talk to your students over the phone, it's generally OK to have your children running around in the background. Most students who go the online route have children of their own, so explaining that you have a toddler or an older child home sick won't faze the student. However, if it's something important, then try to make sure that you'll be able to have the call uninterrupted, whether it's done at night, over the weekend, or while a babysitter is around.

Third, remember that it's a job. Just because you get to do it from the comfort of your home, and sometimes even in the comfort of your pajamas, you are still being held to standards, and you need to treat it just like any other job.

Chapter Twenty-One

A Woman's Journey through the Web

Robert Simpson

My wife, Estelle, senior designer at WebTrax Studio can normally be found in her Oak Park, Illinois, home office in front of her Mac Mini: designing websites, writing proposals, discussing technical issues on Skype with her associates or on the telephone talking with a client about how to build a site that meets their specific needs.

Estelle is a founding member and the leader of WebTrax, which serves mainly non-profits, small businesses, educational groups, unions, and social activist organizations. WebTrax is proud of its pro bono work such as the website and marketing help given to Green Community Connections, a local Oak Park group that holds an annual environmental film festival with an ever-growing audience.

But why would a web designer specialize in websites for this type of client? Such clients usually cannot pay very much and sometimes must ask that the work be done pro bono because their budgets are so tight. And why would a web designer proudly associate herself with controversial and often unpopular ideas and agendas?

As a web design and communications company, WebTrax is a small team based on trust and close collaboration. Its media and marketing professionals work from their various home offices. The kind of trust and close human collaboration Estelle and her team value so highly are shared with their web clients as part of the WebTrax experience. Although WebTrax does maintain a Twitter account, has a Facebook page, and sends marketing e-mails through MailChimp, it relies primarily on word of mouth to connect with new clients. Some clients are attracted to WebTrax because Estelle is an avid environmentalist, feminist, peace activist, union supporter, and gardener. In the warm months visiting clients can easily see the raised beds of vegetables and the rain barrels that surround her modest two-flat.

Estelle became interested in art as a young child and as she grew older, she took classes as New York's Art Students League. The daughter of activist parents who had struggled with poverty in the Great Depression, she can remember being part of such historic events as the 1963 March on Washington where Dr. Martin Luther King gave his famous "I Have a Dream" speech. When she entered college in the turbulent 1960s, she realized what she really wanted to do:

> As a fine arts major at the University of Chicago in the late 1960s, I was drawn into the antiwar and women's liberation movements. I wanted my art to be a part of my political activism and do art within a community that shared my values. I did not want to work for a large corporation or do advertising for the consumer market. I wanted to do art for the social good.

THE BEGINNING

Estelle graduated from the University of Chicago in 1969 with a fine arts degree, when the Internet was the ARPANET and connected one computer lab at Stanford University with one at UCLA. With a handful of other women, she helped found the Chicago Women's Graphics Collective. The Graphics Collective affiliated with the Chicago Women's Liberation Union CWLU), which already had workgroups doing varied projects. These included providing safe abortions before *Roe v. Wade*, battling sex discrimination in employment, making music in a women's rock band, opening up Chicago parks to women's sports, creating consciousness-raising groups, staffing a rape crisis line, publishing newspapers, conducting classes in a women's prison, providing birth control information, and many more projects too numerous to mention.

Working collaboratively with support from the rest of the CWLU, the Graphics Collective distributed tens of thousands of posters all over the planet. Some of these posters are considered feminist classics and are still being sold and displayed at the Chicago Women's Liberation Union Herstory website. My wife relates:

> We worked in an old run-down second-floor office on Belmont Avenue that we shared with the main offices of the Chicago Women's Liberation Union. They later called the area New Town, but in 1973 there wasn't much new about it. We weren't the only artists in the building, though. Downstairs was a tattoo parlor. Still, it was better than having the studio located in my apartment on Newport Street, where there were silkscreen tables in the dining room and a bathroom that doubled as a darkroom. On Newport Street, the Ravenswood El train was right next to the apartment and shook it like the aftershock of a California earthquake. But we were in the midst of a women's revolution and our priorities were clear.

In the Graphics Collective, members held "poster thinks," where they would brainstorm ideas from the basic concept to the rough layout. The finished work came later. Such collaboration meant instant feedback from other skilled artists and production people in the Collective. No names appeared on the group efforts.

EMBRACING TECHNOLOGICAL CHANGE

After leaving the Graphics Collective in 1975, Estelle taught art in after-school programs and became a child care teacher. During that time she partnered with me to form Carol Simpson Productions, and drew cartoons on social and economic issues for the labor, business, and alternative press.

As a high school history teacher on Chicago's South Side, I wrote the gags and distributed the cartoons while Estelle did the drawings. We also worked with artist Rhoda Grossman to produce a cartoon history book, *The Incredible Shrinking American Dream: An Illustrated Peoples History of the United States.*

Wanting to get back into art full-time, Estelle joined Salsedo Press as a freelance graphic designer from 1978 to 1981. After leaving Salsedo, Estelle enrolled at the University of Illinois at Chicago (UIC) and took classes in graphic design, photography, video, and computer graphics. These skills later became important when she turned to web design. She was then hired at the UIC publications office based on a strong recommendation from her design professor, where her electronic typesetting skills were put to daily use.

FROM CAROL SIMPSON PRODUCTIONS TO WEBTRAX STUDIO

Tiring of what she termed "punching someone else's time clock" and the instability of the publishing industry, Estelle decided to expand Carol Simpson Productions into a freelance graphic design studio in 1991. With a six-year-old daughter, Dana, and an infant son, Colin, it was difficult, but she had her mom, me, a child-parent center, and a day care center to help out.

Estelle was aware of the widespread gender and age discrimination in the publishing industry and she wanted to secure a financial future, but soon faced another major challenge. A technological revolution was sweeping through the publishing world and in 1984, a very young Steve Jobs unveiled the Macintosh computer. Then the Pagemaker layout program and Photoshop 1.0 were released. By 1991 pasteup boards, T-squares and even the typesetting computer were made obsolete by the Mac.

Using borrowed money, she bought a Macintosh IIsi, a laser printer, and a scanner. She collaborated with a local Macintosh expert who needed her marketing skills in exchange for teaching her how to use her new computer.

Through hours of studying manuals, my wife mastered QuarkXPress page layout program, Photoshop, and Illustrator.

With the many contacts she had made going back to the days of the Graphics Collective, she was able to build a successful business, even getting design work from the United Nations. I assisted her after teaching during the day, and would help out with production work at night after grading papers and preparing lessons.

The Internet had grown into a global network, but its use had largely been confined to scientists and academics. Mosaic 1.0 allowed the use of pictures and used a relatively simple computer language called HTML, which even non-geeks could learn quickly. The website was born.

In 1992, the Chicago Women's Liberation Union, which had officially disbanded in 1977, entered Estelle's life again. Former members were concerned that the history of the women's liberation movement was being lost. They worried about the huge backlash against women's rights symbolized by the defeat of the Equal Rights Amendment (ERA), Anita Hill's allegations of sexual harassment during the Clarence Thomas confirmation hearings and the scapegoating of low-income women for the nation's economic problems. They discussed how they could share their experience with a new generation of women and talked of writing books and making movies. I suggested a website that would display documents and stories from the Chicago Women's Liberation Union as well as its music, video, and art and agreed to do the initial web coding, and Estelle agreed to design the website. Out of those meetings came The Chicago Women's Liberation Union Herstory Project.

Soon the first version of the Herstory site appeared on the web. After a couple of redesigns, the site grew into a historical archive that attracted attention from women's studies classes and visitors around the globe. Because the women's liberation movement believed the "personal is political," there are deeply moving stories on the site about women overcoming fears and doubts to join in the struggle for equality. The website became a resource that helped writers with their books, filmmakers with their documentaries, scholars with their papers, and journalists with their articles.

Although the Herstory website was getting attention, all work was pro bono. As Estelle gained a better understanding of web design, she decided to put her new skills to work and generate additional income. With the help of her brother-in-law Steve Richter, a skilled programmer who had once worked for NASA, and me, she began designing more sites in 2000.

WEBTRAX STUDIO IS BORN

For a time, web design remained a sideline because of the amount of freelance illustration she was getting from children's textbook publishers. However the illustration market was drying up. Publishers were using more stock photography and stock illustration, putting financial pressure on freelance illustrators.

In 2002 Estelle and Steve formally created a new company, WebTrax Studio. I agreed to work on website production full-time, as I had recently left teaching. Estelle continued doing print design and illustration, but under the WebTrax name, so that she could offer integrated print and online branding.

WebTrax did most of the early sites in what is called static HTML. This was a common practice then, but it meant all the client content was hard coded into the site making it difficult for clients to update their own sites and more complicated for web developers to make major changes as sites grew larger.

Estelle wanted clients to have real ownership over their website and the ability to grow it and make changes without being totally dependent on WebTrax. Steve and I searched for a way to do this. The Macromedia Dreamweaver website software had ways of making site-wide changes, but WebTrax found them to be cumbersome. There was a related program called Contribute that was designed for nontechnical clients to work on their sites. WebTrax tried it but it proved to be troublesome.

The method of coding websites was becoming increasingly complicated and surreal. Originally HTML was fairly simple, but the demand for more complex sites with attractive layouts proved to be beyond its original capabilities and more HTML features were piled on with mixed results. There were competing web browsers like Netscape and Internet Explorer that often displayed the same site totally differently or even totally broken. Steve and I were forced to spend precious hours making sites work with often fragile hacks.

The answer came when the Worldwide Web Consortium (WWC) adopted stylesheets for the web similar to what are found in any word processor. Once web stylesheets were widely adopted, web design became less of a headache and more of a creative process. That still left the problem of how clients could add and edit their own content. Estelle solved this problem when Steve and I investigated Content Management Systems. These stored most of the website in a database while keeping the layout, images, video, and audio in separate online directories. Clients could log in and edit their content using a familiar word processor–like interface without ever looking at HTML code and could upload images and other media as well.

WEBTRAX ADOPTS JOOMLA AND EVENTUALLY WORDPRESS TO BUILD WEBSITES

After testing several different content management systems, WebTrax settled on Joomla; WordPress was added later. Joomla was easy to install and with training, most clients were able to add pages and edit content with only occasional calls for help to WebTrax. It also used a flexible template system so that Estelle could create beautiful designs that would display consistently.

WebTrax began by coding the templates from scratch, but soon switched to commercial templates purchased on subscription from companies like RocketTheme, which proved to be less expensive and more practical. These commercial templates gave Estelle a wide variety of frameworks with which she could add her own color schemes, images and layout ideas.

Joomla had another advantage. It is open source and free to download and distribute, which fits perfectly with Estelle's ideas of a sharing community. Open source maintains a spirit of collaborative work for the greater good. Below is a definition of open source from Wikipedia:

> Open-source software (OSS) is computer software with its source code made available and licensed with an open-source license in which the copyright holder provides the rights to study, change and distribute the software for free to anyone and for any purpose. Open-source software is very often developed in a public, collaborative manner.

Joomla is a project with a large global community to support it. The Joomla core team regularly issues improved versions as well as security updates to repel hackers. Programmers around the world create "extensions" like photo galleries, message boards, directories, product catalogs, data reporting tools, e-commerce and many more. These can be plugged into Joomla and integrated into the overall website. Now WebTrax could create full-featured sites for clients who needed more than a simple online brochure.

The ideals of open source also appealed to Estelle's commitment to social justice because it is widely used in the Global South of Asia, Africa, and Latin America where most of the world's most impoverished nations are. Open source has been vital to these countries for global communication, breaking down the isolation that poverty can create.

Estelle joined the Joomla Chicago, a local user group with regular monthly meetings. Joomla experts and novices alike make presentations about how they create Joomla sites and how they solve problems. There is networking time so that graphic designers like Estelle can talk to programmers, website administrators, and Internet marketing experts:

> I once belonged to a group called Webgrrls, an organization of women in IT. On the Webgrrls e-mail discussion list I read of horrible and degrading treat-

ment from sexist men in the industry. I experienced none of that in Joomla Chicago even though most participants are white males. Anyone may ask questions and there is a culture of mutual respect. Like the global Joomla community, Joomla Chicago is trying to uphold the ideals of open source and I think we are succeeding.

It was through Joomla Chicago that Estelle met Avery Cohen of Metrist Partners and Robert Novak of Aluent Group who have assisted her in many ways. Avery is an expert on search engine optimization (SEO) and digital marketing. Thanks to working with Avery, Estelle can now advise clients on how to appear high on Google search results as well as provide useful tips on digital marketing. Avery is also available to work directly with clients who require more advanced consulting work.

Robert Novak has a team of skilled programmers who are available to build custom Joomla extensions to meet very specific client needs. Normally Estelle prefers to avoid custom programming because of the expense, but when needed, she turns to Robert.

Cassandra West, a former editor at the *Chicago Tribune*, works with WebTrax to help with Facebook and Twitter as social media grows in importance. Estelle met Cassandra through her UIC connections. Ironically, when Cassandra was editing the *Woman News* section of the *Chicago Tribune*, she had interviewed Estelle about the Chicago Women's Liberation Union. Cassandra is also a copywriter, photographer, and videographer; like Estelle, she's an avid environmentalist and gardener.

In the year 2010, WebTrax added WordPress as a content management system for smaller sites that do not require complex extensions. WordPress, which began its life as an open source blogging software, has blossomed into a full-fledged Content Management System. Estelle's daughter Dana, a graduate in illustration and design from Chicago's Columbia College, is the Web-Trax WordPress guru. I had helped Dana build her first website when she was in grade school. By high school she was competent in HTML and was soon posting her illustrations on a gallery she created using open source software. David Marquez also works on WebTrax sites. A political activist on the South Side of Chicago, Estelle met him through her connections at the University of Illinois at Chicago. Steve Richter continues his longtime relationship with WebTrax.

My wife is now gearing up to put more work into the Herstory website. A former member is planning to write a book about the Chicago Women's Liberation Union (CWLU) and an expanded website will be the book's online companion. The CWLU carefully documented its work and while there is already a wealth of material on the website, there are still boxes and file drawers of paper documents that could be added. She hopes to recruit interns from women's studies programs to not only post and organize documents, but to contribute articles. The perspective of young women is important for understanding the women's liberation movement, since we are still far from gender equality and a historical understanding can help achieve that goal. You may visit the Herstory site at http://www.cwluherstory.org . Estelle also plans to continue her pro bono work with Green Community Connections, the Oak Park environmental group. Estelle started WebTrax Studio with the idea that she could build a progressive small business doing work that matters, and she continues to pursue that vision.

Part IV

Personal Aspects

Chapter Twenty-Two

Getting the Most Out of a Virtual Internship

Laura Francabandera

In an era where women have more opportunities than ever before, the rising costs of childcare all too often make it difficult for mothers to have full-time careers. Telecommuting is not for everyone, but virtual internships can often be the entry into a telecommuting career.

FLEXIBLE SCHEDULE

The reason that most people claim for the benefit of working remotely is that they can work wherever and whenever works best for them. Everyone wants to be able to work their schedule around doctor appointments, children's music recitals, or even a dedicated workout time. The unintended consequence of this, however, is that the boundary between work and family life is thin or nonexistent. Mobile phones make this thin boundary even thinner as e-mails and cell service make it possible to work even during the dedicated family times.

THE VIRTUAL COMMUNITY

To many people, the thought of working in isolation engenders fear and uncertainty, but successful virtual internship programs create a corporate culture that spreads beyond the main workplace. Some companies may choose to use instant messaging (both on-campus and off) to create a virtual community. Others recognize the value of face-to-face encounters and ask remote employees to spend a certain amount of time either in the office or video conferencing. The intern or employee also has responsibilities to create community—it cannot be created by only one side, but requires both parties to engage. Beth Gilbert, a virtual intern from San Jose State University interning at Credo, had this to say about the intern's responsibilities: "Being an intern is about gaining skills and experience but you also want to be a benefit to the organization. That's why it's important not just to focus on your own gain but to also focus on doing good work for the internship site" (SJSU, SLIS Department 2013). Even small changes, like adding a profile picture to your instant message account or connecting via social media are easy building blocks of workplace community that require little effort on the part of the intern but go a long way in building professional relationships.

PRODUCTIVITY

Working from home requires a very focused person to be able to ignore the dirty dishes in the sink during "work time" or to be able to work with a baby wailing or babbling in the background. Productivity is often increased because in a virtual environment, the employee has a "greater control over the location, timing, and means of completing one's work" (Gajendran and Harrison 2007, 1534). So while it can be more difficult due to home-based distractions, it is also easier to maximize productivity because you can entirely control your work environment.

Virtual internships have a very steep learning curve in which the intern must learn the basic operating procedures, online tools, and other intranet software. Telecommuting might be the best career choice for some people, and for others, it might be an obstacle (Stout, Awad, and Guzman 2013, 190). For the young professionals, facing the choice between children and career, virtual internships may be the bridge to get where they need to be.

EXAMPLE OF AN VIRTUAL INTERN PROGRAM

While it is helpful to understand the individual characteristic of virtual internships in general, it will help to look at an existing virtual internship program. Credo Reference is a company in the library and information services sector that believes small steps can make a giant difference. They partner with the world's leading publishers to offer an online reference service (Credo Reference 2013). They also have run a successful virtual paid internship program for the past three years employing students from Library and Information Science programs at graduate schools like San Jose State University SLIS, University of Pittsburgh iSchool, and the University of North Carolina SILS. These virtual interns are fully inducted into Credo's corporate culture from weekly company meeting teleconferences every Friday morning (with a different department presenting each week, including the interns) to roundtable discussions with Credo's executive team and thought leaders.

The goal driving Credo's intern program is to have an impact on the next generation of library and information science graduates. It is important to note (when talking about the corporate culture regarding virtual interns) that nearly half of Credo's permanent employees telecommute and only come to the main Boston office a few times per year. Credo's virtual interns work closely with their supervisors to ensure that they get the experience they need. If that requires moving the intern to different departments or other projects, Credo is more than happy to involve its interns on as many levels as possible, even the innovation and thought leadership for which Credo is known.

BEST PRACTICES OF TELECOMMUTING

There are many resources handing out tips to be the best employee in the office. Telecommuting, however popular, typically remains as a footnote within those resources. People have been studying the effects of telecommuting on both the employee and the employer (Sundin 2010). Many studies have put forth some "best practices" that have emerged from the data; things that work well for the greater number of people.

The first practice is to create a workspace. Just because you can connect to the office on the couch, doesn't mean that it is a healthy work habit. To be in a productive mind-set, work in a dedicated space: The home office, a converted closet, or even the kitchen table are all possibilities as long as they remain dedicated only to work during the scheduled time. This also includes getting dressed for the day, setting the cell phone to silent (unless it is a dedicated work phone), and especially turning off the television. Regardless of how you feel in the morning, setting a "get ready for work" routine and sticking to it will vastly improve your workday.

Another tip is to streamline the daily tasks and increase productivity. It can be easy to concentrate within an office setting, but at home, when there are so many distractions, it is important to track the time spent working projects. On the one hand, there will be ample evidence of your productivity throughout the day (not only to a supervisor but also to yourself) but it helps you determine when to "clock off" and realize that the eight-hour workday is finished. Without the pressure of the daily commute or coworkers rushing out of the office at a designated time, it is easy to get caught up in work and lose track of time. Keeping notes of projects completed and the time you spent on them acts like a virtual timecard. You can look back at your day and see exactly where every hour went.

As in the tips above, it is important to be on task for work. It is just as important however to take breaks. Much like on-site employees get government mandated break periods and lunchtime, telecommuters must also take the time to disconnect for a few minutes, set the e-mail or instant message status to "away," and do something other than work. Just be sure to take breaks at an acceptable time, let your coworkers know you are on break, and return when you planned. Bathroom breaks and lunch time both fit into a regular workday, so it is important to fit them in when working from home as well.

When working virtually, it is vitally important to communicate clearly with coworkers. If the bulk of daily conversation is done electronically, via e-mail, text, or instant message, the opportunities for misunderstandings and conflict swiftly rise. As important as "emoticons" are for the modern age, they are certainly no substitute for clear communication. So be sure to keep sarcasm and irony to a minimum in your electronic communications. Just because you are not in the physical office and miss out on the water cooler and break room chats, the distance doesn't mean that you have to miss out on pleasant conversation and social norms. Whether through e-mail, text, or chat, be sure to make personal conversation with your coworkers. This is the best method to combat the isolation that is often felt when working remotely.

Virtual internships and telecommuting are not simply pastimes or something to do when you are waiting for a "real job" to appear. Virtual jobs are just as real as any other and they must be treated with the dedication and enthusiasm they deserve. The tangential benefits of working from home: no commute, distance from bothersome coworkers, and comfortable space must be paid back with an intent and determination to succeed.

LOCATE OR START A VIRTUAL INTERN PROGRAM

As virtual internships increase in popularity, more mainstream companies are recognizing the benefits of working remotely (even if it is only a few days per week) to not only employee morale but to the business in general. Before you start searching for internships, make sure that you have done some intial pre-planning. Thinking through your internship plans before you jump straight into the frenzied search will greatly increase your chances of landing a coveted virtual internship. First, be sure to know what you want out of the internship:

- experience
- new skills
- professional contacts
- a permanent position

Knowing what you want will allow you to refine your internship search based on those parameters. It is also beneficial to do any background research beforehand. If you know which company interests you, be sure to find out as much as you can about the company. This information may give you a head start going into an internship interview. The last item before you start your search is to polish your resume and cover letter. While on-site internships may not rely so much on cover letters, they seem to be a staple when it comes to applying for virtual internships. This is a logical method to evaluate the digital communication skills of the candidates and easily weed out the ones not suited for telecommuting. Once all these steps are done, you have completed your research on the desired company or field, and you've shaken the dust off your resume, it is time to start searching.

WHERE TO FIND INTERNSHIPS

The best places to look for virtual internships are colleges and universities in your field of expertise. Most schools have career departments that curate job lists. Some, like San Jose State University, even notate the ones that are virtual so they are easy to locate. Some college and university career resources are restricted to current students only while some are not. It is always worthwhile to check the website of a college near you for their career resources page, even if you are not a student. Job boards and internship postings are usually prominently located and are easy to find.

If you are a student at an accredited college or university, you might want to check out the U.S. Department of State Virtual Student Foreign Service, which offers over five hundred virtual internships per academic year. These internships range from the managing social media for a small group in Turkey to compiling East African news reports. If you do not go to the college and cannot apply through the system, note the company's name so you can locate it online. Most companies post internship positions in multiple places so if you know the name of the company it may be simple to locate internships.

If you are not a student, public libraries often subscribe to databases (like Hoover's Company Records) that allow you to do background research on a particular company to find out their stance on telecommuting or internships in general. Many libraries also subscribe to career skills databases. Some, like Learning Express Library (2013), not only offer job searches, but also allow you to augment your professional skills and prepare for tests. If you are unsure which resources your local library holds, be sure to call and ask your librarians. They likely can point you to the right place on the website or even give you a list of reliable websites that offer job posts in your area of interest.

There are also many job lists and postings available on the open web that come up in a Google search, whether you are a college student or not. Some are backed by larger, reliable organizations and some stand alone. One example is Career OneStop, which is a job list and career training site that is sponsored by the U.S. Department of Labor (2013). You can find out more about different career paths, search for job openings, and even practice for interviews. FastWeb (2013), for another example, is mostly known as a scholarship finder. It does, however, also have an internship posting section as well. Just be sure to evaluate the company, the poster, and even the job/internship description itself: it is easy to misrepresent a job or position online, and that can have serious consequences when it comes to your safety and your future.

If the company for which you want to intern does not have any virtual internships posted, consider asking about creating a position. Just be sure that you have all the information that you need to present a compelling argument as to why the company should hire a virtual intern: know what your duties might be and explain how you would get them done virtually with the same or better competency than an on-site intern. Again, it is vitally important to have a plan and know how telecommuting will affect you.

Finally, try networking and build relationships by "joining the conversation" in your industry (Bailey 2011, 16). You can ask family and friends if they know anyone who is hiring or who could use an intern. Since you are looking for a virtual internship, you can show off your savvy digital skills and try social networking through Facebook, Twitter, and LinkedIn. You should also attend trade shows, conferences, and job fairs. Not only will this allow you to meet potential employers face-to-face, it will also give you a sense of where the industry is going and a look at your competition. If you cannot find an open position at the particular company for which you want to work, take initiative and contact someone at the company to inquire about positions. Remember, not every intern position makes it to the public job boards.

IN SUMMARY

Before embarking on a virtual internship, it is important to fully understand the benefits and the challenges of working remotely and plan for them. Considering the challenges, virtual internships may not be for everyone. This chapter defined the common traits of telecommuting: a flexible schedule, isolation, impacts on productivity, autonomous, and remote. It is very important to remember that these traits are inherently neither a benefit nor challenge; rather it is the individual response to these traits that determines the value (Clark, Karau, and Michalisin 2012, 38). The benefit of a flexible schedule is often considered a boon for many people, especially mothers of young children, the challenge then is to not let your schedule become so flexible that it infringes on family time. Without strict delineation between work and personal time a flexible schedule becomes a hindrance. Likewise isolation, autonomy, and productivity each can be a benefit with the right mind-set.

This chapter also looked at a model virtual internship program at Credo Reference, where interns worked remotely side by side with permanent employees. The success of a virtual internship rests partly on the corporate culture and how accepting it is of telecommuting (Bernardino, De Dea Roglio, and Del Corso 2012, 297) and partly on the remote employee to stay connected and communicate as an on-site employee would.

To ensure the best chance as a remote intern, there are some best practices that help when telecommuting: Create a workspace, streamline daily tasks, take breaks, communicate clearly, and take the internship seriously. These habits, if all practiced simultaneously, combine to make the optimal telecommuting environment.

Internships can be found on job lists and you can use the many available tools you have at hand (either at the local college or public library) to access company research and other job search tools. If the position you want is not available virtually, consider presenting a case for the company to create a virtual intern position.

There are many reasons to support telecommuting and, at the same time, many reasons why it might not be best fit. The flexible schedule and autonomy makes an ideal situation for a work-at-home parent. A virtual internship may be just the right entry into the wonderful world of telecommuting. No longer should women be forced to choose between children or a career.

REFERENCES

Bailey, Lindsay. 2011. "Fashion Forward: Learning from a Virtual Internship." *Public Relations Tactics*, April.

Benardino, Andre Fernandes, Karina De Dea Roglio, and Jansen Maia Del Corso. 2012. "Telecommuting and HRM: A Case Study of an Information Technology Service Provider." *Journal of Information Systems and Technology Management* 9:285–306. Doi: 10.4301/S1807-17752012000200005.

Casolaro, Nicholas. 2013. "Why Businesses Should Consider Telecommuting." *New Hampshire Business Review*, May 17–30.

Clark, Leigh Ann, Steven J. Karau, and Michael D. Michalisin. 2012. "Telecommuting Attitudes and the 'Big Five' Personality Dimensions." *Journal of Management Policy and Practice* 13:31–46.

Credo Reference. 2013. "About Credo." Accessed December 10, 2013. http://corp.credoreference.com/about-credo/about-credo.html.

Damast, Alison. 2012. "Virtual Internships in Rising Demand." *Businessweek*. Accessed Dec. 10, 2013. http://www.businessweek.com/business-schools/virtual-internships-in-rising-demand-01182012.html.

Ernst, James W. 2011. "Disconnected: The Harsh Reality of Virtual Internships." *Public Relations Tactics,* April.

Fastweb. 2013. http://www.fastweb.com.

Gajendran, R. S., and D. A. Harrison. 2007. "The Good, the Bad, and the Unknown about Telecommuting: Meta-Analysis of Psychological Mediators and Individual Consequences. *Journal of Applied Psychology* 92(6): 1524–41.

Learning Express Library. 2013. http://www.learningexpresshub.com/learningexpresslibrary.

Noonan, Mary C., and Jennifer L. Glass. 2012. "The Hard Truth about Telecommuting." *Monthly Labor Review* June, 38–45.

San Jose State University, SLIS Department. 2013. "SLIS Virtual Internship Blog." Accessed December 15, 2013. http://slisapps.sjsu.edu/blogs/wp/virtual-internship/2013/04/29/tip-of-the-week-25/.

Stout, Marianne S., Germine Awad, and Michele Guzman. 2013. "Exploring Managers' Attitudes toward Work/Family Programs in the Private Sector." *The Psychologist-Manager Journal* 16:176–95.

Sundin, Kirsten. 2010. "Virtual Teams: Work/Life Challenges—Keeping Remote Employees Engaged." Accessed December 16, 2013. http://www.ilr.cornell.edu/cahrs/research/whitepapers/upload/Spring10Mtng_RemoteWorkersEngaged.pdf.

U.S. Department of Labor. 2013. Career Onestop. Accessed December 15, 2013.http://www.careeronestop.org.

Chapter Twenty-Three

How the Internet Has Opened Doors for Women with Disabilities

K Royal

Although there are challenges for individuals with certain disabilities to fully access all the benefits of using the Internet, it creates tremendous opportunities for women with disabilities to succeed in their education, career, and volunteerism. This chapter is written from a broad personal perspective, as my mother, my daughters, and I all have disabilities with ages currently ranging from twenty to sixty-three years. Additionally, I have worked with students of many ages, including those with disabilities, assisting them in various educational, career, and volunteerism aspects.

FIRST IMPRESSIONS

Whereas interactions in person provide for first impressions based on appearance or sound, the Internet eliminates that bias unless an individual chooses to present an initial appearance or sound. For example, a person in a wheelchair who applies or interviews for a job in person may be judged on their obvious disability. Through personal experience, I found that when I used a wheelchair, people treated me as if I lacked intelligence or capability. The same could be said for someone who has a speech, sight, hearing, or other physical impairment, even those whose appearance may be disfigured in some way, whether the disfigurement is truly disabling or not. In some cases, a person's manner of speech is considered in a negative light, be it a speech impediment, second language, or geographical accent. Live in-person first impressions can be negative and result in adverse consequences for the individual.

Conversely, the Internet provides the opportunity for a first impression to be based on what one writes or chooses to present. Like the old cartoon "no one knows I am a dog on the Internet," no one knows who is disabled on the Internet unless the person chooses to disclose that information. There is the potential to be discovered, as information online is rarely completely erased. If it is disclosed at any point online, it is possible for others to find it if they search for it. And as mentioned above, it is not just disabilities that impact a first impression. The Internet also ameliorates one's accent (being from Mississippi, I know discrimination occurs based on accent), height, weight, race, ethnicity, religion, sexual orientation, manner of dressing, body art, hair color—or lack of hair, age, and many other personal factors that may be discerned by meeting in person. Please do keep in mind: what is once online may be forever online. So be aware of your full Internet persona. Guard it well and wield it with deliberate intent.

DISABILITIES DEFINED

In 2006, the United Nations formally adopted the Treaty on Rights for Persons with Disabilities. As of February 2013, there are 129 nations/states that have ratified it and 155 signatories. One of the United Nations' key issues is women and girls with disabilities, recognizing that

> Women with disabilities face significantly more difficulties—in both public and private spheres—in attaining access to adequate housing, health, education, vocational training and employment, and are more likely to be institutionalized. They also experience inequality in hiring, promotion rates and pay for equal work, access to training and retraining, credit and other productive resources, and rarely participate in economic decision making (United Nations 2013) (internal citations omitted).

Many nations define what it means to have disabilities, although often there is not one single definition. Myriad laws and regulations addressing certain aspects of life may provide a patchwork of definitions or may limit the application only to one aspect. For example, a nation may have different definitions of disabilities in its housing laws, employment laws, health laws, and public assistance laws. Although it may be more desirable to have one unified definition, the critical factor is to have the ruling authority recognize that disabilities exist, disability discrimination exists, and there should be protections in place to restrict discrimination.

The U.S. amended its Americans with Disabilities Act ("ADA") in 2008 due to recognizing that the cases interpreting the ADA had veered drastically from the intent of the law. The ADA had become an incredible hurdle for people with disabilities to overcome and heavily favored employers. The text of the ADA "emphasizes that the definition of disability should be construed in favor of broad coverage of individuals to the maximum extent permitted by the terms of the ADA and generally shall not require extensive analysis" (U.S. Equal Employment Opportunity Commission 2013a). In effect, the amended ADA eviscerated years of case law and opened the door for people with disabilities to have equal opportunities and to see justice without the imbalanced fight for rights that we have seen for decades.

Conversely, in Canada, there is no one definition of disability. The Canada Pension Plan requires a disability to be both "severe" and "prolonged" (Government of Canada 2013). "Severe" is defined as a case where "a person is *incapable of regularly pursuing any substantially gainful occupation*" (Government of Canada 2013, my emphasis). Within this definition, each word is also defined by the law. For example, "pursuing" does not mean looking for work, it means actually working. Another key term within "severe" is "substantially gainful occupation." The law states that a substantially gainful occupation is one "that is productive and profitable" as "measured in part by a dollar amount that is set annually and against which a person's earnings are compared." Further, it is not simply the individual's pay that is measured; the government also looks at the individual's functional capacity, productivity and performance (Government of Canada 2013). Canada's medical evaluators will assess the severity of a disability first. If judged severe, they will then assess whether it is prolonged. If not severe, the evaluators do not reach the question of how long the disability has or will last. However, if you work for a federally regulated company in Canada, you will be asked to fill out a form for employment equity that uses this definition:

> Persons with disabilities are persons who consider themselves to be, or believe that an employer or a potential employer would be likely to consider them to be disadvantaged in employment by reason of any persistent physical, mental, psychiatric, sensory or learning impairment (Employment Equity Act 1995, guideline 4).

EDUCATION

In the educational realm, the Internet offers a variety of options. Starting with education and development as an infant, the Internet offers for women both education on raising children as well as on how to assist children with development, whether the child is considered disabled or not. Later, the teenage years are difficult enough without the young individual also dealing with a disability. In this, the Internet offers supplements for high school courses, high school courses online, and elective courses that help students to learn certain skills, indulge personal interests, or gain college credits.

For personal interest, online education is marvelous. Whether you want to know how to change a gasket on a commode, get a knit cap pattern, or learn a new computer programming language, the Internet is unbeatable. Keeping the mind engaged helps keep it functioning.

Online Education Degrees

Certainly another option is to take online degree programs, sometimes called distance education. There are a staggering number of these programs available, from trade degrees to doctoral degrees, but be careful what you choose. If you desire to go the route of an online program, keep these things in mind:

- Make sure the program is accredited through an official accreditation program.
- Explore established colleges and universities, many of which now offer online degrees. These are still more "respected" than strictly online colleges, although some online colleges are strengthening their reputations. There is likely a residence portion of the degree, usually in the summer.
- Check the financial aid. Many online schools are private, for-profit institutions.
- Read the requirements for getting credit and follow all instructions. Do this for both the individual classes and the overall degree.
- Establish yourself with the disability services and use them. Follow the instructions for every course, whether you think you need accommodations in that particular course or not. Do not be afraid to speak up if something is not working.

Reducing the College Burden

Even if you attend a college or university in person, there are some things that can help your education. Although many colleges are strict about allowing students to take courses while still in high school, there are certain alternatives that can assist students with disabilities. The College Level Examination Program ("CLEP") is a good way for students to carve time off their degree plan or to take fewer courses during a semester yet still earn enough credits to graduate on time or early. Essentially, CLEP offers thirty-three courses in five subject areas. Most of these courses are the equivalent of the first two years of a bachelor's degree, when students are taking algebra, biology, literature, and other general requirements. Most tests count for three hours of course credit, although some do count for eight or twelve hours. Colleges and universities that accept CLEP credits will have a list of what they permit, but many will accept thirty to sixty credits of CLEP hours. Generally, one academic year is thirty hours, and students can spread that across fall, spring, and summer semesters. Thus, CLEPing thirty hours eliminates one year of college. CLEP tests are about $80. CLEP is included in this education part because one can study and prepare for the CLEP online even though the actual test is in person, usually at a computerized test center. Accommodations may be granted.

Additionally, many schools also offer the ability to test out of a course. It works like the CLEP: you take a test to gauge how well you know the material. If you know it well enough, they will grant you credit without taking the course. And you may know some of this without studying or you may have taken a similar course in high school, either based on personal or professional experience. For example, there are courses in computer basics: you may be someone who has worked with computer basics for years and could test out of this course. Or, you may have a language skill, such as in the case of my daughter, who was able to test out of American Sign Language, because she knows it so well.

Always look for courses offered online or in alternative formats. Many community colleges especially offer online self-paced, or condensed time-frames. Being able to break up the standard course schedule may help you navigate medical appointments, fatigue, transportation, and other demands on your time, energy, and resources.

Tips for Surviving College in Person

1. Know your limits and respect them. It is okay to push sometimes, but do not push to the point of failure.
2. Get to know the people: there are numerous ways others can assist you and sometimes the smallest bit of aid makes the critical difference.

   - Disability resource office
   - Security/police
   - Parking office
   - Registrar office
   - Office people in your school/department
   - Professors
   - Administrative personnel
   - Financial Aid

3. Do not be too proud or too shy to ask for help.
4. Know the financial aid options and rules for eligibility and repayment.
5. Get involved in a school organization.
6. Don't get involved in too many school organizations.

7. If a course is not going well, know how to withdraw without penalty. There are also ways to drop for medical reasons past the standard drop date—ask the registrar's office.
8. And always turn in the disability form for every class. Even if you don't think you'll need any accommodations for that particular class, something may arise in which you do and it will be too late.
9. How the Internet helps:

- Getting information on all of the above
- Finding the people to speak with for the above
- Following up phone calls with e-mails
- Making a paper trail (e-mail and attachments) of all communications and forms
- Filing a written complaint should things go wrong
- Filing a written compliment when things go right: never underestimate the power of a well-written word

CAREER

In the United States, accommodations are required to be made both for applying for jobs and in the job itself as long as the accommodations are reasonable and do not present an undue hardship for the employer. You must be able to do the job with reasonable accommodations (which is where the ADA amendment discussed earlier really helps those with disabilities). The Internet is one of the most revolutionary tools in job accommodations. The U.S. Equal Employment Opportunity Commission lists various accommodations that can be expected for workers such as job restructuring, leave, and modified work hours (U.S. Equal Employment Opportunity Commission 2013b). The Internet has made restructuring easy and eliminated some previously required leave. By being able to work remotely, workers who are disabled are able to continue working at times that would have been unheard of a few decades ago. For example, those with disabilities can work remotely for part-days, full-time, or alternating days in the office with days working remotely.

In other ways, the Internet has made it possible to use tools to enable some to work that were completely unable to do so. Software, hardware, website accessibility, and assistive tools such as electronic readers and speakers have revolutionized the workplace for those with disabilities. There are many days where I can make it into the office but cannot type; software makes it possible to have a productive day in the office where previously, I might as well have stayed home.

Last, the Internet has made it possible to work completely online either self-employed or as an employee. People with disabilities, as discussed above, are physically invisible online, making online employment attractive and amazingly possible. First, self-employment can run the gamut from writing, developing software, computer aided designing, illustrating, and so many more that we would run out of space in the chapter if I attempted to list them all. And as an employee, many companies use remote workers for convenience, cost-savings, and "follow-the-sun" mentality (meaning service is available twenty-four hours a day). These positions are commonly in customer service. Think of any company that has a help line and you have thought of somewhere to remotely perform customer service work. This includes billing services, such as medical coders and insurance filers.

Career Advancement Tools

Not only is it much easier to have a career with disabilities with the Internet, it is easier to stay current and even advance in one's career. Online classes, not credit courses, but one-time webinars are abundantly available. One can learn new skills, hone current skills, and accomplish any necessary continuing education credits that may be required in the particular career. For example, as an attorney, I am required to have a certain number of continuing legal education credits per year. This is very easy to do online. The same is true for my mother, who is a nurse and a nurse auditor, both of which she is required to obtain continuing education credits for. She also works online, testing certification materials, proposed test questions, and reviewing test scores. My daughters have both used online tools to learn new skills, such as Microsoft Excel, programming issues, and debugging glitches. Seriously, my daughter was sitting in class and the sound would not work for the class presentation so she got online and watched a video on how to fix the problem. It worked and she was the hero! This so impressed the professor that she offered my daughter an undergraduate teacher assistant job.

VOLUNTEERISM

The last category for how the Internet has opened doors for women with disabilities is volunteerism. There are so many ways in which women can volunteer remotely from joining an advocacy group, such as the International Network of Women with Disabilities group, to finding volunteer opportunities that can be done remotely, to actually volunteering online. Three services to use are:

- United Nations online volunteering portal: https://www.onlinevolunteering.org/en/index.html

- Volunteer Match: http://www.volunteermatch.org/
- Interconnection: http://www.interconnection.org/

Each of these organizations lists opportunities for online volunteering and remote volunteering (and there are many others; just look online for "online volunteering"). The key difference is online volunteering actually performs the service online such as serving as an e-mail mentor (I do this both with underprivileged kids and those with Down syndrome), writing policies, advocating, and evaluating websites for certain criteria. Remote volunteering includes doing something at home and sending it in to the organization such as knitting hats and blankets, mailing letters, or making phone calls. The Internet enables volunteers to have the opportunity to connect with organizations, people, and causes they would otherwise not have.

Why would a company want online volunteers? Well, organizations may attract volunteers who have the skills that the organization is missing and cannot afford. Online volunteers help the organizations expand their services without a lot of cost outlay. And do not underestimate the impact this can have. Third world countries often benefit from online volunteers who help with advocacy, organizing drives, maintaining volunteer schedules, communicating with people on the ground, developing business plans and programs, and seeking funding and sponsors. Additionally, online volunteering is environmentally friendly: no car fumes!

CONCLUSION

Were it not for the Internet, my family would not be who we are today: three generations of women who contribute to society and support their families (well, my daughters don't have families to support yet, but they will). We are able to learn, to work, and to volunteer. One must play chess or checkers, or Sudoku to stay sharp. And the Internet opens up the world to us. We can work in Israel, volunteer in the Sudan, and play in Mexico simultaneously. The Internet makes us near whole in mind and spirit, while making the body almost immaterial.

REFERENCES

Employment Equity Act (Canada). 1995. Accessed July 25, 2013. http://laws-lois.justice.gc.ca/eng/acts/E-5.401/page-1.html#h-1 .

Government of Canada. 2013. Service Canada: People Serving People. Canada Pension Plan. http://www.servicecanada.gc.ca/eng/isp/cpp/applicant.shtml .

United Nations Enable. 2013. "Women and Girls with Disabilities. Using Both—the Gender and Disability Lens." Accessed June 11, 2013. http://www.un.org/disabilities/default.asp?navid=13&pid=1514 .

U.S. Equal Employment Opportunity Commission. 2013a. "Notice Concerning the Americans with Disabilities Act (ADA) Amendments Act of 2008." Accessed June 11, 2013. http://www.eeoc.gov/laws/statutes/adaaa_notice.cfm .

———. 2013b. "Enforcement Guidance: Reasonable Accommodation and Undue Hardship Under the Americans with Disabilities Act." Accessed June 11, 2013. http://www.eeoc.gov/policy/docs/accommodation.html.

Chapter Twenty-Four

Reducing the Caregiver's Burden

Darra Hofman

The average family caregiver probably sounds a lot like you, your sister, your friend, your mother, or your daughter: she's a forty-nine-year-old woman, working full-time for pay, and then putting in another twenty hours caring for a disabled or declining relative (Feinberg and Choula 2012). Even when caregivers manage to juggle both employment and caregiving, however, they pay dearly both professionally and financially: 68 percent of caregivers report having to make work accommodations, from arriving late/leaving early, to turning down promotions or even leaving paid employment entirely to meet their caregiving responsibilities (Feinberg and Choula 2012). Women aged fifty and older who leave the workforce to care for an aging family member lose, on average, $324,044 dollars of wages and benefits over their lifetime; caregiving burdens can make the difference between a relatively comfortable retirement and penury (MetLife Mature Market Institute 2011). Given our aging population, increasing diagnoses of developmental and other disabilities among children, and uneven medical and social coverage for professional caregiving, it seems that large numbers of American women will continue filling the family caregiver role. Unlike the caregivers who preceded them, however, modern caregivers have a powerful tool at their disposal: the Internet. The Internet can empower women to remain professionally engaged, create and maintain income streams, and still meet the gruelling, often unpredictable demands of caregiving.

Those demands are ones I know personally. Like many women, I found myself thrust into caregiving without much warning. And like those women, I do whatever is necessary to care for my loved one, regardless of personal costs. Caregiving, beyond the usual child care demands, was the furthest thought from my mind when my son was born. A newly barred attorney, I had every plan to "lean in" and build a successful practice and family, like so

219

many other professional women. However, meeting my son's needs required ever-mounting professional changes; I had to leave behind solo practice for a job with health insurance to cover the appointments in search of a diagnosis. Making appointments from my office on lunch breaks and using every second of paid time off to visit doctors and therapists was the norm. And, like many caregivers before me, I eventually left my career completely to spend my days doing therapy and case managing my son's care. And yet, I couldn't just abandon my professional self, nor could we do without my earning any income. Fortunately, in the two years since I've left full-time employment, I've learned how to use the Internet to remain professionally engaged and earn income. I've also learned how other caregivers use the Internet to maintain their professions and jobs, while creating the flexibility to meet their loved one's needs.

USING THE INTERNET TO MAINTAIN A PROFESSIONAL PRESENCE

For many people, work provides much more than a paycheck. Work is a source of engagement with the world. It provides us with a sense of engagement, accomplishment, and competence. For those who scale back or step out of work completely to take on caregiving duties, the world often feels much smaller. For women facing the loss of those previous islands of competence, the Internet can provide a means to remain engaged and present as a professional.

LinkedIn and Professional Networking

The loss of one's network is one of the hardest blows for caregivers who have to step out of their jobs and careers. It's both a personal loss, limiting the caregiver's social world, and a professional loss, limiting their connections and potential leads to jobs and other opportunities when the caregiver is ready to step back into the workplace. In studies of highly educated professional women, 97 percent of women who "off-ramp" from the careers, often for caregiving reasons, intend to return; only 74 percent are able to do so, and of those, only 40 percent are able to return to full-time work (Hewlett and Luce 2005, 46). Maintaining one's professional network is vital for women caregivers to be able to return to work.

Fortunately, the Internet makes maintaining a network significantly easier than it was in the past. With an e-mail account, a LinkedIn account, and access to relevant professional online mailing lists, a caregiver can stay connected to colleagues and industry news while running around to appointments. Of course, this isn't a passive process. If all you ever do is peruse mailing lists and use LinkedIn as an online resume, it's easy for your colleagues to forget you. Instead, caregivers using the Internet to remain engaged professionally should do so strategically. Some ways to do so include:

- Keeping abreast of developments in one's industry/profession, and using those to touch base by e-mail with important contacts. For example, a former manager of mine is very into leadership theory; when I see an interesting leadership article, I e-mail it to her with a couple of thoughts. It keeps us talking and engaged with one another.
- Be an active part of your LinkedIn groups and mailing lists. Don't just read—talk! Share items of interest, discuss what others have posted, and show that you're still aware and professionally engaged. This needn't be time-consuming; ten or fifteen minutes are more than enough to read and respond to a couple of posts.
- Keep up with your colleagues as people. A quick, "Happy Birthday, Bob! How are you liking the new job?" e-mail or LinkedIn message is an easy way to maintain communication with Bob.
- Above all, use the Internet to keep in contact while demonstrating that you're still part of your former professional world.

Online Platforms

Writers and other creative professionals, who as a group are often freelancers, talk a lot these days about developing an "online platform." For people from more traditional industries, the term might be completely foreign. But anyone whose career might take an entrepreneurial bend would benefit from building an "online platform." In short, an online platform is your online presence—your blog, your Twitter account, your website, and your posts on other people's blogs, Twitter accounts, and websites. By creating a presence on the Internet, you define yourself (and your product, if you're offering one) as a brand, and if you do it well, you define yourself as a brand with value and devotees. Many people think that they don't have anything to say, or anything to offer, but people with successful online presences span the human experience. Stay-at-home moms, preschool teachers, musicians, pastors, and Avon ladies are building online platforms that support them as professionals. All that you really need is:

- A home computer with an Internet connection.
- A blog (WordPress offers free blogs, and setting one up is easy with an online tutorial).
- A Twitter account.
- A message you want to put out there, and a commitment to posting regularly.

This might sound overwhelming. But, if you think of it as marketing, it becomes clear what you need your online platform to do. If, for example, you plan to return to your career as a divorce attorney, and you specialize in collaborative divorce, then your online platform should position you as an expert in that field. You could discuss and analyze high-profile cases and research, guest post on other divorce attorneys' blogs, and tweet about changes in your field. Similarly, if you decide to supplement your income by selling handmade organic cloth diapers, your blog would focus on cloth diapers, their advantages, and news and research of interest to your potential customers. The biggest commitment in building your online presence is time: time to figure out how you want the world to perceive you (and/or your product) and time to create content to support that perception.

Academic/Trade Publications

The goal with both your networking and your online platform is to remain present in your profession as someone who can still contribute, even if caregiving duties have called you away from the workplace. Another way to create such a presence is to develop expertise. Academic publications (if they're relevant to your field) and trade publications allow a caregiver to do exactly that. For me, my first step back toward professional engagement after leaving work was writing a law review article; other caregivers might write small pieces for trade magazines or newsletters. The value of all of these kinds of writing is the same: engagement and a demonstration of expertise. And it's not as hard to do as it might sound; many professions have myriad publications. A Google search for "call for submissions" + "profession name" (for example, "call for submissions divorce law") has helped me find publications that are looking for the kind of articles I can write. Similarly, if you read particular trade publications, check their submission guidelines. These will outline what kind of pieces the publication is looking for, desired length/topics, and where and to whom you should submit. It's quite possible that you can contribute, helping your colleagues with new knowledge, and yourself with a new credential.

USING THE INTERNET TO CREATE INCOME STREAMS

Of course, not every, or even most, family caregivers are professionals. In fact, low-income women are more likely than their higher-income counterparts to step out of work for caregiving duties, perhaps because working simply costs too much relative to their other duties (Giovanetti et al. 2009, 1014). Even high-income women, however, are not immune to financial need: 38 percent of women trying to "on-ramp" back to work said they had to do so because their "household income [was] no longer sufficient for family needs" (Hewlett and Luce 2005, 45). So for caregivers across the spectrum, leaving their jobs means finding ways to bring in income while still meeting their caregiving responsibilities. The Internet, thankfully, makes this much more practical than it was even a decade ago.

Consulting Work

Caregivers with valuable expertise have the possibility of maintaining an income stream by taking on work in their previous field on a consulting basis. Many consultants start with their previous employer as their first client; this can be an especially good option to discuss if the caregiver has not yet left their position. Consulting is easy to position as a win-win from an employer's perspective: they get your work and expertise only on the projects where there's a critical need, without the costs of benefits and potential liabilities that come with having an employee. The Internet makes consulting much more viable for women with the competing priorities of caregiving: tools like email, Skype, and Dropbox let the consultant work collaboratively offsite, oversee production, and troubleshoot problems as they arise without having to be at the office.

Freelance Work

For those who can't or won't continue in their previous field on a consulting basis (for example, I chose not to continue in law because of the potential liability costs), the Internet offers other freelance opportunities in new fields. Since I have an undergraduate degree in English, I offer tutoring, editing, and resume writing services to a variety of clients. While it doesn't bring in a full-time income, this work is flexible, letting me meet my son's needs and be available at the drop of a hat for a therapy appointment while still bringing in extra money. Other caregivers bring in extra money as virtual assistants, web developers, photographers, project managers, and in countless other freelance positions. Some of these caregivers find their work through their professional networks, others through websites like eLance and Sologig. And because the caregiver is working as a freelancer, she can negotiate the terms of the contract; a caregiver can work on her deliverables at night, after her relative is in bed, or can arrange to do her work when someone else is providing respite care. It's not easy to sacrifice that free time to work, but it lets a caregiver bring in income while still meeting her loved one's needs.

Home-Based Sales

The Internet has changed the game for home-based businesses. Another special needs mom I know went through a series of jobs; when her child would have a medical emergency, she would find herself unemployed because she had to take time off to care for him. However, she'd already developed an extensive online following blogging about her son's rare genetic condition. When she decided to start selling Mary Kay cosmetics, she had thousands of potential customers across the country, unlike Mary Kay saleswomen of the past, who had to rely on parties and friends of friends. She is steadily building her income selling to her online followers and friends. Other women have built small home-based businesses selling their handmade goods, such as cloth diapers, cloth menstrual pads, clothes, crafts, jewellery, health and beauty aids . . . the possible products are limited only by the imagination (and, of course, the law in the case of potentially hazardous and otherwise regulated products). These women market their wares through eBay, Etsy, Facebook, and their own websites.

Other women resell items on eBay and Etsy. Some specialize in a particular item or class of items, such as cloth diapers or housewares bought inexpensively from the manufacturer. Others are yard sale queens, finding items from across the spectrum, researching their potential worth and market, and earning good profit margins on a small investment. Although there are upfront costs for building a home-based sales business (inventory, listing fees on eBay and Etsy, postage for shipping items), numerous sellers have found that they can bring in income with little more than a computer, a camera, an Internet connection, and access to a post office.

Blogging

Blogs are useful, not just for creating an online presence, but for potentially generating income. This is dependent on creating a quality blog that attracts readership: regular, well-written posts that are relevant to the readers' interests are the foundation of a profitable blog, and a blog will likely take time before it builds enough readership to become profitable. However, once that happens, a blog can be used to sell advertising, products created by the blogger, affiliate links, and eBooks written by the blogger. For example, women who blog about homeschooling might offer eBooks about how to homeschool, and have affiliate links to the materials they use at home (affiliate links lead a reader to, for example, Amazon; if the reader buys the product from the link, a percentage of the purchase is given to the blogger by Amazon). Particularly influential bloggers often get paid, either in cash or in products, to review and endorse various product lines (you'll see a note at the bottom of such a post stating who the post was sponsored by). Again, beginning blogging requires little more than a computer, an Internet connection, and a commitment to quality content; with "advance post" options, where you upload a post and tell the software when to post it, a caregiver could write a post while mom is in dialysis, and set it to publish Monday morning.

USING THE INTERNET TO MAINTAIN A JOB
WHILE CREATING FLEXIBILITY

The Internet also provides options to those caregivers who can't or don't want to step out of their careers. Flexible hours, telecommuting, and job share arrangements are all made possible by the Internet. Internet access, particularly through smart phones and other mobile devices, lets a caregiver stay up on an account or a project while taking care of their loved one's needs. It facilitates flexible hours by ensuring that the caregiver's "out of office" hours are not the same as "out of touch" hours. It lets job-sharers collaborate and share projects, even when their face time is minimal. And with the advent of technology like Skype, face time can happen even when employees are remote. Some companies, like Telus in Canada, are actively promoting telecommuting for environmental, cost saving, and productivity reasons. And such arrangements are not just for executives or high-level managers; Telus and other companies have found that having their customer service representatives work from home, using the Internet to access their workspace and a dedicated phone line to take calls, improves both productivity and employee morale. Telecommuting can let a caregiver stay with a loved one while still being a productive employee. Such arrangements, which help caregivers meet the needs of both their employers and loved ones, simply wouldn't be possible without the Internet. While, of course, it is possible that an employer would say no to such an arrangement (consider the controversy over Yahoo! revoking its telecommuting arrangements), discussing the possibility would be well worthwhile for a caregiver forced to choose between their caregiving responsibilities and a needed job that is simply not flexible enough.

CONCLUSION

Family caregiving often requires significant personal and professional sacrifices on the part of the caregiver. However, our population demographics, along with various economic and policy pressures, make it highly likely that a substantial portion of American women will continue to shoulder the work of caring for their disabled or aging loved ones. Unlike previous generations of caregivers, however, modern caregivers have a powerful tool available in the Internet. Using the Internet, caregivers can maintain their professional network and presence, find ways to bring in income outside of traditional employment, and even create the flexibility in their current jobs to meet their responsibilities to both family and employer.

The Internet is a tool every caregiver should use to minimize the professional and financial penalties that come with the caregiving role. Although doing so takes initiative, drive, and that most precious resource, time, it comes with a degree of flexibility and freedom almost no other option offers. Blog posts can be crafted on an iPad in a doctor's waiting room; orders can be downloaded and printed while talking to a therapist; clients and colleagues can be e-mailed from almost anywhere with a smartphone. Caregivers who want or need to maintain their professional lives are less and less forced into an either/or situation. Using the Internet, caregivers can continue to offer their hard-won skills and expertise to the marketplace, creating value for themselves and their clients, without having to capitulate to the inflexibility of a job that precludes meeting their important obligations to their loved ones.

REFERENCES

Feinberg, Lynn, and Rita Choula. 2012. "Understanding the Impact of Family Caregiving on Work." AARP Public Policy Institute Fact Sheet.

Giovannetti, E. R., J. L. Wolff, K. D. Frick, and C. Boult. 2009. "Construct Validity of the Work Productivity and Activity Impairment Questionnaire across Informal Caregivers of Chronically Ill Older Patients," *Value Health* 12(6): 1011–17.

Hewlett, Sylvia Ann, and Carolyn Buck Luce. 2005. "Off-Ramps and On-Ramps: Keeping Talented Women on the Road to Success," *Harvard Business Review*, March, 43–54.

MetLife Mature Market Institute. 2011. *The MetLife Study of Caregiving: Costs to Work Caregivers: Double Jeopardy for Baby Boomers Caring for Their Parents*. Westport, CT: MetLife Mature Market Institute.

Part V

Publishing and Writing

Chapter Twenty-Five

Founding an Online Magazine Inspired by Travel Written by Women

Sarah Menkedick

In the fall of 2011, I started *Vela Magazine*, an online magazine of creative nonfiction inspired by travel and written by women. I had just returned from an unpaid internship at a prestigious New York magazine and was disillusioned by a literary world that I found narrow, exclusive, and helmed almost entirely by men. Without solid connections in publishing or a willingness to tackle internship after unpaid internship, gaining purchase in this world can seem almost impossible.

Women in particular are at a disadvantage. The 2011 statistics released by VIDA: Women in Literary Arts, an organization that analyzes how critical and creative writing by women is perceived, show an appalling byline gap at nearly every mass-circulation literary magazine in the United States. More importantly, they reveal what I'd discovered intuitively in New York: these magazines are not only dominated by men, but by male styles and intelligences.

What I wanted, then, was to create a space for women to write what they wanted to write without having to cater to these particular ways of thinking and speaking. I did not, however, want to create a space that would be branded as "female" or "feminine" and cordoned off as such. I did not want the magazine to be a "women's magazine," for and by women and therefore excluded from a larger literary conversation. Rather, I wanted the site to showcase what so many editors and magazines were missing in predominantly featuring men: strong, distinct, and compelling women's voices. I wanted to publish work written by women for a universal audience, work that otherwise might struggle to find a home in conventional publishing, with the goal of advancing women writers' careers.

I discovered that this is the ideal historical moment to take on such a venture. There are still formidable challenges to achieving recognition, success, and above all, financial compensation for one's writing in the current publishing climate, but I firmly believe that it is easier now than ever to break in: not by hoping for a chance from the top but by creating one's own opportunities from the bottom.

GETTING STARTED

The first step, of course, was finding women writers whose work I respected and who would be willing to jump headlong into a new, time-consuming, uncertain venture. But how many women? Two or three seemed too few, and would place an enormous publishing burden on the selected writers, but more than ten seemed unwieldy, and would make negotiations and planning tricky and extenuated. I settled on six, including myself. I wanted all six of us to be at similar stages in our careers, and we all had to write nonfiction and to focus—however tangentially—on travel, since the magazine's tagline would be "creative nonfiction inspired by travel and written by women." I ultimately reached out to an editor and three writers I'd worked with in the past, and to a friend and fellow student in my MFA program. All said yes, almost immediately.

Then I had to find an online platform that suited our sensibility and mission, and get the site itself set up. I opted for WordPress because I did not want the site to look like a blog: I wanted it to look like a professional, literary magazine. Blogger, the other principal platform for writers, is already considered quite outdated; its templates and forms have become the iconic examples of early, clunky, personal blogs. I can't think of a single magazine I read online that uses this platform, which brings me to an important point: know your platform's demographic and its history and identity. Tumblr is extremely popular now, but it's mostly for shorter posts and it is very much designed around images. It's not an ideal choice for a magazine, which will feature lots of text and longer posts. WordPress offers a wide variety of styles and sensibilities—literally, there are thousands and thousands of themes— and it's very simple and user-friendly. It's respected without being strongly associated with a particular group (Tumblr, for example, is generally associated with the young, hip, artistic).

Next: what theme? There are a number of free themes, but lots of websites will be using these themes, so you'll run the risk of looking generic. Beautiful, customizable and unique themes are available for under $100: I chose The Novelist, a theme that really privileged text and actually recreated the texture and experience of a novel on the screen. It allows for a background image—we chose a map—but beyond that is quite simple: a small menu bar at the top, pages that flip like the pages of a book, a clean white background and clear font. For literary sites, where you want your reader to be able to focus intently on the written word, be wary of adding too many widgets and baubles: these are distracting, and more likely than not a reader will get fed up and click away. It's also important for the text to be on a white background and to stand out as the consuming experience: colors or images, and sidebars or columns with clickable buttons and links, easily get distracting and pull readers out of the story. Increasingly, curating sites demand that the stories they feature be viewable on a single page, so after a few months we decided to stop paginating our stories. This is definitely something to take into account: a story with pages is harder to share, harder to get featured on curating sites, and not possible (or very frustrating) to download on an e-reader.

From there, once you've downloaded your theme and begun playing around with your site, you can decide how much customization you want. Do you want to change certain features in your theme? Add others? Greatly modify its appearance? For example, do you want to make square photos circular, or vice versa? You can do a great deal of modifying just with the WordPress site, adding and removing plug-ins and widgets, but to change basic design elements of the theme you'll need to have technical experience with HTML, web design, or coding. If you don't, you can hire someone to do this for you. It's really not necessary, but it can help your site look more professional and distinguished. Even small touches like a professionally designed logo make a big difference, and should cost at maximum several hundred dollars. For some of these considerations, it's not necessary to look strictly to tech professionals: my husband is a photographer with extensive Photoshop training, so we leaned on him to design our logo and to help us pick out colors for the site.

It's also surprisingly easy to learn basic CSS and basic HTML, two types of code that will help you to customize your theme. There are many books on these subjects and, if you're willing to put in the time, training yourself in the basics will come in handy for tweaking small things like colors, fonts, and so on.

Overall, choosing a platform and a theme are very straightforward processes, and do not have to cost anything at all. Spending even $80 for a theme is enough to get a site that's a step up from everyday blogs: it's really not necessary to shell out thousands of dollars for elaborate designs and features. WordPress has so many functions available for free: contact forms, "share" buttons for Facebook and Twitter, and so on, and you can find all of these on the WordPress platform. Really, the only element that could cost money is your site's design, but since literary websites should emphasize text above all and maintain a certain simplicity and elegance, it isn't necessary to worry about having a very complicated or snazzy layout.

Once I had The Novelist installed in WordPress and I'd added the elements I wanted for the site—share buttons, About and Writer pages, and so
on—I wrote a manifesto declaring our mission. We then designed an editorial schedule whereby we'd publish one feature story every Monday, meaning
that each of us would be publishing once every six weeks. Other than the
genre—nonfiction—and the emphasis on travel, we left story topics and
styles wide open, each writer would be free to write what inspired her. Part of
the thrill of starting *Vela Magazine* was not feeling hemmed in by the need to
pitch to specific publications, to cater one's writing to a certain house voice
or style. In the months to come, some of us would write lyric essays, some
narrative journalism, some memoir.

The lessons I learned from this initial process were manifold. Among the
most significant were the following.

1. Cultivate a Community

This is particularly essential when considering starting an online magazine.
Who will read, share, and champion your work? Whose work, in turn, can
you read, share and champion? The success of your magazine and its ability
to advance your career and your standing in the literary world hinges on the
community you build around it.

One of the many advantages of creating a magazine with a number of
other women writers is that each brings her personal network to the venture.
When we launched *Vela Magazine*, each writer reached out to her friends and
connections via social media and personal e-mails, and from the start we
emphasized a sense of community—*Vela* as a space for women writers and a
space to distinguish women's writing—instead of a place to herald personal
triumphs. As time has gone by we've come to focus even more on developing community, creating a Facebook group for women writers, inviting wom-
en guest writers, and featuring a weekly "Women We Read This Week" post
on our blog.

This is all part of what has been called "literary citizenship," and its
current exemplar is Cheryl Strayed. There is a reason, beyond the obvious
quality of her work, that Strayed has become so popular: she is an advocate
for the tens of thousands of unknown, emerging, and struggling women
writers who make up literary communities across the United States. She is
constantly highlighting and lauding the work of other women writers, encouraging those who are coming up, and reminding a press that likes to
create a neat divide between failure and success that she was successful well
before the publication of her bestseller. I have found that on the days when I
start to despair about where my writing is going, about whether it's all worth
it and what I'm doing, I find solace in all the women who've faced the same
questions and who will offer their support. And in fact, *Vela's* most success-

ful blog posts deal with questions of process, success, insecurity, and doubt that plague so many writers. This is where our community coalesces, shares stories and resources, and provides encouragement.

Cultivate, in essence, a place where writers and readers can congregate, feel themselves welcome, and support one another.

2. Be an Oasis

While the web is teeming with content, and there is a perpetual frenzy to create the next "viral" post, the online world of serious, thoughtful, literary writing is still quite small. I've come to believe that in a digital age in which people are perpetually bombarded with bits of information, this kind of in-depth literary writing, which takes time, care, sustained reflection, and attention, is like a soft warm couch on which to take refuge. It embraces, nurtures, reassures. Perhaps surprisingly and counterintuitively, there is a wide audience hungering for it. The number of online literary magazines and websites curating literary fiction and nonfiction has mushroomed in recent years. And with the growth of the tablet market, more and more people are reading, and more and more people are looking for profound, unique, long-form writing online.

What this means for women writers, and particularly for emerging women writers, is that it's easier than ever to get one's work before an audience without relying on an editor at an extremely competitive and exclusive publication to accept and publish it. This is not to say that these institutions are now irrelevant or should no longer be respected, but rather that writers are not nearly as dependent on them as they were ten years ago. If an independent online magazine can establish a reputation for consistent quality, and can earn praise from respected institutions and/or figures, it can offer its writers the kind of exposure and attention they need to advance their careers without expensive internships and academic credentials.

It's paramount, however, for online magazine editors and writers not to get distracted by the detritus of the web. It's important to have faith that insightful, contemplative, serious writing *does* have an audience and a home online, and to remember that building it will take time and care. It's very tempting to cave to ubiquitous pressures for page views, traffic, Facebook "likes," comments, shares, tweets, or other common but frequently deceptive indicators of "success." These are the standard measurements of achievement on the web, but they do not apply in the same way to literary writing. Online and in print, the audience for this work is by nature not mass, and it's important for the integrity of the work and the publication not to get confused in struggling for this particular type of online fame.

A magazine that aims higher, looks further down the road and wants to showcase its writers' literary talents should avoid writing for keywords, search engines, or the kind of whimsical popular attention that attends "viral" content. This does not mean ignorance of how to market online content, but rather a refusal to sculpt the work completely to marketing models. I have seen a number of magazines launch with daring, compelling, powerful literary writing and slowly slip into "link-baiting," a vain and empty process of mining viral topics for links and attention. I worked as an editor for one of these magazines for two years: as the publication began to earn more money from advertising and to expand, the pressure to earn more page views, traffic, shares, and likes grew so intense that it completely eclipsed the fundamental goal of providing good writing. The magazine bled talented writers and editors, who grew increasingly disenchanted with the confines of what a mass audience would be compelled to quickly skim and share, until finally the site became a content mill. A byline from there is now essentially meaningless.

This many sound extreme, but the pull of online popularity is intense. It's perhaps comparable to that of a popular clique in high school. On the one hand, you know you're smarter than those kids, you don't really want to be friends with them, but oh, what you would give for their attention, just one invitation to a party . . . and then once you're there, sick from cheap booze and feeling used and inferior, you realize your error. Such is the pull of the Internet: a "like" is quick and easy, a superficial stamp of instant approval. Real respect is much harder to earn, and much less easy to spot. It is what the editor of Longform.org called "eyes on your work." Editors' eyes, the eyes of people who know and search for excellent writing. You can't feel or spot the eyes until an opportunity arises.

3. Find your Niche

Since all of us were avid travelers and some of us had worked as travel writers or editors, we defined *Vela* as a magazine of "creative nonfiction, inspired by travel, written by women." Also, since our writing styles and genres within creative nonfiction were very distinct, we wanted to place ourselves clearly within a niche, gaining a following and expanding outward from there. This turned out to be a critical decision: all of the initial press we garnered came from the travel sections of newspapers or magazines, and/or bloggers and writers who focus predominantly on travel.

We were concerned, though, about being boxed in thematically, and about being stigmatized as yet another travel blog: hence, the "inspired by" caveat. This single phrase has allowed us the best of both worlds: we can gain press and recognition via the vibrant travel community, about which most of us are passionate and where we have strong connections, and yet we don't feel obligated to stick to the conventional and recognizable forms of travel writing. A lot of topics and ideas can filter through the sieve of "inspired by": all writing, to some degree, is travel writing. All of it asks the reader to undergo a journey, to consider some degree of foreignness. Still, we are careful to check with one another to ensure that a particular piece doesn't stray too far from our focus.

In publishing, agents and editors will often demand that authors define their books in one sentence. This has always seemed insane to me—400 pages in one sentence? —but I've realized how important it is for *Vela*. For better or worse, in an age and a context in which succinct wit might be the utmost virtue, it's critical to be able to sum up the work with a line that is unique and memorable without being too narrow and constrictive. It can take a great deal of collective strategizing to arrive at this line, and it can feel frustrating, but it's surprisingly comforting to return to: it's the mermaid at the helm of your ship.

GAINING TRACTION

My initial goal was to use *Vela* as a portfolio site to promote the work and the careers of the six featured writers. This functioned very well: several writers were contacted by editors who'd read their work and offered them assignments, several stories were anthologized in *The Best Women's Travel Writing* and chosen as best nonfiction reads of the year by curating sites such as Byliner.com, and a number of *Vela* pieces became the basis for writers' book proposals and/or fellowship applications. During this period, we utilized a number of strategies for promoting one another's work:

- sending published stories to known curating sites such as TheBrowser.com, LadyJournos.com, Byliner.com, Longreads.com and Longform.org
- Tweeting one another's work, sharing it on Facebook, and submitting it to sites such as StumbleUpon, Reddit and Digg
- Writing relevant blog posts on our own sites or on sites for which we blogged regularly
- Writing connected blog posts on *Vela*'s blog
- Creating a Facebook group and a Facebook page on which to share and discuss stories

However, as *Vela* gained traction and readership it became clear that in order to keep growing we would need to bring in new voices. First of all, the burden of publishing one new, highly polished story of exceptional quality every six weeks had begun to weigh on each of us. It was limiting our abilities to publish elsewhere, and some of us worried about our writing falling into set patterns. We also wanted to encourage and offer exposure to other emerging women writers, with the philosophy that we live in an era of friends in low places; an era of building from the ground up, and horizontal instead of vertical loyalty.

So we began to reach out to women whose work we respected, and whose vision and voices we thought would fit with *Vela*'s. Most were very enthusiastic, and we published our first guest writer story three months after initially soliciting pieces. The response was overwhelming: there *had* been a demand for new voices, for a departure from our set schedule, and we saw it immediately. We also saw that the reputation we'd built over a year of publishing and promoting our own writing had set the scaffolding in place to begin supporting other women writers: we had enough of a reputation to offer other writers a solid platform, exposure, and most importantly, a strong community.

During this time we also began to dedicate more time to short essays about the publishing industry and the craft of writing on our blog, with the aim of becoming a center of conversation about writing, reading, and women in publishing. These essays also became a space for emerging women writers to publish, and strengthened our identity as a magazine taking on the byline gap in innovative ways.

Essentially, in this transition the six original *Vela* writers became contributing editors. Initially, I was worried that this would thrust the six of us into the background, and that *Vela*'s impact on our careers would not be as great. But one night, following a reading at the University of Pittsburgh, I had a conversation with one of the founders of Longform.org that changed my mind.

"You'll earn much more of a reputation and much more prestige putting out a great magazine than having a great portfolio site," he told me. The thought of transitioning from the latter to the former was terrifying, but I recognized that it was crucial. Otherwise, our site would've become stagnant and predictable, and its ability to catalyze our careers limited. As we've slipped into more editorial roles we've realized that we can have the best of both worlds: we can publish our own work, build a bigger and stronger community, and impulse an up-and-coming generation of women writers.

During this phase of development, we mapped out the following strategies to expand *Vela's* audience and core group of writers without becoming overburdened by submissions and editorial work:

- Putting an "invite" form on our blog asking people to recommend great writing by women, and then reaching out to those writers
- Reaching out to the writers whom we feature on our "Women We Read This Week" posts to see if they'd be interested in contributing
- Personally inviting friends and colleagues whose work we respect and asking them for their recommendations of other writers

- Opening for submissions for a limited ten-day stretch and promoting this brief period intensively
- Holding a contest judged by a renowned women writer with a cash prize

The unifying theme of all of these strategies is the belief that our success is other women writers' success, and vice versa. The Internet demands connectivity. That connectivity can be alienating and overwhelming, but it can also be empowering: it can give women writers the strength to overcome the significant hurdles to their success.

Chapter Twenty-Six

Founding and Running Sheila Bender's Writing It Real

Sheila Bender

In 2002, I founded an online magazine entitled *Sheila Bender's Writing It Real* as an outgrowth of my work teaching writing at colleges and universities and writing instructional books for Warner Publishing, Writer's Digest Books, *Writer's Digest Magazine* and other presses. In addition to instructional writing and college and university teaching experience, I had been a writing coach for an online business, Accepted.com. My job as one of the editors on the team was helping candidates applying to MBA, law, and medical programs understand how to shape their personal experience into compelling essays for their applications. I was comfortable as a classroom teacher, writer, and contracted online editor and coach.

So what made me venture into this new territory of running an online business? The synchronicity of being married to a computer network engineer and watching a news magazine program with him about a woman entrepreneur who was business manager, techie, and content creator for the successful entertainment site she'd started in the Los Angeles area.

"Do you think I could deliver my instructional material about writing through a website?"

"Of course you can."

For months, we discussed what that would look like and settled on the idea of weekly instructional articles that would be archived on the website. It would be fun to be able to have my work out there so much more quickly than the year-and-a-half production schedule books then had. Subscribers would pay a yearly fee and have access to all of the articles we'd posted. I wanted the site to be advertisement free, easy to navigate, and have a quiet feel, things I thought writers I worked with would appreciate.

Next, we engaged a designer and programmer team, and my husband worked with them to ensure the site had the qualities important to me. He worked with me to "populate" my website with a store of articles in categories we created (The Working Writer, Revision Diary, and Literary Gallery, among others). When he asked me if I thought I'd ever run out of things to write about at one article a week, I confidently said no. How do you run out of material when it concerns a passion?

In October 2002, we launched Writing It Real.com. I had once shared an airline row with a woman who identified herself as a marketing consultant. "I make people famous," she said to explain her job. "I made John Edward of television's 'Crossing Over with John Edward' famous."

It didn't take me but a beat to tell her I'd like to be famous. I knew that having established publishers or not, it is very much up to authors to promote their work.

"What would you call your venture?" she asked.

Because my niche was in writing from personal experience, the phrase "writing it real" occurred to me.

As my launch approached, I contacted her, but found her fees too high for our shoestring budget. I started instead with my own large e-mail list of students, friends, and colleagues. Before too long, several hundred people paid me $25 each for a subscription to a year's worth of weekly articles on writing and the writing life.

Now, ten-plus years and two major website redesigns later, I still don't think I'll ever run out of topics for the magazine. But I may run out of time to learn how to use all that is available for the delivery of my work.

Over the years, as the Internet and computer software developed the ability for groups to "gather" in the "cloud" (a formation of computing services delivered over the Internet) in virtual classrooms, I added online classes to the weekly articles I provided. As more people wanted to learn directly from my responses to their work, I also added tutorials by e-mail, phone consults, manuscript evaluations, and developmental editing.

Here are some of the technologies I use:

Google Groups, Nicenet, and Moodle are sites where teachers and students can post lessons, courseware, and enrichment material and hold chats via posts. It is possible, too, to create restricted groups on Facebook that allow a group to correspond and post writing and responses. Each of these places in the "cloud" provides space for online class participants to respond to one another's writing. Although the services are designed to be easy to access, users do have questions and often need support in figuring out the system. Screen share software such as Glance or Team Viewer, available free over the Internet as downloads, allow my page administrator and tech support person (still my husband and cofounder) to control a participant's screen (with her permission to do so for that session only) so he can demonstrate how to use the classroom site.

For clients who want me to edit their work, I use, as I did in my Accepted.com days, Track Changes, an editing tool that comes with Microsoft Word. I also insert editorial comments along the right-hand side of a document—using the Comment function. These two functions allow me to demonstrate edits for students and clients that show the process of editing—what I've moved around, what I've deleted, what I've reworded, and what I suggest adding to a poem, essay, or story. I can attach documents to posts in our Google Group with the tracked edits showing so everyone in the class benefits from following along. When I work on an individual's book manuscript, I read on the screen now, inserting detailed comments without having to worry about the legibility of my handwriting.

I have on occasion used Dragon Naturally Speaking software to translate my spoken comments into type. This saves wear and tear on my wrists, but I do have to correct the typing when the software doesn't translate what I said correctly. Speaking is very different than communicating in writing. In speaking, you are typically watching and/or hearing the response of a student and adjusting your words; in writing you don't have that option and must be more careful to communicate perfectly the first time. For that reason, online I prefer to write my comments. I am, however, grateful for the speech dictation option that software supplies—when I've had some bouts of tendonitis I could keep on working.

Even online, though, I sometimes respond to work "in person" using Skype, Google Plus, or GoToMeeting, as well as other sites that offer venues for no-cost "face-to-face" or "voice only" conversations. (If you use them often or with large groups there are fees in some cases). In addition, having an Internet phone (I use Vonage for its low unlimited-calling monthly fee) allows me to hold telephone conferences with individuals (easy because the person on the other end has only to pick up her phone when it rings and doesn't have to be online). If I need to call out of the country, I use Skype. When calling computer-to-computer over the Internet, Skype is free, and when calling someone's phone from your computer, the Skype rate is very inexpensive for both in-country and out-of-country calls.

In addition to writing my weekly articles, I am equally as busy teaching creative writing. I also work in association with other sites dedicated to facilitating writing: iajw.org, writers.com, and storycircle.org, among others. I enjoy "meeting" with students who are not yet members of my own website this way and expanding the "locations" in which I facilitate writing.

Masters of Fine Arts programs have invited me to work with their students. I have mentored a graduate student in Alaska via phone and e-mail, and I have ridden the ferry across Admiralty Bay to teach for Whidbey Island's Northwest Institute of Literary Arts. I provide in-person teaching at writer's conferences and retreats where online students have requested my participation. Sometimes, program directors find me directly through my website. Other times, program organizers know my books and then learn about Sheila Bender's WritingItReal.com, where they read about how I teach.

Over the years, I've presented in Washington State at Centrum Foundation's Port Townsend Writers' Conference, the Chuckanut Writers' Conference, and the Edmond's Write on the Sound Writers' Conference. I've been invited to teach out of state, too, in California, Arizona, Texas, Oregon, and Illinois at conferences as well as literary centers. Though I imagined before we launched that I'd write half the day and garden, read, and exercise the other half, I do enjoy the blend of online and in-person teaching and, of course, each feeds the other: I redesign as online classes ones that I developed for in-person seminars and presentations, and I gather new members and contributors for my website when I meet writers at retreats and workshops. It is always a bonus when I also get to meet those I've previously worked with only online.

Although I haven't run out of topics for my weekly articles and I've expanded my offerings, there are many more writing sites online now than in 2002. Making sure many choose to belong to Writing It Real requires that I differentiate my services from others' and that I network to reach my target audience. My mission is to provide the kind of information, inspiration, and help for which people attend expensive MFA programs. I specialize in helping people write from personal experience—especially in personal essay, memoir, poetry, and sudden nonfiction. To that end, I review books I think writers from personal experience will find valuable, introduce my readers to the work of writers I admire, and show them how I read as a writer, while also providing lessons on self-editing as well as instructional exercises. Some of the articles in the more than five hundred stored in our archives are: "You Are My Heroes—A Letter to Writers," "Writing Between the Lines: A Personal Essay Writing Ideas," "Accepting the Personal in the Personal Essay," "Let Your Writer Self Be with You," and "Navigating the Online Publishing and Promotion World." There are others focused on writing poetry, children's books, and journals.

My first teacher, poet David Wagoner, said we must always learn to write in more than one genre because there are times the poems don't come. I think there are times that, no matter what a person's favorite genre is, a different one proves more fruitful. So having facility with many genres and approaches helps a writer, and I attempt in the diversity of the articles to encourage people to write in many genres.

Sometimes, I think of the women who inspired my thought to do an online writing site: Linda Abraham's Accepted.com is going strong, and she has worked to create a national organization of agencies helping candidates navigate graduate and professional school and learn how write their application essays. I like imagining the woman whose television spotlight inspired my enterprise as having grown now to need employees. Though my organization is still a small one, I have engaged much contracted help. First, in the form of contributors for Writing It Real articles. Among the contributors who have written for Writing It Real are Tarn Wilson, at the time an intern from The Rainier Writer's Workshop MFA program at Pacific Lutheran University in Washington State; novelists Nancy Lamb, Janice Eidus, and Meg Files; essayist Brenda Miller; poet and essayist Rebecca McClanahan; poet Susan Rich; and poet and memoirist Kim Stafford. Novelist, essayist, and editor Judith Kitchen has been very generous in contributing to Writing It Real articles. The same is true of creative nonfiction and fiction writer Jack Heffron, who was years ago the acquiring editor at Writer's Digest Books who selected my book *Writing the Personal Essay: How to Shape Your Experience for the Page* (now with a new publisher and re-titled *Writing and Publishing Personal Essays*). Veteran children's book writers Carolyn Arnold, Nancy Smiler Levinson, and Joanne Rocklin have also generously offered articles.

Sometimes, contributors are current Writing It Real members who let me know they have published. I interview them about their writing and publishing process and offer a sample of their books, as I also do with the established writers. Fame is not important when we learn from one another. It is the sharing of experience that helps others grow and the ability to articulate that experience (though doing that effectively certainly spreads the word about one's achievements). Recent member interviews have been with Penny Holland, who self-published a children's book; Suzan Huney who wrote an oral history from conversations with her elderly aunt; and Thelma Zirkelbach, who edited an anthology of essays by widows on adapting to their new lives.

Sometimes my contributors are people who have interviewed me for their publications and have allowed me to reprint the interviews. Agent Andrea Hurst is one such contributor. One of my members, Leslie Wake, offered to interview me about the writing of my memoir *A New Theology: Turning to Poetry in a Time of Grief*. Her questions stirred many thoughts about how and why I write.

Every time I teach or attend a writing event, I make contact with writers, publishers, agents, editors, and booksellers. I ask many of them if they might be interested in being the subject of a Writing It Real article or being an interviewee (by e-mail) or allowing Writing It Real to reprint something they have already written. Often, they say they'd like to write something new for Writing It Real. I hold three to four writing contests a year and the three winners of each contest have their winning writing published in Writing It Real. Additionally, when I work with a student on developing an essay, I often create (with their permission) an article about revision, showing the first draft, my response, and their developed draft. The mix of contributors establishes a thriving community of writers.

In 2009, my husband and I decided to switch from our custom programmed site design to a WordPress site to make our content management easier and to be able to add new functionality. We engaged Sheila Hoffman of Hoffman Graphics in Seattle, who had redesigned my original custom-programmed site a few years earlier. We needed her to coordinate the WordPress site with a data access program (we chose Digital Access Pass or DAP) to store our membership start and end dates and payment information for all of our services. Today, a second wonderful woman, Ellen Ziskin of FrontOf-TheLineDesign, is our support for site tweaks and additions as well as search engine optimization (SEO), which is the use of an Internet marketing strategy based on how Internet search engines work, what search terms and keywords people type into them, and which search engines any targeted audience prefers using. Advisors on SEO suggest editing content and coding as well as creating back links to other sites to increase any particular site's relevance to specific keywords and to remove barriers to the indexing activities of search engines. Optimizing my site's visibility online when people search for help with writing requires additions and changes in how I word copy as well as how I create descriptions of my posted articles. It requires using "tags" now that I am a WordPress-based site to categorize the articles according to keywords, words search engines use.

WordPress is open-source software and free for anyone to use and any programmer to improve. The plug-ins we use have been coded by enthusiasts to allow WordPress sites to perform what were once difficult tasks. Because of one plug-in, my members are able to view comment boxes and share their responses to articles; because of another there are routine automatic searches for links that no longer work in my archived articles. Yet another allows for easy posting of author photos and bios. Instead of my tech savvy husband having to use HTML to post our articles and create programs to ensure an interactive quality for Writing It Real, I can copy and paste the articles from Microsoft Word to WordPress right onto the server that hosts our site.

Although he no longer needs to fix typos I spot after we have posted because I can do that myself, my husband is still the best formatter of the two of us, and he catches my spacing and style mistakes. It always takes more than one set of eyes on anything going into print to ensure it gets published properly, but our process on Wednesday nights, the night we reserve for getting the new article up online, is so much smoother and so much less time consuming than when we started Writing It Real in 2002.

And that's a good thing because with the leaps forward on the Internet, his job has not gotten smaller. As an extension of our member online tech support via screen share, my husband helps members with any computing issues and teaches them how to use functions on their computers as well as updates their software so their computers run smoothly—very important for writers!

He hosts the Writing It Real site on the server space he rents from Dewahost and goes into action with them if the site goes down. If the site's functions fail, he works with our WordPress expert as well as the people at Digital Access Pass. He offers me support in using Google Groups and other venues effectively, as well as explains how I can effectively help members with their simpler tech questions.

My own on-the-job training is never-ending. In addition to my husband's tech help, I've also engaged a long-distance tutor, John Nemerovski in Tucson, Arizona, who uses screen shares with me to show me how to become proficient with photo manipulation and uploading, keeping a neat desktop, and making screen shots, among other functions that can help me reduce what he calls "workflow annoyances." I make use of social media, too, all during the week with a Facebook Fan Page for Writing It Real (www. facebook.com/writingitreal) that links to a Twitter feed and one for those who write to heal grief (www.facebook.com/anewtheology) as well as a Pinterest page called The Writing Life, on which I frequently post links to Writing It Real members' publishing successes. There is not one writer's conference I've attended recently that hasn't had a session or more on using social media to build a platform so others learn about your work, and learning to use social media effectively is an ongoing process.

The checklist I make today of what it takes to build an online business is much longer than the one I made in 2002. Here are the needs as I see them:

- A copywriter. All websites require written descriptions that grab visitors' and search engines' attention.
- A fast, trustworthy editor. Eyes other than one's own or even the copywriter's own are necessary.
- A person to design your site, whether it is custom programmed or using open source like WordPress. Of course, you can do it yourself, too; there is much information online about creating your own website and using WordPress. Google "create a free website" and "using WordPress" and you'll find many resources.
- A web host that allows your website to be housed on their server. Again, Dewahost is the one with which my husband maintains an account.
- A program for keeping a member database.
- A way to collect funds linked to a PayPal account or to a merchant credit card funds collection system if you are selling services or products.
- A facility with Google tools: Google Groups, Google Calendar, Google Documents, Google Plus, among them.

- A mail manager software program like Mail Chimp, which is free if your mailing list is small, or Constant Contact so you can stay in touch with people interested in your business. A mail manager makes it easy to have a nicely designed newsletter as well as store an archive of all of them and use analytics to find out if people are opening the e-mail and using the links you provide for them.
- Ongoing search engine optimization work so people learn about you.
- Development of an online network of sites and people to ensure links to your site from other sites where your audiences hang out.
- Use of social media to attract people to your online business.
- Development of venues through which you can advertise your website, such as guest blogging and having site administrators interview you.
- Someone who can offer tech support as needed. Websites are not static; broken links need fixing, software updates are required, servers go down, and more.
- Time, lots of it, for learning new tricks for websites, administering your site and for responding to e-mail from your audience.
- Unless you are good at it yourself, a bookkeeper and tax accountant who understand the state and federal tax laws for online business sales.
- Time to engage in the activity you love that fostered your idea for a web business.

Despite all the tasks of the online business, my own creative writing is still at the heart of my work. Writing my own new essays, poetry, and book material keeps me fresh when it comes to helping others through the process. My husband is my first reader and contributes expert edits—a bonus to be sure. Who would have thought that a computer geek would become an excellent editor? I learn a lot about reaching my audience from his questions and from his careful disagreements with my word choices and phrasing. I've continued to write books and that means extending into digital books. When my town opened KPTZ, an all-volunteer FM station, I pitched a show about writing called "In Conversation with Sheila Bender: Discussions on Writing and the Writing Life." Although I am not allowed to talk about my business in my capacity as interviewer, I am constantly finding new people to talk with about writing and those talks spawn articles.

Aired regularly, the programs are also made into podcasts maintained and indexed on the KPTZ.org website. I can provide links to the shows from my site and social media. Program topics have included discussions about MFA programs, agenting, playwriting, learning to present poetry effectively before an audience, creating Lifejournal for Writers software for those who journal on their computers, and becoming a rap poet in middle age, among other topics. By Skype, I spoke with Yesim Cimcoz in Turkey, a Writing It Real member who started a project called Writing Istanbul for those who are not in universities but want to write.

The many forms available for the delivery of my lessons and the lessons of others involved in the writing life to a wide-world audience is gratifying. Accessing my own body of work in the archives of Writing It Real multiplies that gratification. Anytime I want to reference something I've taught, I search with keywords though my website archive of articles, and there are my lessons ready to continue helping people. The Internet is a giant thesis binder that holds my words about what I've learned and what I know.

What's next on my list? Video! I want send video lessons to my members who might enjoy the experience of seeing me teach. Camera, Lights, Action! YouTube, here I come.

Chapter Twenty-Seven

Founding Female Editors

Your Voice, Your Vision, and How to Make It a Reality

Nicole M. Bouchard

As F. Scott Fitzgerald noted, the correlation between an author's purpose of making the reader "see" or become endowed with a deeper understanding, and a magazine's ultimate purpose being to make itself be read (Phillips 1985, 4), we can thus derive that a founding magazine editor's overall purpose or mission is a dual one of vision and visibility. Utilizing the Internet as a vehicle to accomplish this throws open doors on a worldwide scale and creates innovative, cost-effective possibilities that have been made widely accessible for the many voices looking to communicate with their individual niche. Women at various stages of their lives and careers, balancing home, family, and/or work obligations are able to take on exciting new roles whether by delving into a passion, building a haven for focused expression, or becoming entrepreneurs. They often do this from their computer with little more than a plan developed from the thrilling spark of an idea and a very modest investment of time and resources.

Founding editor Margaret Brown of *Shelf Unbound*, a book review magazine that draws over one hundred twenty-five thousand readers domestically and abroad, combined twenty-five years of experience as a traditional magazine editor with a passion for the latest technology and an interest in showcasing small press and independent titles to form a unique online publication with a vivid array of content and dazzling design. Brown encourages those wishing to forge their own paths:

> Before the advent of digital publishing, I would never have considered launching my own business. The amount of investment, and the risk of that investment, was just completely prohibitive. Digital has changed that. I encourage

women to look at their accomplishments and realize that they have the skills necessary to become successful entrepreneurs. It takes experience, hard work, perseverance, and passion. But I have personally experienced that if you follow your passion with unwavering commitment; look upon the many mistakes you will make as positive course correction; and believe that your unique talents, experiences, and interests make you the exact right person for the job, then you will achieve your goals and be personally rewarded beyond measure. Find mentors, and be a mentor. Enjoy the journey. (Margaret Brown, e-mail message to author, March 7, 2013)

The possibilities and forms of execution to embark on such projects are more present today, with so many more user-friendly ways of getting content into readers' hands than there have ever been before.

However, as with any personal or professional endeavor built from scratch, there are natural considerations and factors to weigh in terms of the "how" and just "how much" you are willing to dedicate yourself to the success of your venture. There is freedom and there is sacrifice. There are long hours at certain points on the horizon and the wearing of many hats as an editor who will be responsible for a full compilation. The instrumental keys are in choosing a mode of communication that will suit your purpose, goals and lifestyle, as well as determining whether you alone or a dynamic team of selected individuals will be putting the publication together.

Once you have a vague idea about the kind of publication you want to produce, you can begin putting together a game plan and mapping out the important decisions.

PURPOSE

We'll begin with purpose because it is from this seed of potential that your idea will or will not take root. It is at this early stage where viability comes into play and you can tell through educated estimation whether or not the project is worth the nurturing and cultivation it will take to make it truly blossom. Women are thinking in this age of communication, one in which a Facebook status post can generate a discussion with a hundred people or more in minutes, "What do I want to share, to add? What do I feel I need to say? What message do I have as an individual that isn't already out there or isn't talked about enough?"

To delve into the symbolism of fairy tale literature, this is a time of women of all cultures, ages and socioeconomic statuses being universally heard, the metaphoric apple removed from the throat chakra so that Snow White's voice is uninhibited and she awakens; not to a prince, but to the archetype bearing the other half of herself, her own capacity for action, decision making and independence. Women all over the world are able to connect instantaneously with the power of words at their fingertips, even in situations where they might be physically isolated. The question that arises is, "How do I best use this ability in the most positive sense?"

A more detailed discussion of form (magazines, blogs, newsletters) follows below, but first, you are still in the deciding stages of what you wish to say, how you want to say it and who you want to say it to.

In my five years as editor of *The Write Place At the Write Time*, I've seen shifts and evolutions in many aspects of the publication as we gained new ground, yet our founding purpose of creating a literary magazine with a uniquely personalized approach toward content, contributors and a profound sense of community has not changed. I wanted to use my experiences as both a writer and an editor to give a very human visage to the publishing process. Our collective voice, from our aesthetic to our artwork to the words, would be looking at and highlighting aspects of real life (from the sorrows to the triumphs) through a storytelling lens that would allow for or promote a universal understanding. We gave thought to themes, genres, and language— all that would fit us and all that would not as a mainstream publication.

Our audience started to take shape in our mind's eye before we set out. A good portion of our aim was writers who were also readers; we wanted to nurture, aid, inspire, entertain, embrace and encourage (providing personalized, constructive feedback if needed). We wanted to give hope in what can be a difficult, isolating discipline. We wanted readers, writers, and artists to visit the site and feel as if they'd come upon an artistic safe haven, imbued with a sense of home. Through experience, research, and observation via my immersion in the field, I knew and had seen that there was a need; there was a market of writers and aspiring writers looking for our brand of publication.

In a concise article entitled "How 2 Start Your Own Online Magazine" by Marcia Passos Duffy featured on the site *WOW! Women on Writing*, the notion of choosing a passion and then doing research to substantiate the level of market interest in that passion is advocated (Duffy 2009). Duffy recommends the use of Google Keywords to enter main topics that you'd like to write about and seeing how many searches are done on said topics. Forums are also a great place to look to take a pulse on a topic, issue or theme and see the level of response. Examine your experiences closely and you'll likely find observations about what people are talking about, what issues strike a spark, what niches are left unfilled.

If you feel that you want the responsibility and expression involved in becoming a founding editor, create a list of concepts for your publication and rate them according to three factors:

1. Your enthusiasm or passion for the subject
2. Your experience or knowledge about the subject

3. The estimated viability of the subject in terms of what market it would have

Once you've narrowed your list down to a central concept, focus it further. What do you wish to say or do that is unique? What purpose will your publication serve and how will it go about doing this? Strike a balance between being specific and narrowing your project to the point where there wouldn't be enough content to generate on it or create lasting interest.

FORM

We would be remiss in this section on form if we did not first discuss the role of the Internet that allows for wide reach, low overhead, marketing efficiency, multimedia, go-green practices, many devices providing easy accessibility, and instantly up-to-date communications. The Internet also provides for an unprecedented relationship with the marketplace where editors can instantaneously develop a rapport with their readers and keep attuned to their needs and wants.

Editor April Gray Wilder discusses the transformation of *Fiction Fix*, the diverse literary journal of the University of North Florida and home to the distinctive Gypsy Sachet Award, when it went from print format to online and the benefits of that transformation:

> In 2008 when I became editor of *Fiction Fix*, it was a print journal and the economic situation threatened its future. The existence of the Internet and the growing support and validity of online journals allowed *Fiction Fix* to survive. More than that, being an online journal has allowed *Fiction Fix* to continue to grow exponentially, both in the number of submissions we receive and our number of readers. The Internet now offers (and continues to offer more and more) tools to bring publications to life in digital format. Everything that makes *Fiction Fix* possible is online. . . . Services like Submittable, Drop Box, Tumblr, WordPress, etc., are making it possible for editors of all levels of experience to bring their literary visions to life by matching their dedicated manpower to an everyday expanding amount of resources. I've now come to believe that small (and very good!) journals should have an online presence, even if they aren't completely online. (April Gray Wilder, e-mail message to author, March 8, 2013)

Long-standing print publications such as *Newsweek* have gone digital and other print publications have enhanced their websites to incorporate multimedia features that serve to further enhance their product.

Once you have chosen the Internet as your basic canvas, it comes time to decide on your mode of delivery for your content. In the book, *How to Start a Magazine and Publish it Profitably*, author James B. Kobak points out the importance of matching your purpose to the proper form (Kobak 2002, 20); this involves considering the amount of content to fill a space; reaching the right audience; taking into account the size of your market; and if you intend to turn a profit, addressing the right advertisers.

A magazine is at the top tier of commitment. This is a fantastic outlet to convey a larger vision, yet it implies a good deal of responsibility, attention to detail, and oftentimes interaction with colleagues and contributors to put forth a quality product. There are magazines of all shapes and sizes; you'll want to think about what you'll need not only to start out but also to allow room for growth. Layout, design, assigning tasks, submission calls for art and written works, managing content, submission evaluation, establishing guidelines, setting schedules, editing everything from the aesthetic down to the order of content on a page, promotion, development, creative input, networking with publicists, dealing directly with high-profile interview subjects and maintaining brand across social media are a few of the things on my regular to-do list. They are fueled by passion, excitement and dedication. As a literary magazine that has one main purpose but numerous themes/sections/features speaking to that purpose, we have many facets to consider.

Your project might be quite different and require less, yet what is universal in your job as editor is to oversee every aspect of the publication so that it adheres to consistent standards of quality that your readers will come to expect and recognize you by.

Newsletters

If your primary output will be highly focused with an informative purpose to a limited circulation that you want to actively engage and reach out to directly on a regular, structured basis with more formal structured content (articles, etc.), a newsletter might be your form. Possibilities in a newsletter that cultivates an ongoing relationship with clients could extend to special offers, market surveys, joint ventures, and targeted advertising.

Blogs

In the world of blogs, with more popping up every day, the gift of communication is paired with the challenges of setting yourself apart, maintaining interest, and being seen as an authority even if you're simply conveying the "everyman" perspective. Consider the following three examples, their associated focuses, and how they've distinguished themselves.

Bag Snob, founded by two business undergraduates that shared a passion for bags, is a blog that was intended for their mutual discussions on the latest fashions (Amed 2011). Their starting cost? Twenty dollars. By 2011 they had over 250,000 unique visitors and fifteen income streams. Their descriptive posts are short, sweet, to-the-point, frequent and informative. The ability to quickly share the posts, tag them and organize them in a quick, easy-access blog format serves their purpose.

Julie Powell and her namesake blog, was intended to be a personal, realistic, frank discourse on her goal of working through Julia Child's recipes. Her solitary voice and goal was well-suited to a blog and that format allowed for the commentary and responsiveness she was looking for. The subsequent book and film make this a motivational example of what one voice, striking a chord with its audience, can do.

Tracey Jackson, author, director, producer and screenwriter for films including *Confessions of a Shopaholic*, has her blog *Tracey Talks*, which allows her a platform to comment not only on her experiences but on important current events seen through her perspective. Well-written, thought-provoking and intriguing, it is a natural extension of who she is as a person and a creative brand.

These three examples are all well-suited to their form and work as models of what blogs can be, do, or accomplish.

IDENTITY

When discussing the development of your identity as a publication from the perspective of being an online magazine as opposed to a blog or newsletter, begin with the notion of personifying what your collective voice wishes to accomplish.

Thinking of the ways in which art and literature, artists and writers, writers and their stories, content and readers often come together in unexpected, incredible ways, we touched upon the idea of serendipity in creative endeavors. From this, we would arrive at our name. *The Write Place At the Write Time* stresses the serendipitous convergence of place and time to create circumstances far greater than those originally envisioned or planned for. Much of our existence has been wrought with serendipity, whole issues coming together with strong, unifying themes that we hadn't purposely intended, and it is in this way that we feel faithful to our original premise.

Create a checklist against your purpose so that your logo, name, aesthetic, guidelines, language, content, and communications cohesively reflect a clear, consistent identity that is effectively your brand. The standards and tone should be consistent as well. This isn't to say that you won't branch out into new territory and try different things; what it means is that the essentials can be depended upon, that they will reflect your fundamental vision. With a clear understanding of who you are as a publication, it will be simpler to further narrow down your market and, if you intend to have advertising, your clients.

In terms of individuality, just as every person is unique though they might share similar traits or backgrounds, see to it that your publication has a distinctive personality. Similar to the way in which writers are encouraged to read extensively, research the greats, the publications you admire, research those closest to the basics (size, general category) of what you'd like to do with your publication, research the publications you wouldn't want to emulate and then put all research aside. From a mix of knowledgeable exposure and innovation about ways that you might do things differently, create something of your own, reflecting your signature style, views and experiences.

EXECUTION

Once you've determined your purpose, form, and identity, all you have left to do is get yourself in gear for the execution of your idea. At this juncture you will make decisions and put in place detailed plans concerning design, cost/budget, publication schedule, obtaining a domain, choosing a hosting service and obtaining legal counsel to set forth publication terms (author rights, permissions, etc.).

A good place to look to that may influence design, budget, and domain (price) is your hosting service. A simple Google search can return comparative results on which hosting packages consumers rated the highest based on value, ease-of-use, and function. Think about your level of design experience, whether you will want to implement HTML and to what level you want to be involved with design. Wanting more than an inflexible template that was filled with standard spaces that could affect layout choices, I chose a hosting service that would allow complete freedom and creative control (every single detail down to the colors of the borders around images is painstakingly pondered) without requiring extensive HTML experience. It was a slightly more expensive option but still reasonable with ample room for growth in the website package I chose (room for the amount of pages, e-mail boxes and features I *would* want as opposed to what I'd need starting out).

For domain names, consider again your purpose and the need to set yourself apart. We chose .org because of the not-for-profit status and the humanitarian focus on the arts.

Your design should be both functional and personalized as appearances make strong impressions and it will be the outer manifestation of the vision behind the magazine. Make your design an experience.

The publication schedule has to strike a balance between the needs and interests of your readership and the amount of time you can dedicate to running a magazine. A regional online entertainment magazine with performance reviews would need a more frequent publication schedule so that readers could, for instance, read the review of a play and then decide to get tickets before the show moved on.

To obtain legal advice or answer your questions, there are many free resources for writers and publishers whether in the form of comprehensive sites, forums, or copyright lawyers willing to consult with you. In addition to research, I took the direct route and spoke to a lawyer about all that I wanted to do and asked a few basic questions. The most important piece of advice that he gave me was to make sure that I thought through even unlikely circumstances and made terms to allow for them in case they arose at a later time. From there I set in place terms that would be writer friendly and that I felt would also protect the originality of the magazine's content. Each issue of the magazine is also copyrighted; this is another option for editors to contemplate.

Giving birth to your project is no small feat; surround yourself with encouragement and willing helpers.

The Review Review, a publication that gives a backstage pass to the world of literary magazines with a lively, engaging voice was founded by editor Becky Tuch around 2008. She discusses the importance of reaching out to your network to actualize your vision:

> This project really would not be possible without my friends, all of whom I have leaned on in some form or another in launching and growing this project. Who does graphic design? Who does computer programming? Who does marketing stuff? Who blogs? Who can design a logo? Who knows about web hosting? One of the most rewarding aspects of this project is that I discovered so many talents among all the people I know, and I absolutely was not shy to ask for help from anyone and everyone. (Becky Tuch, e-mail message to author, March 19, 2013)

Once you are live, it will be your duty to let the right audience know you're out there.

Through the previous steps, you've continued to define your market and have likely seen where they frequent; think of forums, cross-promotions you can do with noncompeting sites, getting your publication listed as a resource, doing a targeted e-mail campaign and developing a list, flyers placed prominently in applicable locations that have to do with your theme and encouraging word of mouth. More ideas will come your way as you mature, but the pivotal part is getting started.

MAINTENANCE AND GROWTH

Each editor comes to know that of the many balances to be struck in magazine publishing, the one most vital to survival (and seemingly contradictory) is that between adaptability and consistency. There are fundamental visions, purposes, standards and basic identities that ought to stay the same; however, an editor keeping in touch with the times, with their readers, and with industry changes, will know when to shift, revitalize and change course as necessary. Part of the enjoyment in having your own publication is trying new things, expanding, adding features, and then gauging reader response to see what resonates. The lines of communication between a publication and its audience need to stay open. A good part of maintenance (keeping what works) and growth (expanding into new territory) comes from a solid rapport with your readers.

From here you can continuously fine-tune the publication and streamline your goals based on collected feedback paired with your own observations. Encourage feedback through discussions and surveys and consider rewarding participants by entering them in product giveaways or sending them publication merchandise (pens, bookmarks, etc.). It's not about inundating your audience with major changes in every issue or cluttering the site with features. It is about strategic trial and error with a bit of innovation. Being online allows for a good deal of innovation as publications experiment with video, podcasts and even interactive technology providing customized experiences designed by the reader. There are also growing numbers of ways to reach readers and make your publication available.

Cynthia Reeser, founding editor of *Prick of the Spindle*, a comprehensive journal with a strong emphasis on quality, speaks of the evolution of the publication and the role of the Internet in its growth:

> We've built our audience online, and *Prick of the Spindle* was intended initially to be an online-only journal. Partly because of its visual appeal and partly because of the quality of writing we feature, the journal has grown and expanded beyond my initial vision for it. We are now a 501(c)(3) nonprofit organization and are looking at securing grants; we have a print edition (a biannual publication, whereas the online edition is quarterly), and we were the first literary journal to create a Kindle magazine edition (this is a different animal from a Kindle eBook). I see only more growth ahead for the journal, and I know that *Prick of the Spindle* would not be anywhere near what it is today without the Internet as a launchpad. (Cynthia Reeser, e-mail message to author, March 26, 2013)

Along with the global access the Internet provides, it can also provide numerous marketing and expansion opportunities.

Free marketing opportunities can take various forms (that may include aforementioned cross-promotions, joint ventures and social media). Consider social media mentions and link exchanges with reputable entities that provide information, goods, or services that would benefit your readership. Offline opportunities for networking might involve joining organizations or associations that tie in to your magazine topic or your work as an editor. There are also events, tradeshows, and conferences that you may choose to attend or send business cards and flyers to be displayed at. You may eventually host events for your own publication (whether in person or online) in the form of launch parties, courses or workshops.

However you might choose to grow your publication, whatever directions might beckon to you in the future, it all begins with an idea and enough passion to bring into fruition. You have a voice and it can be used in a myriad of ways to inform and inspire. For founding female editors, there has never been a better time to bring your vision to life. Your readers are waiting . . .

REFERENCES

Amed, Imran. 2011. "The Business of Blogging: *Bag Snob*." *The Business of Fashion*, May 24. www.businessoffashion.com/2011/05/the-business-of-blogging-bag-snob.html .

Cooper, Steve. 2006. "Start Your Own Magazine." *Entrepreneur*, June 6. www.entrepreneur.com/article/160238# .

Duffy, Marica Passos. 2009. "How 2 Start Your Own Online Magazine." *WOW! Women on Writing*, www.wow-womenonwriting.com/34-How2-StartEzine.html .

Kobak, James B. 2002. *How to Start a Magazine and Publish It Profitably*. New York: M. Evans and Company.

Phillips, Larry W., ed. 1985. *F. Scott Fitzgerald on Writing*. New York: Scribner.

Chapter Twenty-Eight

Self-Publishing in a Male-Dominated Publishing World

Leanne Olson

Women are unequally represented in the traditional publishing world, which "remains dominated by a narrow, privileged few" (Cochrane 2013). The big five New York–based publishers: Penguin Random House, Simon & Schuster, HarperCollins, Macmillan, and Hachette tend to stick with the tried-and-true, which often means male writers. "Large houses . . . tend to favor blockbusters or best-sellers and do not aggressively pursue more modest or unconventional books" (Campbell 2011, 332).

VIDA: Women in Literary Arts is a grassroots organization that was founded in 2009 to address some of these issues. Their mission statement refers to "the need for female writers of literature to engage in conversations regarding the critical reception of women's creative writing in our current culture" (VIDA 2013b). Each year, they publish "The Count," a set of charts displaying the number of women included in various American literary publications, as book reviewers, as essay, fiction, or poetry authors, as authors of books reviewed, and as interview subjects. This year's iteration of The Count found that publications featured more men than women, in nearly all cases. With some the divide is significant: 83 percent of *Harper's Magazine* reviews were of books written by men, and the *New Republic* featured nine book reviews written by women, with seventy-nine written by men (VIDA 2013a).

A study by Ruth Franklin (2011), senior editor of the *New Republic*, was inspired by VIDA's work. She found that women writers were represented poorly in literary publishing houses, with works written by women ranging from 45 percent to well below 25 percent of total works published. "If more men than women are publishing books," Franklin explains, "then it stands to reason that more books by men are getting reviewed and more men are reviewing books." Robin Romm, a VIDA member, journalist, and author of a memoir and short stories, also discusses the 2010 version of the VIDA study, and agrees: "The gatekeepers of literary culture—at least at magazines—are still primarily male" (Romm 2011).

Considering that women make up an equal population of readers, these statistics are appalling. Women buy more books in print and digital format, with 57.9 percent of American women buying at least one book in a year compared to 41.2 percent of men (Norris 2013a, 207–8). Cochrane (2013) posits that the reason may be men's lack of interest in writing by women. She notes that in a 2005–2006 study by Jardine and Watkins, men and women were surveyed about their favorite authors and most recently read books. Male readers unwaveringly chose male authors (nineteen out of their top twenty authors were male, and four of their five recently read books were by men) whereas women followed authors of either gender. Women writers are pigeonholed by publishers into women's fiction or genre fiction, and their writing is not seen as "important" in the same way as a man's (Franklin 2011; Romm 2011). But even some women writing in male-dominated genres such as science fiction, fantasy, or horror use pen names or initials to avoid turning off male readers. Joanna Rowling, for example, was urged by her publishers to use the gender-neutral J. K. Rowling (Larsen 2013).

How do women get around this problem, while keeping their sales and self-respect intact? While some aim to change traditional publishing from within, others have turned to self-publishing.

WOMEN AUTHORS AND SELF-PUBLISHING

Self-publishing, or independent publishing, is the publication of a work by the author without the participation of a publishing house. The author makes all decisions relating to production, marketing, and distribution.

There has been a recent splash of established female writers making the change from major publishers to self-publishing. Polly Courtney left Harper-Collins over the marketing of her books as chick lit, a genre notoriously not taken seriously. "I'm not averse to the term chick lit but I don't think that's what my book is. The implication with chick lit is that it's about a girl wanting to meet the man of her dreams. [My books] are about social issues—this time about a woman in a lads' mag environment and the impact of media on society, and feminism" (quoted in Flood 2011). After finishing her three-book contract with HarperCollins, she chose to return to self-publishing. Courtney believes that part of the problem is "There's a feeling that any author should be grateful for any attention they can get from any publisher—that they should take what they can get." Novelist Michele Gorman confirms that "publishing houses do tend to take a single broad brush approach to books by women, for women, and we as writers don't have creative control over our covers or our titles." This treatment is turning off male readers. Author Maureen Johnson tweeted, "I do wish I had a dime for every email I get that says: 'Please put a non-girly cover on your book so I can read it— signed, A Guy,'" and even bestseller Jodi Picoult is frustrated, asking "Why is it 'domestic fiction' if a woman writes about family/relationships, but if a man does that, it's Pulitzer-worthy?" (quoted in Flood 2013).

Self-publishing, by contrast, gives complete creative control: women can choose the title, the cover, and the marketing plan. New writers also see this as appealing. Science fiction author Michelle Proulx self-published her first novel:

> I think I made the decision to self-publish around the time I received my 40th negative response from an agent I'd queried, along the lines of, "We're sorry, but we don't have time to sift through all our submissions, so while we're sure your story is great, we just don't have the time or manpower to look at it right now." . . . when I realized how long, arduous, depressing, and potentially futile the agent querying process was, it became clear to me that self-publishing was the way to go. Not to mention I've always liked the idea of being self-suffi-cient and accomplishing things through my own hard work, so self-publishing really turned out to be the perfect fit for me. (e-mail message to author, August 30, 2013)

It requires an entrepreneurial spirit, but self-publishing can appeal to a wom-an seeking to publish on her own merits, with her own vision.

THE WEB AND THE RISE OF SELF-PUBLISHING

Self-publishing is a growing field, and e-books are driving this rise. E-books became a viable market in the United States with the birth of Amazon's Kindle in 2007, and are now "the fastest-growing segment" of the industry (Campbell 2011, 329). In Canada, the popularity of e-readers and digital media is continuing to increase (Conference Board of Canada 2012).

As bookstores close down, it's harder for new authors to find success with traditional publishing. Department stores and drugstores are becoming the sales points for selling print books (Norris 2013b, 12–13), and they primarily carry known, best-selling authors (Norris 2013a, 2–3). When publishing digi-tally, authors need not purchase print copies upfront or convince brick-and-mortar stores to take a chance on their book. Campbell (2011) explains that "because e-books make publishing and distribution costs low, e-publishing has enabled authors to sidestep traditional publishers" (332).

Self-publishing is finally being taken seriously by the industry. Self-pub-lished authors may now join the Writers' Union of Canada (announced in

June 2013), and the American National Writers Union. With the web, it's easier to obtain reviews that speak to a book's legitimacy, and self-published books are even making the best-seller lists. Amazon founder Jeff Bezos noted that "Sixteen of the top 100 best sellers on Kindle today were self-published" (Friedman 2012), and on April 30, 2013, *Digital Book World* (2013) reported that five out of the top ten bestsellers were self-published, and four of those five authors have female names.

Women writers, free from the constraints of traditional publishing houses, are finding success in self-publishing: Amanda Hocking sold millions of copies of her self-published paranormal romances, and *New York Times* best-selling young adult science fiction writer Keira Cass (2012) began her career with self-publishing. Major self-publishing bestseller lists compiled by Jason Boog, with data taken from Amazon, Barnes & Noble, and Smashwords from the week of August 26, 2013, were over 50 percent filled with female writers. Eighty percent of the authors on the list of self-published bestsellers from Amazon had distinctly female names (Boog 2013).

These wild successes are the exception, not the rule, and Harper (2011) compares the chances of making millions in self-publishing to the chances of winning the lottery (248). However, the same could be said about a traditional publishing deal. Self-publishing is hard work, but now the web makes this significantly more achievable.

PUBLISHING YOUR BOOK WITH THE WEB

Where to start? The main types of self-publishing choices are:

- True self-publishing, in which an author handles all aspects of publication herself.
- Vanity presses, which publish for a fee. These are generally scams, with the author unable to recoup her investment. These companies make money from the author rather than the reader.
- Print-on-demand (POD) services, which print books as needed from digital files. Fees are taken as the books sell. Examples include Lulu, CreateSpace, and iUniverse.
- e-book publishing, which the author can handle herself or use a service that provides templates and converts the book to formats for various e-readers. Barnes & Noble, Amazon, and Smashwords offer these tools.

To avoid scams, speak to other writers, search the company online, and visit sites such as Writer Beware, maintained by the Science Fiction and Fantasy Writers of America. Legitimate POD and e-book services may offer additional services with fees, such as editing, cover design, formatting, and marketing, though Carnoy (2012) cautions against ordering all services from your POD/e-book company. If you're doing the work yourself, many have online communities where authors share tips and tricks.

Whether you plan to do the work yourself, use a self-publishing service, or contract it out, take into account:

- Editing. Have a professional look over your text. To hire freelance, get recommendations from authors or writers unions. The Independent Editors Group, for example, are New York-based freelancers who critique, advise, and edit.
- Formatting. Templates for interior format are available from publishing services or your word processing software.
- Copyright. If you use an image or quote from lyrics or a poem, you may run afoul of copyright restrictions. Read up on your country's laws, for example through the U.S. Copyright Office or the Copyright Act of Canada. National writers' organizations provide publications with tips.
- Cover design. The web makes finding beautiful images for book covers easy. Stock image websites such as iStockPhoto, ShutterStock, and Dreamstime offer royalty-free (pay once, use multiple times) photos and allow downloading watermarked images to test layouts before paying. These sites have advanced search capabilities (you can search for scenes, type of model, and even concepts), and allow downloading watermarked images to test layouts before paying. If you're a prolific user, a subscription may work, but for a new author, starting out by purchasing an image at a time is more financially feasible. If you have time but no budget, free images are available through the Creative Commons search portal, which will search popular image sites (Flickr, WikimediaCommons, etc.) for images with your preferred licensing. The creator of the work decides which rights they will share, and many professional-quality photos are available if you credit the artist. If you are unsure, contact the rights holder. Bestselling romance author Roni Lauren advises, "Assume that something is copyrighted until proven otherwise" (Loren 2012).
- Register an International Standard Book Number, especially if you plan to sell in print. This thirteen-digit number uniquely identifies books. Cost varies; in the United States go through Bowker at ISBN.org and in Canada, the Canadian ISBN Service System (CISS).

With self-publishing, the details are up to you. For a busy author with a day job or children, using a full-service e-book or print-on-demand publisher may be worth the money and slight loss of control. For an author with a tight budget and a DIY sensibility, the ability to design everything herself can be freeing.

SELLING YOUR BOOK WITH THE WEB

The cliché of the self-published author is a lonesome figure with a trunk full of prepaid paperbacks, driving from bookstore to bookstore. But while selling your book online requires dedication (this isn't a get-rich quick scheme) the prevalence of handheld devices and wireless Internet access means that marketing your book can now be done on lunch breaks, on public transit, or while the baby is napping. An article in *Writer's Digest* cautions would-be authors who are not net-savvy. They list several requirements for self-published authors: comfort online, a current website and online identity, the willingness to experiment with online marketing, and a platform from which you can reach readers (Friedman 2011).

Self-published books can be sold online in a variety of places:

- Major book distributors such as Amazon and Barnes & Noble offer free services for authors with statistics and sales tracking, such as Amazon's AuthorCentral.
- Smashwords is the largest online distributor for independent e-books; it allows you to sell online and become a part of their catalog for retailers.
- Your own website, though handling money this way adds a few extra challenges. Whether or not you sell books yourself, make sure you have a professional-looking website that links out to your books. You can design it yourself or hire a designer, host it for free using tools such as Blogger or WordPress, and register a domain (YourName.com) for as little as $10/year.

To determine a price, investigate the market: there is no standard for e-books, and pricing varies significantly. Similar books in the genre of the length and format can lend insight.

Include extras that let readers find out more about your book, such as subject keywords, a summary/blurb, excerpts, a table of contents, and an author biography. Here, you don't have to hide behind a male pseudonym: use your personality to connect with readers. Take advantage of the web's variety of low-cost methods to promote your book:

- Social media tools such as Facebook, Twitter, Google+, and Pinterest. Pay attention to where your readers are. Self-published author Michelle Proulx says, "Perhaps the best advice I can give is 'know your audience.'" Make marketing data work for you. Romance writers or cookbook authors may want to get on visual, female-oriented Pinterest, and if you're a science fiction writer, don't neglect the male audience on Google+. YouTube can be used to post book trailers, created using software on your computer or free options on sites such as Animoto, which provides templates and even copyright-free music.

- Social networking schedulers such as HootSuite. These allow you to schedule posts across a variety of social media tools. Work in advance to post automatically while you're at the office and catch the afternoon web-surfing crowd, or in the middle of the night for readers outside your time zone.
- Blogging. Regular blogging on topics related to your writing, sneak peeks, or interviews with other authors, can keep readers interested. Triberr allows you to connect with similar bloggers, and promote each other's work.
- Virtual book tours. Before the web, book tours were time-consuming and expensive. Now, you can set up a virtual tour across blogs run by readers, writers, and reviewers of relevant genres. These involve author interviews, book excerpts, and giveaways (readers love giveaways). You may wish to use a marketing service such as AuthorBuzz or Goddess Fish. You will still have to write the content, but they'll do the legwork, and a starter tour can be quite cheap.
- Book-lover sites. At Goodreads, LibraryThing, and Shelfari, readers catalog their book collections, post reviews, and discuss their favorites. Authors can participate, buy ads, or even sell their book from their site.
- Review services. Many bloggers will review your book if provided with a free copy, and some major reviewers such as Kirkus Reviews and *Publishers Weekly* will review your book for a fee. While they won't guarantee you a good review, it's another way to get your book in front of readers (Fry 2011).

Promote where it comes naturally to you, and to your target readers. Johnson (2011) states that "on the web, marketing has quite literally become conversational" (203). Speaking the language of your readers can hook them before they've read your book. If you're witty, on the run, and have a smartphone, try Twitter. If you enjoy longer conversations and have the time, share your thoughts with readers on your blog. With persistence, research, and the web on your side, you may become the next self-published sensation. After writing that book, self-publishing should be easy by comparison.

REFERENCES

Boog, Jason. 2013. "Rachel Van Dyken Leads Self-Published Bestsellers List." *Galleycat*, August 26. http://www.mediabistro.com/galleycat/rachel-van-dyken-leads-self-published-bestsellers-list_b76805.

Campbell, Richard, Christopher R. Martin, and Bettina Fabos. 2011. *Media and Culture: An Introduction to Mass Communication*. 7th ed. Boston: Bedford/St. Martin's Press.

Carnoy, David. 2012. "Self-Publishing a Book: 25 Things You Need to Know." CNET, June 13. http://reviews.cnet.com/8301-18438_7-10119891-82/self-publishing-a-book-25-things-you-need-to-know/.

Cass, Kiera. 2012. "About." *Kiera Cass*. http://www.kieracass.com/about-me/.

Cochrane, Kira. 2013. "Has Virago Changed the Publishing World's Attitudes Towards Women?" *Guardian*, March 14. www.theguardian.com/books/2013/mar/14/virago-changed-publishers-attitudes-women.

Conference Board of Canada. 2012. *Canadian Industrial Profile Summer 2012: Canada's Printing Services Industry*. Ottawa, ON: The Conference Board of Canada. Conference Board of Canada E-Library, accessed July 8, 2013.

Digital Book World. 2013. Self-Published E-Books Dominate Best-Sellers List. *Huffington Post*, April 30.http://www.huffingtonpost.com/2013/04/30/self-published-ebooks_n_3187084.html.

Ebert, John D. 2011. *The New Media Invasion: Digital Technologies and the World They Unmake*. Jefferson, NC: McFarland & Co.

Flood, Alison. 2011. "Novelist Ditches Publisher at Book Launch for 'Condescending' Treatment." *Guardian*, September 15. www.theguardian.com/books/2011/sep/15/novelist-ditches-publisher-book-launch.

———. 2013. "Coverflip: Author Maureen Johnson Turns Tables on Gendered Book Covers." *Guardian*, May 9. www.theguardian.com/books/2013/may/09/coverflip-maureen-johnson-gender-book.

Franklin, Ruth. 2011. "A Literary Glass Ceiling?" *New Republic*. February 7. www.newrepublic.com/article/books-and-arts/82930/VIDA-women-writers-magazines-book-reviews.

Friedman, Jane. 2011. "Should You Self-Publish After a Near-Miss?" *Writer's Digest*, May 11. www.writersdigest.com/editor-blogs/there-are-no-rules/general/should-you-self-publish-after-a-near-miss.

Friedman, Thomas L. 2012. "Do You Want the Good News First?" *New York Times*, May 19. www.nytimes.com/2012/05/20/opinion/sunday/friedman-do-you-want-the-good-news-first.html?pagewanted=1&_r=0.

Fry, Patricia. 2011. *Promote Your Book: Over 250 Proven, Low-Cost Tips and Techniques for the Enterprising Author*. New York: Allworth Press.

Harper, Steven. 2011. *Writing the Paranormal Novel*. Cincinnati, OH: Writer's Digest Books.

Johnson, Christopher. 2011. *Microstyle: The Art of Writing Little*. New York: W.W. Norton.

Larsen, Kari. 2013. "Why J. K. Rowling Used a Pseudonym." *PennLive*, July 18. www.pennlive.com/entertainment/index.ssf/2013/07/jk_rowling_is_robert_galbraith.html.

Loren, Roni. 2012. "Bloggers Beware: You CAN Get Sued for Using Pics on Your Blog." RoniLoren.com. July 20. www.roniloren.com/blog/2012/7/20/bloggers-beware-you-can-get-sued-for-using-pics-on-your-blog.html.

Norris, Michael, and Simba Information. 2013a. *Business of Consumer Book Publishing 2013*. Stamford, CT: Simba Information. Available from MarketResearch Academic, accessed August 8, 2013.

———. 2013b. *Trends in Digital Trade Book Retailing 2013*. Stamford, CT: Simba Information. Available from MarketResearch Academic, accessed August 5, 2013.

Romm, Robin. 2011. "Why It Matters That Fewer Women Are Published in Literary Magazines." *Slate*, February 2. www.slate.com/blogs/xx_factor/2011/02/02/ vida_study_fewer_female_authors_published_in_literary_magazines.html.

VIDA. 2013a. "The Count 2012." *VIDA: Women in Literary Arts*, March 4. www.vidaweb.org/the-count-2012.

———. 2013b. "Mission and History." *VIDA: Women in Literary Arts*. www.vidaweb.org/about-vida/mission.

Index

About the Editor and Contributors

Carol Smallwood coedited *Women on Poetry: Writing, Revising, Publishing and Teaching* (2012), on *Poets & Writers* magazine's list of Best Books for Writers and *Women Writing on Family: Tips on Writing, Teaching and Publishing* (2012), and is the author of *Lily's Odyssey* (2010); *Bringing the Arts into the Library* (2014), her sixth book for the American Library Association; and *Divining the Prime Meridian*, her third poetry collection, forthcoming from WordTech Editions. Carol's library experience includes school, public, academic, and special, where she has worked in various capacities including administration and as a consultant. Carol has founded and supports humane societies.

* * *

Julie N. Adkins is an assistant professor in the College of Education at Ashford University in Iowa. She holds a PhD in education with an emphasis in professional studies from Capella University. Dr. Adkins worked as a fourth- and fifth-grade elementary school teacher for six years before transitioning into a career online in higher education. Since then, she has continued to share her knowledge about best practices with future teachers. Dr. Adkins appreciates the flexibility that a full-time online professorship affords her, as she attempts to balance a professional career and raising a family.

Kara Poe Alexander, associate professor of English at Baylor University, Waco, Texas, obtained her PhD in English rhetoric and composition from the University of Louisville. Kara teaches courses in professional and technical writing, literacy studies, advanced composition, and digital writing. Her research examines the intersections of writing, teaching, and technology. Her work has appeared in several academic journals and edited collections, including *College Composition and Communication*; the *Journal of Business and Technical Communication*; *Technical Communication Quarterly*; *Computers and Composition Online*; *Kairos: A Journal of Rhetoric, Technology, and Pedagogy*; and *Composition Forum*.

Jill Andrew has an MA in women and gender studies from the University of Toronto, New College and is a PhD candidate. She is a columnist; international speaker; educator; and media consultant on female body image, equity, and leadership, and founded BITE ME! Toronto Int'l Body Image Film & Arts Festival and Curvy Catwalk Fashion Fundraiser, and is cofounder of FatintheCity and the Body Confidence Canada (BCC) Awards. Jill participated in Canada's inaugural Governor General Women's Conference, received the Michele Landsberg Media Activism Award, and was awarded the Soroptimist Foundation of Canada Grant and induction into Humber College's School of Social and Community Services Alumnus of Distinction Hall of Inspiration. See www.BiteMeFilmFest.com and www.FatinTheCity.com.

Aurélie Athan, PhD, is a researcher and member of the faculty within the Department of Clinical Psychology at Teachers College, Columbia University, and cofounder of the Women, Sexuality, and Gender Project. Dr. Athan is also the founder of KHORAI and the Maternal Psychology Laboratory, which studies the transition to motherhood as a developmental niche within the female lifespan trajectory, as part of the broader task of illuminating the overall psychology of women, the domain Freud once described as a "dark continent."

Amy Barnickel is a lecturer at the University of Central Florida (UCF) in Orlando, Florida, who holds a bachelor's degree in English and French from the University of Wisconsin–Milwaukee, a master's degree in English language arts education from UCF, and a doctoral degree from UCF in texts and technology. She is the assistant editor of *Studies in Art Education* and the editor for KlynnAcademics.com. Formerly a writer/liaison for UCF's president, she has two decades of executive-level writing experience. Amy is a feminist who encourages education, assertiveness, and pursuit of success for all women.

Sheila Bender earned a master of arts in creative writing at the University of Washington and holds a master's degree in teaching. Combining her love of writing and teaching, she founded Writing It Real in 2002 with her husband Kurt VanderSluis. Since then, the website has allowed her to facilitate the writing of those who use personal experience in essays, stories, poetry, and memoir. She has authored a dozen books on writing; several collections of poetry; a memoir; and, recently, an e-book on healing grief through writing. Learn more on http://writingitreal.com.

Emily Bent, PhD, is assistant professor in women's and gender studies at Pace University in New York City. She serves as the co-chair of the Working Group on Girls, a coalition of over eighty national and international non-governmental organizations with representation at the United Nations. She earned a doctorate in global women's studies from the National University of Ireland, Galway, in 2012. Her research explores the complexities of global girlhoods and of *girl* as a political subject of feminist inquiry.

Nicole M. Bouchard is the founder and editor-in-chief of *The Write Place At the Write Time*, member CLMP (Council of Literary Magazines and Presses). She is a Letters member of the National League of American Pen Women. Her credits include *The Gunpowder Review, The Pen Woman, The Storyteller, Trail of Indiscretion*, and *The Review Review*. She served as a speaker on the Small Press Panel at the Fourth Massachusetts Poetry Festival and was profiled for her literary and journalistic work on *Creative Women Today*. For a more extensive bio, see the About Us page at www.thewrite placeatthewritetime.org.

Debbie Carpenter, MAEd, serves as a full-time remote faculty member for Ashford University in Iowa and began her career in the field of elementary education, having taught for both Riverside Unified and Poway Unified School Districts in Southern California. She obtained her master of arts degree from San Diego State University and currently supports bachelor's-level students as they pursue careers in the education field. Debbie's memberships include the Association for Supervision and Curriculum Development, and she volunteers regularly for both the Poway Unified School District and Junior Achievement of San Diego and Imperial Counties.

Kathleen Clauson, MA economics, is a library operations associate at Western Illinois University. Clauson spent five years in Santiago, Chile, as assistant financial controller at Bank of America and as a business consultant for the American-Chilean Chamber of Commerce, publishing feature business articles and economic forecasts. Clauson publishes extensively—short fiction, essays, book reviews, and in two anthologies, *Handling Job Stress: Tips by Librarians,* and *How to STEM in Libraries*. Clauson is also the owner of a small home-based online business and enjoys the success of a top-rated "power seller."

Having worked in a library since she was thirteen, **Melissa Cornwell** is the new distance learning librarian at the Kreitzberg Library at Norwich University in Northfield, Vermont. She has a graduate degree in library science from the University of Illinois, Urbana-Champaign; her BA in English literature is from Southern Illinois University, Carbondale. Melissa loves all things cat and library related. She hails from Illinois and is a new resident of Vermont with her sandals and Midwestern accent. A tea, manga, and crime drama addict, Melissa can be found atwww.melissacornwell.org.

Judy Donovan, EdD, remote assistant professor at Ashford University in Iowa, earned her doctorate in instructional technology and distance learning from Nova Southeastern University; an MLS from Indiana University/Purdue University, Indianapolis; a master's in educational leadership from Western Michigan Univerisity; and a master's in early childhood education from Grand Valley State University; she also holds secondary, elementary, and library media certification. She has also completed master gardener training and volunteers at gardening events. Judy has published in several journals and books, presented at many conferences, and is past president of the School Library Division of the Association for Educational Communications and Technology.

Aisha Fairclough is a Toronto-based lifestyle television producer and is cofounder and editor of FatintheCity, and the Body Confidence Canada (BCC) Awards. Aisha's credits include television shows on Food Network Canada, Slice, TVO, HGTV, Much Music, CTV, CBC, and TLC International. Her most recent story producer credit was *Million Dollar Neighbourhood* (Season 2), which aired on the Oprah Winfrey Network (OWN) Canada. Aisha is also one of the co-owners of Glad Day Bookshop, the world's oldest LGBT bookstore. For more information visit www.fatinthecity.com and www.BiteMeFilmFest.com.

Laura Francabandera is the senior e-learning technology coordinator for Credo Reference, a reference database company dedicated to more effective research. She received her MLIS from San Jose State University. She has presented at American Library Association conferences and contributed a chapter to *The Machiavellian Librarian* (2013). Straight out of graduate school, she took a virtual internship with Credo Reference that became a permanent position, telecommuting from her home office in Sacramento, California, to Credo's headquarters in Boston, Massachusetts. Her husband, Brandin, studies ethics at Fuller Seminary and they have two young children, Elijah and Judah.

Mariana Grohowski is a PhD student at Bowling Green State University in Bowling Green, Ohio. Her research examines the cultural ideologies and literate activities of female veterans of the U.S. Armed Forces. She has taught courses in first-year writing and service learning, and has worked as a writing consultant in a university writing center. She earned her MS in rhetoric and technical communication from Michigan Technological University. She is the vice president of Military Experience and the Arts, an organization that fosters healing for veterans through writing and other forms of self-expression.

Marie Hansen, MLIS, is a master of arts student in the Department of Clinical Psychology at Teachers College, Columbia University. Combining her background in information and library science with her work as a psychological researcher, Marie helped developed the KHORAI live series at the New York Public Library. In addition to enhancing public psychological literacy, Marie's scholarly interests include psychoanalysis and premenstrual syndrome, postpartum hallucinations, and biopsychosocial approaches to women's reproductive health.

Alexis Hart is an associate professor of English and the director of writing at Allegheny College in Meadville, Pennsylvania. A United States Navy veteran, Hart has published scholarly work on veterans' issues, and was the co-recipient, with Roger Thompson, of a Conference on College Composition and Communication (CCCC) research grant to study veterans returning to college writing classrooms. She is cochair of the CCCC Task Force on Veterans and codirector of research for Military Experience and the Arts. She received her PhD from the University of Georgia.

Darra Hofman, an author and legal scholar, obtained her BA (English literature) and her JD from Arizona State University. She has appeared in the *William and Mitchell Law Review*, the *Tulane Journal of Law and Sexuality*, and the *Denver Law Review* (forthcoming), as well as contributing to *The End Was Not the End* (Seventh Star Press, 2013). Her legal scholarship focuses on bioethics, particularly the ethics of medical decision making for caregivers and other surrogate decision makers, while her fiction is focused on questions of autonomy and individual agency.

Kanina Holmes works in Ottawa, Ontario, an assistant professor at Carleton University's School of Journalism and Communication. She has a bachelor's in journalism from Carleton as well as a master's degree in international affairs. Kanina worked as a reporter and producer in radio (CBC), television (CBC, Global, CTV), and also as a print correspondent for Reuters. She teaches television and print storytelling, journalism studies, and ethics. She is currently working on a PhD in human geography at Queen's University. Her research focuses on gender and online space and online social media by Canadian military spouses.

Hailing from Alabama via Thailand, **Jenny Ungbha Korn** attended Princeton, Harvard, and Northwestern before attending University of Illinois at Chicago, where she received an outstanding graduate student award from her department and two leadership awards from the university. Jenny Korn has appeared in video, online, radio, and print stories revolving around race, gender, and online identity, including NPR, CNN, SXSW, Colorlines, and more. Her research examines race and gender within Facebook, Twitter, YouTube, Chatroulette, blogs, and e-mail. Please feel free to connect with Jenny Korn via Facebook at http://facebook.com/JenKorn, LinkedIn at www.linkedin.com/in/jennykorn, or via Twitter @JennyKorn.

Sarah Menkedick is a writing instructor and MFA student at the University of Pittsburgh. Prior to returning to the United States for graduate school, she spent six years living, teaching, and traveling abroad. Her work has been published on Amazon's Kindle Singles, *The Common*, World Hum, *Perceptive Travel*, qarrtsiluni, and Matador Network, among other online and print publications. She was the recipient of a 2012 Ohioana Award for a writer under thirty. She is the founder of Velamag.com, an online magazine of creative nonfiction inspired by travel and written by women.

Tasha Muresan, MA, is a graduate of the Department of Clinical Psychology at Teachers College, Columbia University, in New York City. She is a member of the Maternal Psychology Laboratory and managing editor of *KHORAI*, an online newsfeed of reproductive and maternal mental health. Tasha's main scholarly interests include Jungian psychology and female psychosocial development along the lifespan. Accordingly, her graduate thesis explored motherhood archetypes through folklore and fairy tales. Alongside research in both maternal and positive psychology, Tasha is preparing for doula certification, which will allow her to assist women in birth and labor.

In 1984 **Chris A. Olson** became an entrepreneur and launched Chris Olson & Associates, a consulting firm working exclusively with information service and knowledge professionals. As the principal consultant, Chris advises on marketing, branding, and communications in knowledge management settings. She established her business website, ChrisOlson.com, in February 1996, a year before Google and when the Internet had a hundred thousand sites. Chris has a BA in art history, an MLS in library science, and a master's in business administration (MBA). She's a Special Libraries Association fellow and enjoys working in her gardens overlooking Chesapeake Bay.

Leanne Olson is a librarian at Western University in London, Ontario, Canada. She obtained her MLIS at Western University and her bachelor of arts in Drama at Queen's University in Kingston, Ontario, Canada. She has been writing in various genres since she could hold a pencil. Some of her work includes performed plays, articles published in consumer magazines such as *Together Family* and *ADDitude*, and romance e-books published under a pen name. She is currently self-publishing a book based on her blog, and surviving a hectic term as treasurer on the London Writers' Society Executive.

Amanda Peach, reference and instruction librarian at Berea College in Berea, Kentucky, obtained her MLIS from the University of Kentucky. Amanda has previously published on the topics of QR codes and urban literature in the journals *The Reference Librarian* and *Kentucky Libraries* and along with her coauthor Debbra Tate, she received the 2012 Award for Outstanding Article in *Kentucky Libraries*. She is the mother of three amazing girls and in her free time volunteers as a Girl Scout troop leader. She is a big fan of hearty soups, mystery novels, and tattoos.

Denise Powell is the founder and editor-in-chief of The Voices Project (www.thevoicesproject.org), an online literary venue for women to express their voices through poetry to promote social change. She holds dual BA degrees in English and journalism from the University of Iowa and was a student of the university's Undergraduate Poetry Workshop. Her writing has appeared in various publications including Earthwords (University of Iowa Undergraduate Review), Lethologica, The Pulchritudinous Review, and Poetry Pacific. Recent works can be found on her poetry blog, www.writingsbydcp.blogspot.com.

Liz Webler Rowell joined Benz Communications after spending eight years at Hewitt Associates. Her writing has appeared in *TLNT* and *Employee Benefit News*. She has a BA in English and African studies from Smith College and an MFA in writing from the School of the Art Institute of Chicago, and has a daily practice of stepping away from the computer to breathe fresh air. A Midwesterner who now lives thirty miles from where she grew up, Liz has left her forwarding addresses in two foreign countries and four states.

K Royal, CIPP/US/E (Certified International Privacy Professional), is a nurse and attorney with degrees from Mississippi College, University of West Alabama, and Arizona State University. With over twenty years of professional experience in the legal and health-related fields, Royal has a particular interest in health and technology such as telesurgery, bioethics, and privacy. She has been recognized as a Forty-under-40 recipient for Phoenix, as an educational leader through the YWCA, and a top pro bono attorney in Arizona. Royal is currently an in-house counsel and finishing her PhD from the University of Texas at Dallas.

Jennifer Ann Russum is a PhD student at Arizona State University studying rhetoric and composition, specifically in online contexts. Her dissertation is a long-term study of "mommy bloggers," which looks at how mothers are writing, reading, and socializing in the blogosphere. Jennifer also teaches undergraduate composition classes on topics such as: pop culture, digital communities, the research process, and creative nonfiction. When she is not researching or teaching, Jennifer can be found writing on her personal blog, *The Arizona Russums* (www.theazrussums.com).

Lura Sanborn, research and instruction librarian at St. Paul's School in Concord, New Hampshire, has a master's degree in library and information science (Simmons College) and an undergrad degree in Women's Studies (University of New Hampshire). She is a regular reviewer for *Library Journal* and has written articles related to teaching research, building digital library collections, and the construction of digital libraries appearing in the *Journal of Academic Librarianship, School Library Monthly*, and *eContent Quarterly* as well as a chapter for *E-Learning in Libraries* (2013). In her position, Lura is responsible for the Ohrstrom Library blog and research LibGuides.

Katherine Sanger, an English professor for various colleges and universities, earned an AA in general studies, a BS in information technology, an MA in liberal arts, an MA in English literature, and a post-master's certificate in college teaching. She is currently working on her MFA in creative writing with the University of Tampa. Her fiction and poetry has been published in various e-zines and print publications, she has edited the e-zine *From the Asylum*, and she writes nonfiction for various websites. She's a member of Broad Universe, Science Fiction Poetry Association, and SFWA.

Robert Simpson, resident of Oak Park, Illinois, is a retired history teacher and former web production worker with a degree in English from the University of Maryland–College Park; urban education from the Catholic University of America in Washington, D.C.; and history from Northeastern Illinois University. He belongs to the National Writers Union and the Freelancers Union and is a past member of the HTML Writers Guild and JoomlaChicago. He is active in the Chicago labor movement, and blogs at the *Daily Kos*,

Open Salon, and *ZNet*. Robert believes in the power of the Internet to influence social change.

Jennifer Sintime is a freelance writer based in Toronto, Ontario. After obtaining a BA in philosophy from York University in Toronto, she attended the University of Toronto for a certificate in Freelance Writing. Former junior communications officer and content writer for HedgeStone International, Jennifer is currently writing for the 100 Women Who Work Project. Referred to the project by the Women in Work Boots graphic designer, Jennifer started writing for *Women in Work Boots Magazine*, the online network for women in the trades founded by Jill Drader, in 2013.